Identities and Interests . . . .

Identities and Interests

Race, Ethnicity, and Affinity Voting

...... Randy Besco

UBCPress · Vancouver · Toronto

28 27 26 25 24 23 22 21 20 19   5 4 3 2 1

Printed in Canada on FSC-certified ancient-forest-free paper (100% post-consumer recycled) that is processed chlorine- and acid-free.

Library and Archives Canada Cataloguing in Publication

Title: Identities and interests : race, ethnicity, and affinity voting / Randy Besco.

Names: Besco, Randy, author.

Description: Includes bibliographical references and index.

Identifiers: Canadiana (print) 20190119535 | Canadiana (ebook) 20190119551 | ISBN 9780774838924 (hardcover) | ISBN 9780774838931 (softcover) | ISBN 9780774838948 (PDF) | ISBN 9780774838955 (EPUB) | ISBN 9780774838962 (Kindle)

Subjects: LCSH: Voting – Canada. | LCSH: Minorities – Political activity – Canada. | LCSH: Race – Political aspects – Canada. | LCSH: Ethnicity – Political aspects – Canada.

Classification: LCC FC104 .B47 2019 | DDC 324.971 – dc23

Canada

UBC Press gratefully acknowledges the financial support for our publishing program of the Government of Canada (through the Canada Book Fund), the Canada Council for the Arts, and the British Columbia Arts Council.

This book has been published with the help of a grant from the Canadian Federation for the Humanities and Social Sciences, through the Awards to Scholarly Publications Program, using funds provided by the Social Sciences and Humanities Research Council of Canada.

Printed and bound in Canada by Friesens
Set in AlternateGothic2, Scala Sans, and Minion by Artegraphica Design Co. Ltd.
Copy editor: Lesley Erickson
Proofreader: Lauren Cross
Indexer: Marnie Lamb
Cover designer: David Drummond

UBC Press
The University of British Columbia
2029 West Mall
Vancouver, BC V6T 1Z2
www.ubcpress.ca

This book is dedicated to
my great-grandparents Leon and Franka Bezkorowajnj,
my mother Anne Cauley,
and my son Arthur Besco.
We are always who we are, with others.

Contents

Figures and Tables

TABLES

Acknowledgments

The first people I want to recognize are the candidates and voters whom this research is about. Sometimes with quantitative research, it is easy to forget that the figures and plots we make represent their hopes and fears, desires, and intentions. Or, we plot their indifference and carelessness, which have consequences as well. This distance from their experience is especially the case for candidates, who pour months or years of their life into a career that demands an extraordinary amount from them. Political life has its rewards, to be sure, but it has high costs as well. Yet, we need someone to stand for office, and those that do so need to be held to account, but they also deserve our respect and recognition.

No book springs up from nowhere, and different people inspired each turn in the path of this book. In more or less temporal order, I should thank Jason Kenney, whose campaign to bring visible minority Canadians into the Conservative party made me realize what an important part of electoral coalitions they are in Canada. Tim Uppal's experience in the 2011 election made it abundantly clear to me that even with the general rules of electoral politics – local candidates don't matter much and ordinary people pay little attention – a minority candidate could still provoke an extraordinary reaction, both in terms of rejection and loyalty. André Blais' presidential address, and the "prize" of explaining visible-minority support for the Liberal Party made me think this was an academic project worth doing. At the first academic conference I attended, CPSA 2011, I saw Karen Bird present a candidate experiment that found no affinity effects between South Asian and other minority voters, which immediately caught my interest. My reading brought me to Paula McClain and Matt Barreto's work, which was my first serious introduction to Latino and African-American politics research. In a search for explanations, I read Paul Sniderman and discovered social identity theory, which was electrifying. I was convinced groups and identities mattered for intrinsic reasons, not just as a matter of a concrete payoff, but I could never really explicate, why, exactly, identities affected behaviour. Social identity theory gave me a firm motivational grounding and a simple yet sophisticated theoretical framework. Later, Leonie Huddy's work introduced me to the broader field of social identity and social categorization research. Finally, Steven Greene's adaptation of Fred Mael's Identification with a Psychological Group Scale provided the final piece – I then had a question, a theory, and a measure.

I owe a debt to all of these academics, but there are others who deserve more direct thanks. When I received my letter of admission to a PhD program, I thought I had been offered a great supervisory combination: Keith Banting would provide experience and expertise in diversity issues, and Scott Matthews would bring enthusiasm and a knowledge of electoral behaviour. I don't think I truly realized how lucky I was until years later. I owe them thanks not only for years of providing advice and support but also for doing far more than they were really required to do. Although, I admit at the time I didn't always appreciate why I needed a whole extra reading list of classic works, or why they needed to read a third draft and have me do yet another round of revisions. Specifically, I would like to thank Keith for his support throughout my dissertation and still to this day. His insistence on asking "why does it matter?" will stay with me for the rest of my career. It was in Scott's MA class that I really learned the concept of social science, and it was him who encouraged me to apply to grad school. He was a dedicated supervisor who ensured that we met regularly, despite the distance, and was always there to help when I ran into difficulties. I now count Scott as a colleague to look up to as well as a friend, and I hope I can live up to his example with my own students.

Special thanks also go to Elizabeth Goodyear-Grant, who provided years of advice and support, both on this project and in other areas of my life. Her participation in the survey made the project in its current form – and perhaps the rest of my career – possible. The conclusion of this book is largely a response to Will Kymlicka's questions, which I always appreciated. I also want to recognize Todd Alway; Bill Moul, my first methods teacher; and Peter Woolstencroft, who introduced me to the study of Canadian politics so many years ago. Finally, thank you to Erin Tolley, who has provided sharp advice, helpful feedback, and inspiration. Working with her has been a highlight of my career on at least three occasions so far and no doubt more to come. She is not only a superb colleague but a wonderful friend and the funniest political scientist I know.

Graduate school involves somewhat solitary work, but I had a wonderful set of colleagues, including Andrea Collins, Aaron Ettinger, Megan Gaucher, Edward Koning, Matthew Mitchell, Bailey Gerrits, Jeff Rice, Charan Rainford, Iain Reeve, Leah Sarson, and Beesan Sarrouh. Thank you for five excellent years. I still miss lunch in the lounge. I should also thank the research assistants and students who helped with this work, including Mdu Muzinga, Andy Kim, Christopher Lamm, Keenan Aylwin, Tanya Bandula-Irwin, Brindan Baskaran, Emily Bailey, Chris Casher, Kelsey Champagne, Amanda Cohn, Sarah Dorrington, Justice Durland, Alexandra Haberfellner, Cathrin Hughes, Emeleigh Gauthier-Moulton, Sianan Irvine, Henrieta Lau, Jessica Lau, Mason Levesque, Claire McNevin, Brandi Rees, Patrick Pereira, Rachel Kane, Sarah Kim, Kelvin Kwok, Milena Gligorovic, Britney Foerter, Anna Majetic, Jacqueline Palef, William Simonds, Rebecca Snider, Scott Tinney, Olivia Vozza, Rebecca Wallace, Beatrice Weng, Meredith Williams, John Woodside, Eriq Yu, and apologies to those whom I have somehow missed. The first draft of the book was done during my term at the Center for the Study of Race, Ethnicity, and Gender in the Social Sciences at Duke University. Having an entire term free to dedicate to writing was an extraordinary help and for that I am thankful to Paula McClain and Kerry Haynie, as well as to Dick Engstrom for his advice and company. And thank you to the anonymous reviewers, who made this a much better piece of research than I could have done alone.

Lastly, my thanks go out to Laurel, who is the best partner in life and academics that anyone could ask for. She read many drafts, put up with my late nights spent working, and gave me the time and space to finish the book. Writing and publishing a book is a long road, and no doubt every author gets tired along the way – thank you, Laurel, for encouraging me when I needed it most. And to Arthur – you were born hours after I submitted revisions, so I feel as though you are inextricably linked with this work. Thank you for always bringing a smile to my face, even when work seems overwhelming.

Identities and Interests

1
..... Introduction

As global immigration continues to transform the electorates of democracies, the political activity of racialized voters will have increasingly powerful effects on political life. Racialized Canadians are now approaching 20 percent of the Canadian population (Statistics Canada 2011), and there is little doubt that this upward trajectory will continue. Therefore, electoral districts with large and diverse racialized populations offer a preview of our future political demography. These ridings are also key electoral battlegrounds (Marwah, Triadafilopoulos, and White 2013), which means even relatively small levels of influence can produce dramatic changes in power at the national level, including determining who governs. A growing racialized population will also make racialized leaders far more influential. These demographic changes will mean more racialized candidates, public officials, and party leaders, and increasing weight in electoral coalitions. Already, as will be shown, one in four electoral districts have at least one racialized candidate, and a growing number have multiple racialized candidates.

Racialized citizens will be increasingly important political actors, yet there is surprisingly little research on the electoral behaviour of racialized Canadians in Canada or, indeed, on racialized voters in any democracy other than the United States. While there is a great deal of research on immigration, multiculturalism, integration, and attitudes toward racialized people, the subject of racialized citizens as active participants in electoral politics has been somewhat neglected. In part, this is because the backlash of the majority against the minority, in the form of discrimination and hostility, tends to be the focus of attention. Ethnic minorities are also difficult to study: standard surveys generally do not include a large enough sample of ethnic minorities and certainly not enough data to study subcategories such as specific ethnocultural groups. Nonetheless, ignoring the political behaviour of racialized citizens is no longer a viable option. As globalized immigration increases ethnic diversity, the electoral choices of racialized minorities are becoming increasingly important: we can't understand politics without understanding the political behaviour of racialized citizens.

This book examines the role of racial and ethnic identities in politics. Specifically, it explores how and when people identify with ethnic and racialized groups and the role they play in the political support that racialized candidates receive from racialized citizens. It is a truism in political commentary that voters support candidates who are like themselves – be it their region, language, or gender – often referred to in the political science literature as affinity voting. Yet the extent of this phenomenon among ethnic groups, and the motivations for it, is still not well understood. People identify in many ways, but which identity groups matter, and when? Affinity effects can have wide-ranging implications, including those that are explicitly electoral but also those that are broadly political and social. In terms of electoral politics, coethnic affinity voting could form an essential base of support for racialized politicians, influence party leadership races, and act as an important counterbalance to discrimination by white voters. The data examined here show that there were 1.6 million racialized Canadians that could cast a vote for a racialized candidate in the 2011 federal election: in other words, coethnic- and racialized-affinity effects are potentially widespread and affect many voters. Similarly, these psychological effects could impact many other forms of political and social action, such as social movements, issue-based advocacy groups, and immigration settlement programs.

Three central themes are explored in this book. The first is voting behaviour: Are voters more likely to support candidates of their own racial or ethnic group or candidates of other racialized ethnic groups? Does affinity voting produce rainbow coalitions or more narrowly focused support from single ethnic groups? The breadth of affinity voting effects is a major determinate of the size, and therefore, political influence, of these coalitions.

The second theme is the motivation for this affinity behaviour: why do racialized voters support racialized candidates? This question cuts to the heart of our understanding of democracy and citizenship: when citizens vote, what are they doing? This question is part of a wide-ranging debate about whether electoral politics are fundamentally expressive or instrumental (Achen and Bartels 2016; Huddy, Mason, and Aarøe 2015), which has important implications for democracy and citizenship. Two types of motivations are explored in this book – interests and identities – which can express themselves in a series of different mechanisms.

The third theme of this book is the structure of race and ethnic identity: how people identify and how ethnic and racial groups are defined in Canada. Ethnic and racial groups can exist at multiple levels, such as specific cultural identities, as ethnic identities (such as those used by Statistics Canada), and as superordinate racialized "ethnic minority" identities. Racialized Canadians can and do identify with all of these groups. These higher- and lower-order identities are connected, but the strength of higher-order identities is weaker, as nested-identity theory would suggest. While the state-defined Statistics Canada ethnic categories are, in some sense, artificial, Canadians do identify with these categories, and immigrants start to do so quickly. More subtly, racialization and the normalization of whiteness in Canada seem to result in a racial schema (Roth 2012) in which nonwhite ethnic groups are defined as a unified "minority" or "immigrant" social group. It appears that this categorization is internalized by racialized Canadians themselves.

Coethnic versus Racialized Affinity Voting

There is a good deal of evidence that voters are more likely to support candidates of their own ethnicity. However, nearly all research is from one country and focused on two specific groups: black and Latino voters in the United States (e.g., Barreto 2010; Philpot and Walton 2007). Although there is some emerging research out of Canada (Bird 2015) and the United Kingdom (Fisher et al. 2015), as of yet, evidence is scarce for affinity voting outside the United States or among other ethnic groups. This is particularly important given the long history of bitter racial conflict in the United States and the fact that racial issues continue to play an explicit role in modern elections. The extent to which findings of coethnic affinity voting in the United States are generalizable to the rest of the world is not clear.

It is also unclear whether affinity voting is limited to the candidate's own ethnicity (coethnic affinity voting) or applies to all racialized voters (racialized affinity voting). The breadth of affinity voting is a key factor in the potential size and influence of rainbow coalitions of different racialized ethnic groups, given the diversity of racialized populations in most Western democracies. Understanding the relationships among racialized ethnic groups is especially important in Canada, since Canada's population of racialized minorities is not only large but also diverse. According to Statistics Canada, the largest racialized ethnic category is "South Asian," and it makes up only 25 percent of the racialized minority population (Statistics Canada 2011). Moreover, diversity is reflected at the electoral district level. As Chapter 7 will show, the ethnic group of a racialized candidate is almost always a minority of racialized voters – that is, voters of the candidate's ethnic group are usually outnumbered by voters of other racialized ethnic groups. To a great degree, the influence of rainbow coalitions and the success of racialized candidates may be conditional on the degree of affinity (or discrimination) among different racialized ethnocultural groups.

Previous research suggests that racialized citizens may well discriminate against other racialized groups. The limited evidence from studies on black and Latino Americans suggests that there is conflict between ethnic groups (Meier and Stewart 1991; McClain et al. 2006). Of course, political conflict, as defined here, includes discrimination against candidates or opposition to policies favouring particular ethnic groups rather than violence or persecution. Still, these effects may have important consequences. One broad concern relates to the capacity of citizens to build coalitions among racialized communities and, therefore, these citizens' ability to address important shared policy concerns. Postcolonial theorists sometimes advocate for strategic essentialism, an approach that suggests that oppressed peoples should sometimes adopt broad, essentialized group identities for pragmatic political reasons. For example, Asians in Britain might consider themselves "black" for the purposes of building a useful political coalition (Modood 1994). While such group identities inevitably erase distinctions and homogenize differences, they can also help build support for important political projects (Spivak 1987). Similar concepts have been used by activists around the world, including influential leaders such as Jesse Jackson, who famously called for a rainbow coalition of black, Jewish, Arab, and Hispanic Americans, along with other social groups (Jackson 1984). Advocates for rainbow coalitions make the claim that racialized communities of all kinds often share similar experiences and needs, including issues related to immigration, racism and discrimination, and the recognition of foreign credentials. Yet the viability of rainbow coalitions may depend on the attitudes of racialized minority groups toward one another rather than on commonly held issues of concern. If different racialized ethnic groups see one another as out-groups, it follows that issue coalitions will be much harder to build. Therefore, identity may undermine issue coalitions.

A lack of solidarity among racialized communities (when voters are more likely to support candidates from their own ethnocultural background than other racialized candidates) may also put all racialized candidates at a systematic disadvantage. Research suggests a correlation between the number of racialized citizens in an electoral district and the nomination of racialized candidates (Tossutti and Najem 2002; Black and Hicks 2006). Counterintuitively, racial diversity may be a disadvantage for racialized candidates in ridings where their ethnic group is only a plurality. As noted earlier, in Canada this is the situation for racialized candidates in almost all federal electoral districts. If racialized voters prefer white candidates to candidates from racialized communities *other than their own,* then this preference may have a systematically negative impact on candidates from *all* racialized communities. Put another way, racialized candidates may split the racialized vote in a way that white candidates do not.

Nonetheless, the prospects for rainbow coalitions are not so bleak as they first appear. Conflict between Latinos and African Americans is not universal; there are examples of political cooperation (Browning, Marshall, and Tabb 1984; Saito 1998). While specific ethnic identities may be chronically accessible, broader racialized identities may be influential in the right context. This suggests that we should not presume that interminority conflict is inevitable; rather, we should pay careful attention to the context and to the way that ethnic and racial identities are defined.

Effects on Party Leaders, Nominations, and Social Movements

The psychological principles that apply to voting for a local candidate also imply a wide range of effects on other types of political and social behaviour, such as those related to party leaders, nominations, and social movements. Perhaps the largest affinity effects would occur if a racialized leader of a major party were elected. That party leaders are influential in elections around the world is well established (Bean and Mughan 1989; Bittner 2011; Gidengil et al. 2007; Garzia 2017; Watenburg 1991). Therefore, if affinity voting affects local candidates, it is very likely that those effects would be even stronger and more widespread in the case of party leaders because they are prominent in campaigns, the media, and advertising, and knowledge and salience of their characteristics is very high. Voters would be aware of the leaders' ethnicity, and the general concept of ethnicity would likely be salient in the election (an important factor in the degree of influence that ethnic identification has on vote choice). Media often report on the candidates' race, gender, or other characteristics that make them exceptional, particularly if they are a "first" in some way (Tolley 2015).

In Canada, a racialized party leader would be considered newsworthy, and even if the leader downplayed his or her ethnicity, there would be much public debate about whether the country was ready to elect a racialized prime minister. Furthermore, a racialized party leader would likely produce at least some prejudiced or discriminatory attacks, which would also receive media coverage. These debates and media coverage itself would increase the salience of ethnicity. In addition, voters (quite correctly) think that party leaders are important and that the attributes of leaders are an important factor in vote choice. Party leaders in Canada are particularly powerful, even compared to other Westminster systems, making them even more important.

Party nominations and leadership races are also likely to be shaped by coethnic- and racialized-affinity effects. While there has been no systematic study of affinity voting in these contexts, there is widespread anecdotal evidence suggesting that minority candidates regularly win nomination meetings with support of coethnic party members. In fact, minority candidates have been so successful that there are periodic complaints from other party members and calls for party leaders to reform the nomination rules to restrict voting to citizens or, at least, to long-time party members (*Kamloops This Week* 2005; CBC News 2008). Party leaders have consistently declined to intervene, to the benefit of minority candidates who often win nominations with the apparent support of coethnic party members.

Affinity voting for both party leaders and in nomination contests is likely to produce long-lasting effects. Early research on ethnic voting (such as among Irish and Italian immigrants) showed clear preferences for in-group candidates, but it also revealed that early support and "first" candidacies produced long-lasting changes in support for parties (Wolfinger 1965). When the first candidate of an ethnic group runs for a prominent political office, they attract a substantial amount of support for their ethnic group to that political party. Wolfinger (1965) suggests that these first candidacies can be a form of critical election. There is debate about how many generations these effects will last for (see Dahl 1961; Parenti 1967; Barreto and Pedraza 2009), but Wolfinger argues that these effects can persist for three or four generations, perhaps more. In part, persistence likely depends on the degree to which party competition reinforces and reproduces the link between the party and the ethnic group. The socialization of partisanship, however, provides another long-term mechanism. Since the partisanship of parents strongly influences the partisanship of their children (e.g., Jennings, Stoker, and Bowers 2009), initial partisanship based on ethnic ties might extend for multiple generations, well after strong ethnic identification has faded.

Initial affinity voting is also likely to lead to a long-term increase in participation. When people join a party or express support for a party (via voter ID calling, door knocking, social-media monitoring, etc.), these actions can result in a long period of party contact. The voter enters the party's support and GOTV lists, and they are called, mailed, or have their doors knocked on to remind them to vote. The sophistication of political data analytics is sometimes overstated (Hersh 2015), and Canadian parties have fewer resources than US parties; nonetheless, these standard techniques do have important positive effects on voter participation (Green and Gerber 2015) and are regularly employed in Canada. Contact is likely to continue indefinitely (or at least until the party is informed that the voter no longer supports it). As anyone who has been on a party mailing list knows, parties keep data forever, and given the near-zero cost of communication technologies such as email and auto dialing, they will continue to use it even with no subsequent confirmation of interest. As a result, recruitment through affinity effects may result in a lifetime of increased participation.

Affinity effects, particularly the role of coethnic identity and higher-order racialized identities, also have important implications for social movements and issue coalitions. Group identities are a crucial way for social movements to overcome collective-action problems (Brewer and Silver 2000; Klandermans 2002), particularly among marginalized or "low-power" groups (Simpson and Macy 2004). Because generating identification is difficult, movements that link to existing identities are more likely to mobilize people. For more narrowly defined cultural national groups, however, linking to a narrowly defined identity inherently limits the size of the potential coalition. Given the diversity of Canada's racialized population, this is a serious problem. A natural response is to build a broader coalition that incorporates more groups, but to do this effectively at the mass level, I argue, requires a superordinate identity.

There is essentially no research on multiethnic social movements in Canada, but research elsewhere reveals that multiethnic and multiracial movements can be especially effective. Many of these movements are in large cities where immigrant populations and African Americans have formed political coalitions (Pulido 2006), but there are also nationwide examples, such as Martin Luther King's multiracial campaigns (Mantler 2013). In fact, even movements based on standard racial or ethnic groups are usually coalitions of national groups, such as Chinese, Japanese, Korean, and other Asian Americans (Espiritu 1992). The Black Lives Matter movement in the United States was borne out of a relatively homogeneous African American population, but a similar movement in Canada draws on a "black" population composed of people who have many different national origins, yet the majority still view "black" as their primary racial identity (Black Experience Project 2017). Clearly, there are reasons why certain identities are more appropriate for certain movements and issues; in general, however, higher-order racialized identities apply to more groups, providing a broader basis for social movement mobilization. Although the research presented here focuses on affinity voting and local candidates, there is good reason to believe that affinity effects can also be found in many other forms of political and social behaviour.

Interests and Identities in Racialized Politics

If racialized voters are more likely to support racialized candidates, why do they do so? That is, what is the motivation behind affinity voting? Here, the role of race and ethnicity is part of a larger debate about the meaning and content of politics, about whether political actions are fundamentally instrumental or expressive (Fiorina 1976; Huddy, Mason, and Aarøe 2015). Within an instrumental understanding of politics, citizens cast ballots and take action as a means to some end – to change public policy for the better, to further their own interests, or to be consistent with what they believe is right. An alternative interpretation is that politics are expressive – citizens act to express their identities or to support their group's status, regardless of changes to government policy. As Achen and Bartels (2016, 4) put it, "even the most informed voters typically make choices not on the basis of policy preferences or ideology, but on the basis of who they are – their social identities."

Despite evidence demonstrating that people tend to vote for a candidate of the same ethnicity, little research explores why they do so. What does exist suggests notionally heuristic explanations, but it does so without testing the mechanism (e.g., Philpot and Walton 2007; Stokes-Brown 2006; L. Sigelman and C. Sigelman 1982). More than thirty years after initial experimental studies on affinity voting, there is a clear need for a more sophisticated theoretical account of coethnic affinity voting and empirical examinations of the psychological mechanisms that the account proposes.

Potential explanations for affinity effects can be divided into two general categories: identity-based explanations and interest-based explanations. These categories are not necessarily mutually exclusive – both interests and identity can influence coethnic affinity voting, and one might serve as a mediator for the other. Nonetheless, they form distinct motivational accounts. As defined here, interest-based explanations involve rational, relatively intentional motivations, such as policy or ideological preferences or a general sense of self-interest. Identity-based explanations, on the other hand, involve expressions of group identity or bias produced by in-group favouritism.

The classic explanation for the effects of candidate race is interest-based heuristics: a candidate's race is a piece of information that tells voters about the candidate's likely positions and future actions (e.g., Popkin 1991, Lau and Redlawsk 2001). This is the core of instrumental politics: electing a candidate of one's own group is not a goal in itself but a means to some end, such as supporting a policy that favours the voter or is consistent with the voter's beliefs. Interests could produce affinity voting in multiple ways. For example, a voter might have a general sense that voting for the candidate of her ethnic group is in her own best interest, however she defines it. Influential theories of group consciousness provide accounts of this kind: group identity alone does not affect behaviour; rather, there must be a perception of inequality that political action can address (e.g., Miller 1981). Similarly, proponents of the closely related theory of linked fate argue that discrimination and oppression tie the interests of the individual and the group together (e.g., Dawson 1994). Since the candidate's ethnicity implies that he or she will pursue policies that benefits the group, group consciousness and linked fate lead to affinity voting (McConnaughy et al. 2010).

A second type of interest-based explanation posits that voters can stereotype candidates ideologically – that is, they might believe that the candidate's ethnicity tells them something about his or her general ideological position (e.g., McDermott 1998). Or voters might adhere to stereotypes about specific policy positions such as immigration or racial inequality based on the candidate's ethnicity. All of these explanations can be thought of as the link between descriptive and substantive representation, where the descriptive characteristics of legislators are an important indicator of the substantive policy that they will pursue, and affinity voting is a product of the voter's desire for that policy.

Identity-based explanations imply a quite different account of politics. That is, voter self-identity has an independent effect on their choices, separate from their interests or the policies a candidate would implement. Perhaps the most prominent identity in political behaviour research is party identification, and it is now recognized that the traditional direction of causality is often reversed: party identification affects issue positions (Goren, Federico, and Kittilson 2009), perceptions of the economy (Gerber and Huber 2009), and leader evaluations (Bittner 2011) rather than the other way around. Psychological theories of identity provide an important account of why self-identity itself can affect choices. In particular, the arguments set out here draw on social-identity theory, which focuses on the relationship between the self and the status of the group (Tajfel 1981). The central insight of this theory is that identification links the self and the group. The successes and failures of fellow group members become our own successes and failures, and we are motivated to perceive in-group members as superior in all kinds of ways. This link between self-esteem and group success can produce a number of important effects, including a straightforward desire for a candidate of the same ethnic group to win, persuasion effects stemming from increased source credibility, and voting as a way to express membership and loyalty to the group. While interest-based effects have received the most attention by scholars of affinity voting, I argue that identity effects are far more influential than is commonly held.

Racial and Ethnic Identities

If identities are important for affinity voting, which racial and ethnic groups do people identify with? At a more fundamental level, if people support candidates who belong to their own group, how is that group defined? These questions are complicated by the social construction of identities and the potentially infinite number of groups. As a result, identification is the product of two processes: the long-term definition of identity groups and the short-term selection of which groups a person identifies with at a given moment. Since the research that follows manipulates the short-term context and explores its effects on how people behave, it can shed light on how racial and ethnic groups identify and how ethnic and racial categories are defined and understood.

Long-term definitions of ethnic and racial categories do not exist separate from society, nor are people free from constraints in how they identify. It is hardly surprising that a person's individual experiences – including socialization, family history, and country of birth – are naturally important to how they identify. Less obvious, but equally important, is the way that society defines what ethnic and racial categories and identities mean and how they are (apparently) logically structured. For example, a woman might know that her family originated in Guatemala and, therefore, that Canadian society and the state bureaucracy defines her as Latin American. She has two plausible ways to identify – as Guatemalan or as Latin American – alongside definitions of who fits into those categories, what Roth (2012) calls a racial schema. Simultaneously, this racial schema rules out other identities, such as being black. These categories may appear logical but are in fact produced and enforced by social processes involving social power (Waters 2006), the state (Thompson 2016), the media (Tolley 2015), and the expectations of other individuals (Ujimoto 1999). The difference between the Canadian and US censuses illustrates this: in the United States, people are categorized as black Hispanics or white Hispanics, whereas in Canada black and Latin American are exclusive categories.

Nonetheless, the existence of bureaucratically defined categories, such as "Latin American," does not mean that these labels are psychologically meaningful. Just because people recognize that they objectively fit into that category does not mean that their internal sense of self-identity is defined in those same terms. Self-reports of group membership are what Verkuyten (2005, 61) calls "identity as a social fact," which is both conceptually and empirically different from a subjective sense of self-identity. While there are connections between the two, there can also be a great deal of variation.

In the analysis that follows, one important consideration is the ethnocultural categories used by Statistics Canada. These categories are used by the state, not to mention in academic research. In addition, they are also useful mid-range identities – narrower than the general "ethnic minority" category but still large enough to be politically important. However, despite their use by the government, it is unclear if they have any real weight in the self-identification of ordinary Canadians. Do these ways of defining ethnic groups have real psychological impacts? In the terms of identity theory, are these identities easily accessible to many Canadians, and do Canadians readily categorize themselves as belonging to these groups? I argue that Canadians do in fact identify with Statistics Canada ethnic categories, but this identification is something that needs to be empirically investigated rather than assumed.

The short-term process that determines how Canadians identify in a given moment is also crucial, because many different identity groups can be psychologically meaningful to the same person. The woman in the above .example could identify as Guatemalan or as Latin American, but her identify might also be influenced by her gender, religion, class, language, province of residence, her status as a parent or child, political party, or place of employment. In fact, each of us could identify with a potentially infinite number of groups, a great many of which could be important and politically influential. Yet all these possible identities cannot be active at the same time. While priming theory and framing theory show how some considerations are made "top of mind," and thus much more influential (Iyengar and Kinder 1987), self-categorization theory explains which group we identify with in a given moment (Turner et al. 1987).

One important set of factors that determine how a person identifies in a given moment are short-term contextual factors. For our purposes, the most important are those related to electoral context: the candidates with which the voter is presented. The candidates might all be white; one candidate might be of the same ethnicity as the voter; there might be a racialized candidate of a different ethnic group. These different choice contexts might make different identities salient – that is, the candidate context helps determine which identity in-groups are relevant and how a person identifies while making the choice between candidates. I argue that a candidate of the same ethnic group as the voter will make the voter more likely to identify with that ethnic group than with some other identity.

A less obvious situation is when a candidate is of a different racialized ethnic group. Do racialized Canadians see one another as members of some broader group of "racialized people" or "ethnic minority"? Racialized identity is more difficult to study than specific ethnic group identities because it is less concrete or real, in the sense that it lacks the institutional and social markers of more specific ethnic groups (e.g., associations and traditions; see Goette, Huffman, and Meier 2006) or even a generally accepted name. In the analysis that follows, this way of identifying is not measured directly and is inferred from behaviour. Nonetheless, I argue that a choice between a white candidate and a racialized candidate of a different ethnic group will lead voters to identify with a more general racialized or ethnic-minority identity and to support the (racialized) in-group candidate.

This is an important empirical finding in its own right, but it also has far-reaching implications for Canadian society. A racial schema where people understand ethnic groups as, among other things, bifurcating society into white and nonwhite or racialized or nonracialized is not inevitable or natural. Nor should we assume this is the case; rather it needs to be empirically established. Returning to our example of the Guatemalan Canadian voter – why should she see a Chinese candidate as an in-group member and the white candidate as part of an out-group? The implication is that the dominant racial schema in Canadian society defines racial and ethnic categories this way, dividing society into racialized "ethnic" people and nonracialized white people. It would be less surprising if white people held this view, but the evidence presented here suggests that this structure of ethnic and racial identities is also inculcated and internalized by racialized people.

A simple thought experiment will help highlight the importance of these processes. Imagine the different ways that racial- and ethnic-identity categories – that is, different racial schemas – could be structured and defined (Roth 2012). One possibility is viewing racial and ethnic groups as equally distinct, what we might term a cultural equality structure. Such a society would be a collaboration of many cultures, all of which would be equally deserving of respect and participation. In this way of thinking, ethno-cultural groups have meaning and importance but are all equally "distant" – that is, all other ethnic groups are equally different from one's own group. In this scenario, it would not be surprising if citizens showed a preference for candidates of their own group and considered all other ethnic groups out-groups. However, in a society where ethnic identities are structured as simply a series of separate groups, there would be no natural alliance or sense of commonality among nonwhite ethnic groups.

A second possibility would be a racialized society in which some citizens are racialized and others are not. In this kind of a society, white Canadians would be normalized ("not ethnic") while others would be considered "ethnic" Canadians. Society would not be composed of distinct but equal cultural groups; it would be bifurcated into those who are ethnic and those who are not. Even if there were many specific ethnic subgroups, racialized groups would be viewed as part of some superordinate grouping. In contrast, white, European-origin Canadians would be part of another separate group. While the Canadian national myth of multiculturalism implies a society of equal ethnocultural groups, the evidence presented in this book tells a more complex story: Canadians are loyal to specific ethnic groups, but they also think in terms of white and nonwhite.

Structure of the Book

Chapter 2 begins with an evaluation of the existing empirical research on affinity voting and then sets out a number of potential theoretical explanations. These explanations fall into two broad categories based on their core motivation: interest-based explanations and identity-based explanations. Each category contains a number of different mechanisms or subtypes, including general group interest, ideological stereotyping, and policy attitudes (as types of interest-based explanations) and self-esteem, persuasion effects, and expressive voting (as types of identity-based explanations). In addition, I apply these explanations to two major scenarios: one in which the candidate and voter are of the same racialized ethnic group (which I refer to as coethnic affinity voting) and one in which candidates and voters are racialized but of different ethnic groups (which I refer to as racialized affinity voting).

The basic pattern of affinity voting is explored in Chapter 3 using a national survey sample of Canadians, including a large oversample of racialized respondents. The centrepiece of the survey is a voting experiment involving a set of fictional candidates. The results show evidence of greater support for candidates of the same ethnic group, relative to a white candidate (i.e., coethnic affinity voting). There is also some evidence of affinity voting for candidates of different racialized ethnic groups (i.e., racialized affinity voting).

In the chapters that follow I examine several explanations for affinity voting. Chapter 4 presents the argument that self-identification is a key concept for understanding identity effects. In-group bias and expressive voting turn on identifying with a group, not merely on cognitive recognition of an "objective" group membership. Thus, we require a measure of ethnic self-identification. I set out an adaptation of the Identification with a Psychological Group Scale (IDPG) and explore its demographic predictors.

Ethnic self-identity – the IDPG scale – is linked to affinity voting in Chapter 5. If identity is an important cause of coethnic affinity voting, then strength of ethnic self-identification, as measured by the IDPG scale, ought to interact with the effects of candidate and voter ethnicity. This means that people who strongly identify as part of an ethnocultural group will be more likely to support a candidate of that group. Conversely, those who are members of an ethnic group but do not identify with it are likely to be indifferent, or even opposed to, candidates of their ethnic group. The analysis suggests that this is the case: the IDPG measure of ethnic self-identification has a strong, positive relationship with coethnic affinity voting. Although weaker in the latter case, this positive relationship obtains for both coethnic and racialized affinity voting. Chapter 5 concludes with an analysis of an open-ended question: "Why did you support that candidate"? The responses were coded into a series of categories related to different explanations for affinity effects and examined qualitatively. The results confirm the importance of identity; many respondents explicitly said they had voted for a candidate because of his or her ethnicity, while others described making more generalized racialized references, such as to minority or immigrant status.

The second set of explanations for coethnic affinity voting – interest-based explanations – are explored in Chapter 6, where I test the role of ideological stereotyping, policy attitudes, and perceived self-interest. The concept of ideological stereotyping explains coethnic affinity voting by suggesting that racialized candidates are stereotyped as being ideologically left-wing. Racialized voters are purportedly also left of centre, suggesting that what appears to be the effect of ethnicity may actually be a product of ideological preferences and stereotyping (McDermott 1998). I tested this account by asking respondents questions about perceived candidate ideology but found no evidence of ideological stereotyping. A different explanation might be about specific policies rather than general ideology: if people who want more immigration support a racialized candidate as a way to pursue that policy preference, then the apparent effects of identity might instead be a result of policy preferences. I test this for various policy attitudes, including immigration, racial inequality, government job creation, and crime, but there is little evidence that policy preferences are related to affinity voting.

Finally, I examined what I refer to as general group interest. In this account, voters believe that a candidate of their ethnic group will act, in some diffuse, nonspecific sense, in their interest. Voters may not have a sophisticated or coherent account of what general group interest is at stake, but they may, nonetheless, have a vague sense that the candidate who shares their ethnic group membership will better serve their interests. I tested this explanation using question wording that primed self-interest considerations but that had little or no effect. Lastly, I reviewed the results of the open-ended question, revealing that many respondents explicitly cited candidates' ethnicity and minority or immigrant status as a reason for supporting them. Conversely, respondents hardly ever mentioned ideology, policy, or interests. Although they often mentioned the influence of the party when the candidate had a party affiliation, there seemed to be no connection to candidate ethnicity. In sum, while there is strong support for the effect of identity, a series of tests found little or no support for interest-based explanations.

Finally, Chapter 7 examines whether affinity voting is likely in Canadian federal elections and how widespread it might be. I evaluate three factors: party labels, the distribution of candidates, and the geography of racialized voters. Some research suggests that the effects of candidate ethnicity are significantly diminished when party cues are present (Kam 2007). If this is the case, the findings for affinity effects in Chapters 4 and 6 would be significantly less important – perhaps applicable to municipal politics or other nonpartisan settings but not to provincial or federal elections involving clear party affiliations. To test this, I examine how respondents reacted to the presence or absence of candidate party affiliations. Contrary to Kam's findings, I found no evidence that the presence of party labels attenuated the impact of candidate ethnicity, a finding that suggests that, at least at a psychological level, there is no reason affinity effects should not apply widely to both partisan and nonpartisan elections.

The second half of Chapter 7 examines two new sources of data: a data set of the ethnicity of candidates in the 2004, 2006, 2008, and 2011 Canadian federal elections and census data on ethnicity at the federal riding level. This data shows that racialized candidates are widely distributed rather than concentrated in a small number of ridings. In fact, approximately one-quarter of ridings have at least one racialized candidate. Finally, I used census data to compile the number of racialized Canadians in these ridings, and the findings indicate that affinity voting, as explored in this research, may apply, in principle, to some 1.6 million racialized Canadians. Moreover, an examination of the level of ethnic diversity at the riding level makes it clear that most racialized candidates face electorates in which their ethnic group is, at best, a plurality. In other words, few racialized candidates compete in ridings dominated by a single ethnic group. This highlights the importance of racialized affinity voting, and its role in rainbow coalitions.

2
Framing and Explaining
..... Affinity Voting

To understand coethnic and racialized affinity voting in electoral politics we need to understand why, and under what circumstances, it occurs. This chapter sets out a social-psychological framework for group identification and describes a series of possible explanations for affinity voting. I explore two basic voter-candidate combinations: coethnic affinity voting and racialized affinity voting. Further, two categories of potential explanations are set out: interest-based explanations and identity-based explanations. As will become clear, there is reliable evidence of affinity voting for candidates who are of the same ethnicity as voters (e.g., McDermott 1998; Barreto 2007; Fisher et al. 2015). Unfortunately, there is little research on racialized affinity voting; to fill this gap, I draw on research that focuses on more general attitudes among different ethnic groups.

Assessing the role of racial and ethnic groups requires understanding how race and ethnicity function as social identities. They are socially constructed and influenced not simply by an individual's personal history and experience but also by the views and action of others and by widely accepted social definitions of these categories – the dominant racial schema. People have a great many identities, and the way they actively identify at a given moment is a product of two factors: the centrality of that identity to the individual and the context at that time. Many racial and ethnic identities are nested in the sense that membership in specific lower-order groups implies membership in higher-order ethnic or racialized groups. Rather than being competing categories, they reinforce each other when individuals identify with both.

Explanations for affinity voting fall into two general categories, interests or identities, which are classified according to their central motivation, although their operation might include various mechanisms. Interest-based explanations, at their core, assume that people are motivated by utility maximization and that ethnicity is a useful heuristic, although the way it maximizes utility varies in different accounts. There are a number of mechanisms through which such reasoning could influence candidate choice, such as the use of policy and ideological stereotypes or diffuse concepts of general group interest.

Identity-based explanations are motivated by the expression and maintenance of identity group status. Social identity theory shows how identity can motivate people through in-group bias and a desire for positive group attributions, independent of more concrete interests (Tajfel 1981). Despite widespread adoption in social psychology, so far there appears to be only a few studies that examine identity-based explanations for affinity voting (Barreto 2010; Fisher et al. 2015; McConnaughy et al. 2010), and the measures they use have significant drawbacks.[1] To provide a clearer theoretical foundation for the causal effects of identity, I examine a number of theories that explain how identity might influence vote choice, including bias in perception of candidate attributes, persuasion effects, and expressive voting.

Finally, I consider the Canadian context. Given that most research on affinity voting focuses on black and Latino Americans, what should we expect elsewhere? Taking our limited knowledge about the causes of affinity voting into account, it appears that Canada (and many European countries) has relatively good prospects for interminority coalitions. In addition, the electoral system in Canada militates against local candidate effects (Carey and Shugart 1995), suggesting that if there is evidence of affinity voting in these data, it may well imply larger effects for party leaders in Canada and for other countries with similar social and demographic structures but different electoral systems.

Group Identities, Racialization, and Normalization

Group identities are social, not only in that they are about groups of people but also in that they are socially shaped and defined: rather than being freely chosen by the individual, identities are deeply influenced by the behaviour and expectations of others, including other individuals and the state (Hogg and Abrams 1988). The impact of government on social definitions of identities is often difficult to see because people are socialized to accept them at a young age. However, immigrants provide dramatic examples of how individual opinions are affected by the weight of social expectations. Waters (1999) describes immigrants from the West Indies to the United States as being sometimes shocked to see themselves categorized as black since they are used to identifying with their nationality. While concepts of race are, to some degree, transnational (Thompson 2012, 2016), Roth (2012, 12) argues that "racial schemas – the bundle of racial categories and sets of rules for what they mean" also vary substantially from country to country. As a result, just as immigrants learn and assimilate in other ways, they must fit their experiences into the racial and ethnic categories of their new country.

The views of others also have a more immediate impact because categorization by others affects our self-categorization and behaviour in that moment. Ujimoto (1999) describes how, when he was viewed as Japanese by others in a conversation on public transit, he accepted and took on the role. While there is certainly some agency in these actions, they are not without consequences: rejecting the assumptions of others can lead to confusion and social conflict even in simple, personal conversations, not to mention categorization by the state or social institutions. Similarly, an antiracist advertising campaign in Toronto from 2016 features photos of a white man talking to a woman wearing a hijab. He says, "go back to where you came from." Her response: "Where? North York?" (*CityNews* 2016). The idea that a woman wearing a hijab could be from a suburb of Toronto is subversive in part because it challenges the man's categorization of her as an immigrant and a foreigner.

Rejecting the categorization of others or challenging well-established definitions of racial and ethnic groups can lead to sanctions. In the language of role identity theory, not conforming to the norms and expectations of a role can result in stigmatization because nonconformity is seen either as violating role identities (Stryker 1980; White and Burke 1987) or as a norm violation (Abrams and Hogg 1990; Cialdini and Trost 1998). Counterstereotypical behaviour that violates expectations about cultural or racial groups can cause backlash (Phelan and Rudman 2010; Rudman and Fairchild 2004). Not only can racialized people face sanctions from white out-group members, but their own in-group members are likely to punish those who violate group norms (Marques, Yzerbyt, and Leyens 1988). While much of this research focuses on responses to external behaviour, norm enforcement can also have an effect on internal self-identification since people are motivated to bring their beliefs in line with their own behaviour (e.g., Janis and King 1954, Harmon-Jones et al. 2018).

Racialization is an especially important way that identities are shaped – and imposed – by others. It is the process by which a person is defined as having a race. Advocates of the concept emphasize that race is a process rather than an attribute (e.g., Hawkesworth 2003), in part because it de-naturalizes the category: if people can be racialized, then it is possible for people not to be racialized. The definition of who is racialized is the product of broad social and historical processes, including state policies (Thompson 2016) and media coverage (Tolley 2015). As Blumer (1958, 3) puts it, the construction and definition of racial groups is a product of experience, and it is a "fundamentally collective process." However, this collective process reflects power relations – who is racialized in Canada reflects the viewpoints of overwhelmingly white social, political, and media elites.

Some people are normalized rather than racialized: they are treated as the standard or default category, which is assumed rather than stated. In con-temporary Canadian society, being white or having European origins is usu-ally normalized. While the concept of a norm is old, the emphasis on racial norms and on how being part of the normative group confers privilege while not being part of it produces harms and disadvantages, emerged more re-cently, particularly in whiteness studies (e.g., Frankenberg 1993; Dyer 1988; Lopez 2006; Clark and Gardner 2009). Driedger (1989) notes that white (northern European) Canadians rarely mention their skin colour when de-scribing themselves, yet they are very conscious of the race of non-white people. Similarly, drawing on student discussions, James (1999) argues that white Canadian students resist and avoid defining themselves as white. The result of the normalization of whiteness is that white people are often treated as not having a race or ethnicity – it is simply not noticed or perceived as not a "real" or relevant categorization.

Of course, normalization is about perception: in fact, white people do have a race or ethnicity, and whiteness is not always the norm (white people can, and are, racialized in some circumstances or by some people). Racialization and normalization are often two sides of the same coin, although not neces-sarily so. Nonetheless, the empirical reality is that in Canadian society the ethnicity of white people is commonly invisible, while racialized nonwhite or non-European groups are noticed and noteworthy, often resulting in ref-erences to people or things being "ethnic" or "multicultural." The alternative categories, "not ethnic" and "not multicultural," do not have commonly used terms and sound incongruous to the ear, making the point that the categor-ies are implicit rather than explicit, assumed rather than stated.

The effects of normalization and racialization in politics are widespread. In 2011, for example, a leaked document detailed the Conservative Party's plan to pursue "ethnic voters," which ranked electoral districts in terms of the number of visible-minority residents and presented a list of "very ethnic" electoral districts that the party needed to win (Castonguay 2013). The subtext is that some voters have an ethnicity while others do not. Although the leak was widely mocked as a gaff, the attitudes it revealed are present in general media coverage. Tolley (2015) shows that media coverage of visible-minority candidates in Canada often mentions their ethnicity, while media coverage of white candidates does not: their ethnicity simply goes unmentioned. Similarly, Gershon (2012) found that media coverage emphasizes the race of black candidates for Congress but not that of white candidates.

Waters (2006) argues that whiteness allows a much greater freedom to identify, or not, with a heritage, nationality, or other groups. Racialized people, by contrast, have much less freedom to not identify because of how often they are classified and treated as ethnic group members by others, even in simple conversations about hair, clothing, or food or through questions such as "Where are you from?" The processes of racialization and normalization, I argue, are important for affinity voting because they can lead to people identifying other racialized people as fellow in-group members. Nonwhite ethnic groups have no obvious commonality aside from who they are not: racialization itself produces this commonality.

Multiple Identities: Centrality and Context

All people have multiple identities, including gender, nationality, class, or ethnicity. They actively identify in different ways at different times. In the voting booth, we might identify as a citizen; when we are with our parents, as a child; and when in the classroom, as a teacher or a student. In some ways, it is more useful to say that people do not *have* identities but rather that they *identify* in a given way at a given moment. The way a person identifies at a given point in time involves a negotiation between (long-term) centrality and (short-term) context. In political science research, these two factors are often conceptualized as having an identity and making an identity salient (e.g., Campbell et al. 1960). While these two ways of thinking about identity often lead to similar conclusions, I refer to centrality and context because, as the minimal group paradigm shows, identity can be created instantaneously and arbitrarily. Tajfel (1971) famously divided people into "minimal" groups – such as by their (supposed) ability to count dots – and found that even these trivial and temporary categorizations produced in-group bias. Moreover, the various gradations of specificity and combinations of groups make even "real" social groups infinite in number. Yet, at any given time, most of these infinite number of possible group identities have no influence on behaviour, because a person cannot possibly have them all in mind, rendering the idea of "having" identities simultaneously trivial and overwhelming.

We should instead focus on the way people identify in a given moment as a function of how 1) long-term beliefs about their own lives, the views of others, categorization by the state, and other pieces of information map onto 2) the short-term context of a given situation, especially the other people involved and the categories provided. As Spears and colleagues (1999, 61) put it, identification is "the crystallization of past contextual influences and ongoing alliances." As a result, identities are simultaneously fluid and stable. Many important social facts and personal beliefs are unlikely to change even over years and decades, but the meaning they hold for identification changes based on the context.

These long-term factors influence the centrality of an identity to an individual's self-concept. The centrality of an identity denotes "the significance of a particular component [identity and] its location in the self-concept structure – whether it is central or peripheral, cardinal or secondary, a major or minor part of the self" (Rosenberg 1979, 18; see also Cameron 2004). The centrality of an identity is a product, among other things, of knowledge about expectations of others, personal experience, social history, and repeated self-categorization in the past (Oakes 1987, 1996). Different psychological theories have similar concepts, such as prominence (McCall and Simmons 1966), importance (Stryker 1980), schematicity (Bem 1981), strength of identification (Deshpandé, Hoyer, and Donthu 1986), and so on (see Morris 2013). The term I use is centrality, but the core concepts are quite similar. Crucially, identities that are more central have a higher activation potential – that is, people will actively identify with a group more strongly and more frequently if it is more accessible for information processing (Higgins 1989). As a result, if an identity is highly central to a person's self-concept, a given context will produce a larger effect on his or her behaviour. The way people identify at a given moment, and the effect this identification has on their behaviour, is a product of the context and centrality.

The short-term context also helps determine which of their many identities people actively identify with in a given moment. Comparators, such as other possible in-group members, are one important context. However, there are many contextual factors that might be important: the issue at hand, the kind of decision, the location, the nature of recent media coverage, and so on. Identification varies between different people because of centrality, and it varies in the same people over time because of context.

Multiple Identities: Nested

Since people have multiple identities, the relationship between them can be important. Sometimes, they are unrelated, such as when someone is both a student and a Canadian. Often, though, they are nested, or hierarchical. Many of the studies on this topic fall under the rubric of organizational research, focusing on cases where employees are general employees of a company but also members of specific units or teams (e.g., Ashforth and Johnson 2001; Ashforth, Rogers, and Corley 2011; Foreman and Whetten 2002), but the theory has also been applied to national identities and European identity (Medrano and Gutiérrez 2001).

Two findings are especially relevant. First, lower-order identities tend to be stronger. Ashforth and Johnson (2001) explain that higher-order identities are generally more inclusive, abstract, and distal, whereas lower-order identities are more exclusive, concrete, and proximal. These lower-order identities structure people's daily lives in concrete ways and likely produce more common self-categorizations, implying that the most specific cultural, ethnic, and national identities are the most likely be the strongest (in the sense of being central to people's self-identity) and that higher-order ethnic and racialized identities are likely to be weaker.

In addition, lower-order and higher-order identities often reinforce each other. Since they are at least somewhat overlapping, lower-order identities can lead to generalized identification (Ashforth and Johnson 2001). But this is not always the case: identities at different levels can be viewed as antagonistic or threatening. When higher-order identities are viewed as threatening, lower-order ones (assimilatory identities, for example) are weakened. This is what happens with national and regional identities, when the national identity is seen as assimilatory and hostile. However, in general, lower- and higher-order identities should be correlated: people with strong lower-order identities should also have strong higher-order identities.

Concepts and Terminology

The terminology of race and ethnicity is contested and varies widely between countries, but more importantly, it reflects debate over the meaning and nature of identity. The concept of group identification used here defines identity as fluid: it is the product of both centrality and context, and it is social rather than individual in that it is deeply influenced and constrained by external factors rather than being a purely autonomous choice. The racialization and normalization of ethnic groups are key factors in identification related to racialized affinity voting. The terminology reflects the fact that this study focuses on the effects of ethnic identities rather than on their formation. Nonetheless, the concept of identification used here draws on both aspects of identity and process.

In the analysis that follows, the terms *ethnicity* or *ethnocultural background* refer to specific backgrounds such as "South Asian." While the term *ethnicity* could apply at many levels of specificity, the empirical analysis here draws on the categories used by Statistics Canada (discussed in detail in Chapter 3). European-origin Canadians are referred to as white in the text (though not in the survey questions), although this term is not used by Statistics Canada. Of course, the terminology of ethnicity changes over time. Earlier – though not that much earlier – studies used *ethnicity* to refer to different countries and parts of Europe (e.g., Black 1987; Berry and Kalin 1979). The study of European Canadian ethnic identity, or the ethnicity of whiteness, however, is a research agenda all on its own (e.g., Baldwin, Cameron, and Kobayashi 2011; Jacobson 1999), and this study does not focus on the behaviour and attitudes of white respondents. Nonetheless, the term *white* is useful because it points toward a group that is usually unnamed and nonracialized and, thus, in some sense it de-normalizes whiteness.

It is certainly true that specific groups are influential at community levels. South Asian community groups, for example, are often organized around specific regions of origin (the Punjab, Gujarat, and so on). The fact that multiple identities are possible, however, does not require us to reject the concept of ethnic identities. In fact, a major part of this project is to address whether ethnocultural groups as defined by Statistics Canada are meaningful to Canadians. Keep in mind the connection between knowledge and context: when presented with these categories, do Canadians categorize themselves accordingly? Do they do the same when presented with candidates? Perhaps terms such as *South Asian* will be meaningless – for example, respondents of Pakistani origin may not identify themselves as South Asian. If people do identify with them, then these categories deserve attention, and the question of their meaning and influence is an important one. Finally, it is certainly plausible that analysis of more specific group identities would find even stronger effects than in the present study. Nonetheless, ethnicity, as it is used here, is a useful compromise: large enough to be politically important yet distinct from general racialized status.

When referring to nonwhite ethnicities as a group, I employ the term *racialized*. Being racialized is not a naturally existing state of affairs, nor is it a permanent one. In other circumstances, such as a Chinese-origin candidate running for office in China, that candidate would probably not be racialized because Chinese ethnicity would be normalized. Nonetheless, these Chinese and South Asian–origin candidates are referred to as "racialized candidates" because in current Canadian society they *are* racialized, in the sense of how they are understood by society rather than by some innate characteristic. There is some danger in using this terminology (and some irony in converting a term used to emphasize process from a verb into an adjective – see Dhamoon 2011), but it is difficult to entirely separate the terminology of the research from the way concepts are understood in society. Alternative terms such as *nonwhite* are equally as problematic or, in the case of *minority*, misattribute the concept of interest. The aim here is to use this language to represent empirical social reality while recognizing that this social reality is constructed and not natural or necessary. The electoral implications of this fact – that these candidates and voters are racialized – is one of the major points of investigation.

When I discuss other research, I adopt the terminology used in that research, including terms such as *Hispanic* and *Latino* and *black* and *African American*. For attitudinal research on conflict between racialized ethnic groups, such as blacks and Latinos in the United States, the phrase generally used is *interminority relations or conflict,* though only research dealing with racialized minorities is discussed here. British research generally refers to *ethnic minorities. Visible minority* is an official Canadian term that refers to people who are nonwhite and non-Indigenous; it is used in reference to government data where appropriate.

The terminology in existing research on affinity also varies. Generally, *affinity* refers to liking or attraction, while *affinity voting* is defined as the propensity to vote for a candidate of a particular group. Research on African Americans generally refers to racial affinity, although the analyses focus only on African American respondents (e.g., McDermott 1998). By contrast, for Latinos, the term *coethnic candidates* is commonly used (e.g., Barreto 2007) when discussing Latino candidates, as does Fisher et al. (2015) regarding minorities in the UK. However, there is no term for affinity between different racialized ethnic groups. Given these considerations, this study uses *coethnic affinity* when describing voters as being more likely to vote for candidates of the same ethnicity. For voters being more likely to vote for racialized candidates of a different ethnicity, the term *racialized affinity* is used. This effect, I argue, stems from racialization and normalization, and it is this point of commonality that defines the group. Therefore, I avoid using alternative terms such as *minority affinity;* they would be misleading because affinity affects are not caused by minority status. The terms I employ have the advantage of being general rather than specific, and they distinguish between the two types of affinity, directing attention to the key level of analysis in the study.

Social Groups, Candidates, and Vote Choice

At the most general level, ethnic groups are a type of social group, and the importance of social groups to voting behaviour has been clear since researchers engaged in early election studies (Berelson et al. 1954; Lazarsfeld, Berelson, and Gaudet 1944). Converse's (1964) classic analysis of voter ideology had pessimistic conclusions about voters' abilities but at the same time pointed toward the role of groups in compensating for voters' informational shortcomings. In fact, he suggested that social groups are "objects of high centrality in the belief systems of the less well informed," the less well informed being, of course, a category including most citizens (Converse 1964, 234). Attitudes toward social groups, Converse suggested, are a key determinant of specific opinions and decisions. Voters use their general orientation toward social groups rather than sophisticated ideologies to determine their opinion on specific policies.

Evidence for the influence of social groups on political opinion extends across a wide range of public policy areas, including affirmative action (Kinder and Sanders 1996), social welfare programs (Kluegel and Smith 1986), political tolerance (Kuklinski et al. 1991), AIDS (Price and Hsu 1992), and war (Kam and Kinder 2007). That attitudes toward social groups influence political opinions is, as Kinder (2003) puts it, indisputable. The effect of social groups on vote choice has been the subject of a wave of recent research. Research on partisanship has focused on its nature as a social-group identity, rather than as a form of ideological voting or a "running tally" of judgments (Greene 1999; Huddy, Mason, and Aarøe 2015). In their influential book *Partisan Hearts and Minds,* Green and colleagues (2002) argue that partisanship is a product of the association of social groups with parties – union members are Democrats, business people are Republican, and so on. Similarly, religion (Layman 1997), gender (Gidengil et al. 2005), immigrant status (DeSipio and Uhlaner 2007), class (Evens 2000), and attitudes toward various social groups play an important role in vote choice. In fact, Achen and Bartels (2016) argue that the influence of social groups on vote choice is so dominant that it is a defining feature of elections in modern democracies.

Voters draw on their attitudes toward social groups when they assess candidates – that is, the candidate's membership in a social group allows citizens to express their attitudes toward that group by supporting or opposing the candidate (Campbell et al. 1960; Achen and Bartels 2016). In turn, people's opinions of candidates are affected by attitudes toward the social groups to which the candidate belongs. In addition, the inclusion of a candidate with a particular social-group membership makes the presence of that group in the electoral coalition more difficult to ignore. The salience of a social group in politics and the strength of identification with that group are crucial determinants of the group's influence on political decisions (Campbell et al. 1960; Junn and Masuoka 2008).

Coethnic Affinity Voting

A candidate's social-group membership affects political decisions because it influences attitudes among voters of the same ethnicity. While *affinity* can be generally defined as liking or attraction, the focus here is on affinity voting, which can stem from gender (Dolan 2008; Goodyear-Grant and Croskill 2011), age (Sigelman and Sigelman 1982), geography, language, or religion (Cutler 2002), but by far the most common claims are about race and ethnicity. Early American studies on racial affinity (which looked at black candidates and voters) found supporting evidence in experimental analysis (Sigelman and Sigelman 1982; Piliavin 1987), survey data (Sigelman and Welch 1984), and aggregate data (Karnig and Welch 1980). Block-voting analysis rooted in redistricting discrimination court cases usually focuses on white voting against minority candidates, but it also demonstrates block voting among black and Latino voters who support candidates of their own ethnic group (Barreto 2007). More recent experimental data has also confirmed these dynamics (Philpot and Walton 2007; McDermott 1998). All else being equal, black voters are much more likely to support a black candidate than a white candidate.

Studies of American Latinos show similar results: Latino voters are also more likely to support Latino candidates than white candidates (Barreto 2007, 2010; McConnaughy et al. 2010; Manzano and Sanchez 2010; Stokes-Brown

2006). These effects may be quite strong. For example, as noted in the Introduction, in an analysis of real election data (rather than experimental or survey evidence), Barreto (2007) found that Latino candidates received between 75 and 90 percent of the Latino vote, regardless of whether the Latino candidate was Republican or Democrat.

Outside the United States, a study by Fisher and colleagues (2015) pairs data from the Ethnic Minority British Election Study with candidates in the 2011 British Election. Although the authors found that Pakistani voters were more likely to support Pakistani candidates, there was no evidence for coethnic affinity among black or Asian voters. In similar designs, during the 2014 Toronto municipal election, racialized voters during the election were more likely to support Olivia Chow, the Chinese-origin candidate (Bird et al. 2015), and racialized city councillors (McGregor et al. 2017). In addition, using fictional candidate experiments, Bird (2015) and Goodyear-Grant and Tolley (2017) found affinity voting for South Asian and Chinese candidates, respectively. British and Canadian data support the general conclusion of research on affinity voting, as well as voting literature more generally: voters are more likely to support candidates from their own ethnic or racial groups.

Explaining Coethnic Affinity

Explanations for coethnic affinity voting fall into two categories: interest-based or identity-based. The key difference between the two explanations is the original causal impetus they describe – the core motivation – which can produce affinity voting through a number of different mechanisms.

INTEREST-BASED EXPLANATIONS

Unfortunately, most of the research on coethnic affinity voting demonstrates that it exists, but it does not investigate its causes. Often, this means simply suggesting that voters are drawn to candidates who are like themselves (Sigelman and Sigelman 1982; Sigelman and Welch 1984) but failing to state the reasons why. Other studies suggest either that the politicization of race increases affinity effects or that the effects are driven by policy goals, but the mechanisms underlying these explanations rarely receive careful empirical testing (e.g., Philpot and Walton 2007; Stokes-Brown 2006; Sigelman and Sigelman 1982). For instance, Stokes-Brown (2006, 631) argues that "racial self-identification may affect cost-benefit calculations" but does not test that explanation.

While interest-based explanations can manifest in a number of different forms, the assumed motivation is simple – utility maximization – and the proposed psychological process is relatively rational and cognitive. Here, I consider three interest-based explanations of how voter and candidate ethnicity can be linked to vote choice: policy stereotyping, ideological stereotyping, and general group interest. The policy stereotyping argument suggests that candidate ethnicity is a mental shortcut for finding out information about candidates' positions on specific issues. In other words, ethnic-minority voters might assume that ethnic-minority candidates are more likely to support immigration, adopt antiracist policies, or support welfare programs. Thus, similarities in demographics are – in the mind of the voter – a good indication of similarity in policy opinions. Voters may use a candidate's ethnicity as a heuristic for their position on these policies, making them more likely to support racialized candidates.

Another interest-based explanation for affinity voting is ideological stereotyping, of which there are two versions: racialized candidates are seen either as left-leaning or as ideologically "closer" to the racialized voter. While ideological effects do not reflect self-interest in a narrow sense (Chong, Citrin, and Conley 2001), ideological stereotyping is classified as an interest-based mechanism here since it is a relatively conscious, utility-maximizing strategy. This classification is consistent with how ideology is defined in the literature on rational choice and spatial voting. Broadly speaking, citizens have policy goals, but the high cost of being fully informed makes the vote choice difficult. Ideology helps solve this difficulty. As Downs (1957, 98) argues, "a voter finds party ideologies useful because they remove the necessity of relating every issue to their own philosophy ... with this shortcut a voter can save himself the cost of being informed upon a wider range of issues." Of course, even in the rational-choice literature, a one-dimensional, left-right spectrum is not the only plausible construction of ideology (e.g., Enelow and Hinich 1982). In Canada, the place of francophones and Quebec complicate the role of standard left-right ideology in politics (Johnston et al. 1992; Johnston 2008). Nonetheless, it is reasonable to assume that the left-right spectrum is a widely held conception of ideology, encompassing most economic and social issues.

One influential study suggests that left-leaning ideological stereotyping drives affinity voting. McDermott (1998) argues that black candidates and female candidates are ideologically stereotyped. When stereotypes of candidates and the opinions of voters match – for example, when female candidates are stereotyped as left-leaning and female voters are also left-leaning – the result is demographic affinity. Using a survey experiment that manipulated the gender and race of hypothetical candidates, McDermott (1998) found that self-reported ideology influences vote choice, even when controlling for attitudes toward gender and race. Specifically, female and black respondents were more likely to support female and black candidates, respectively, even when controlling for attitudes toward those specific attributes (i.e., attitudes toward women and blacks). As a result, McDermott argues that racial and gender affinity must stem from the ideological stereotyping of the candidates.

Unfortunately, the category used to measure ideology in McDermott's (1998) study was "liberal" for female candidates but "do more for Blacks" for black candidates. It is not clear that black voters supporting a candidate because he or she will "do more for blacks" reflects ideology, broadly defined. It might very well be a measure of general group interest or symbolic attitudes. Still, ideological stereotyping is a plausible explanation for affinity voting, and it does hold for women candidates. Certainly, it is very possible that racialized candidates are stereotyped as left-leaning (Sigelman et al. 1995; Jones 2014; though see Weaver 2012), but McDermott's study does not provide clear evidence on that point.

If black and Latino candidates are stereotyped as left-leaning in the United States, can the same be said of racialized candidates in Canada? While there is no research addressing this question directly, there are long-standing associations between the Left and diversity and welfare issues, both of which are often linked to race. Left-wing parties, and the Liberal Party of Canada in particular, are clearly associated with diversity and multiculturalism. More insidiously, racialized minorities are commonly associated with welfare and government assistance in the public mind (e.g., Bobo and Kluegel 1993; Gilens 1996, Winter 2008). While there is less evidence of this kind of stereotyping in Canada (though see Harell, Soroka, and Ladner 2013 on Indigenous people and welfare), it is plausible that the same associations exist. Certainly, visible minorities tend to support the Liberal Party (Bilodeau and Kanji 2010; Blais 2005) and, in fact, ethnic minorities are reported to support parties of the Left in countries around the world (Bergh and Bjørklund 2011). There is also evidence that racialized Canadians hold left-wing policy opinions, particularly on redistribution and minority rights, though less so on social questions, such as gay marriage and the role of women (Soroka, Johnston, and Banting 2008; Soroka et al. 2013).

The argument can also be made from the other direction – that is, parties of the Right are associated with opposition to diversity and multicultural-ism, both globally and in Canada. While the Conservative Party of Canada under Stephen Harper did not reject official multiculturalism (though some argue it did attempt to reform its meaning; see Abu-Laban 2014), previous incarnations of the party did. The Reform Party included the repeal of the Multiculturalism Act as part of its party platform, and a survey of Reform Party activists found that 96.8 percent disagreed with the statement "the federal government should increase its efforts to further multiculturalism" (Archer and Ellis 1994). Indeed, Jenkins (2002) argues that anti-minority and anti-immigration attitudes played a major role in increasing support for the Reform Party in the 1993 election to the extent that, nearing the end of the campaign, they were nearly as influential as attitudes about the welfare state. While the position of the Conservative Party of Canada is certainly quite different from that of the Reform Party, it would not be surprising if this history continued to inform the party's image. Certainly, partisans of the Left continue to be more positive toward diversity, as 2.1 illustrates. According to the 2011 Canadian Election Study, only 22 percent of Con-servative Party identifiers believed that more should be done for racial min-orities, as compared to 35 percent of Liberal Party identifiers and 47 percent of New Democratic Party identifiers. Of course, the association of minor-ities with the Liberal Party in Canada is probably weaker than the associa-tion of African Americans with the Democratic Party in the United States. Still, there are plausible reasons to think that, in Canada, racialized candi-dates are likely to be stereotyped as left-leaning and that racialized citizens are also likely to be left-leaning in their political ideology.

TABLE 2.1

"How much should be done for racial minorities?," by partisan identification

	More (%)	Less (%)
NDP	47	9
Liberal	36	11
Conservative	22	21

NOTES: Cell entries are percentages of total respondents, and percentages are rounded. Categories combine "Much/Somewhat More" and "Much/Somewhat Less"; other responses not included.
SOURCE: 2011 Canadian Election Study.

General group interest, the third mechanism for interest-based motivations, refers to when voters think a candidate of their own ethnic group will act in their best interests in some diffuse, nonspecific way. There is little research that examines a direct link between interests and coethnic affinity voting – perhaps the only example is Goodyear-Grant and Tolley (2017). Drawing on realistic group conflict theory and group threat theory, they suggest that coethnic voting should be higher among voters whose ethnic group makes up a smaller portion of their neighbourhood, or who have lower income than others in the area. In fact, that turns out not to be the case: there is no evidence that coethnic voting is conditional on economic or cultural threat.

Most research in this area suggests that interests and coethnic voting are connected, but less directly. Perhaps the most influential account of this kind is group-consciousness theory, which suggests that group identity must be politicized to have an effect on political behaviour (Verba and Nie 1972; Miller et al. 1981; for reviews, see Chong and Rogers 2005; McClain et al. 2009). The related theory of linked fate emphasizes that when voters believe their fate is linked to the fate of the group, as a result of discrimination and oppression, they are more likely to act in the group's interest (Dawson 1994; McClain et al. 2009). Most notably, McConnaughy and colleagues' (2010) interest-based heuristic account holds that Latino ethnicity is a cue that communicates that the candidate will take policy positions that benefit the ethnic group, thus leading to coethnic voting. In testing the role of interests, they use a measure of linked fate. This is a measure that asks respondents if they believe that what happens to Latinos in the country as a whole has something to do with what happens in their own lives. In contrast to the null effect of identity, linked fate is strongly correlated with voting for the Latino candidate.

How exactly should we interpret the results of studies on group consciousness and linked fate? A close examination of the literature leads to two conclusions: 1) interests are the primary motivation for action in group-consciousness theory, and 2) a major concern of group-consciousness theory is how identity is linked to politics. The latter is significant when explaining political participation but less so when applied to affinity voting. First, what does it mean when group interests or group consciousness affects a person's behaviour? Early research on group consciousness examined its effect on political participation and supported the argument that group identity needs to be transformed into group consciousness. The paradigmatic case was

African American participation, which was substantially higher than socio-economic status would predict (Verba and Nie 1972; Olsen 1970; Shingles 1981). In a particularly influential piece, Miller and colleagues (1981) argued that the effect of group identity on political participation required the presence of multiple factors, including system blame, dissatisfaction with the group's position, and polar affect (in-group preference and out-group hostility). Simply identifying with a group, such as identifying as African American, should have little effect on political participation. Since then, most research on group consciousness has similarly emphasized the requirement of a combination of factors, usually identity, group deprivation, and belief in collective action (e.g., Chong and Rogers 2005; Lien 1994; McClain et al. 2009; Sanchez and Vargas 2016).[2] The general argument has been that group identity alone should have no impact on politics; some combination of conditions is required.

In group consciousness theory the motivation of inequality is group specific: rather than being an effect of a general attitude of opposition to inequality, it is a reaction to one's own group being disadvantaged. That is, the voter is motivated to reduce inequality (deprivation) because it applies to the group (group identification). Put another way, identification determines who is affected; inequality or deprivation determines why they take action.

Although the motivating factor of inequality or deprivation is not precisely or narrowly defined, most research on group consciousness and linked fate refers to an interest-based motivation. Michael Dawson's *Behind the Mule: Race and Class in African American Politics* (1994) is perhaps the most influential study and presents a theoretically developed account that explicitly argues that consciousness is rooted in utility maximization; in fact, Dawson (1994, 64) formalized this theory with a rational choice analysis.[3] In addition, Miller and colleagues (1981, 495) note that group consciousness is described in Marxist terms, that "fundamental differences exist between the interests of one's own group and those of the dominant group." Lien (1994, 364) says group consciousness requires a belief about one's "own ethnic group getting fewer opportunities than most Americans." Lee (2008, 442) refers to "the belief in shared interests, in-group favoritism, the sense of relative deprivation, and the systemic attribution of blame for unequal opportunities and outcomes," while Wong, Lien, and Conway (2005, 547) describe group consciousness as relating to "deprived group position." McConnaughy and colleagues (2010, 1201) note that the coethnic candidate will "represent the interests of their ethnic group." These definitions all make clear the important role that interests play in in-group consciousness.

Some research on group consciousness cites a generalized concern for status or standing rather than more concrete interests. Notably, Chong and Rogers say group identity requires beliefs about the "group's status" (2005, 350), while McClain and colleagues refer to the "group's social standing" (McClain et al. 2009, 476). This connection to group status complicates matters somewhat. The first issue is that social-identity theory and group-consciousness theory point to quite different status effects. Social-identity theory suggests that all people are intrinsically motivated to maintain positive group status. Status differences matter, but the effects on behaviour are not straightforward. Most notably, low group status might reduce identification (exiting the group) rather than motivating action to improve group status, while high-status groups are especially likely to show effects of identity such as in-group bias (Tajfel and Turner 1979). Group-consciousness theory says precisely the opposite: it applies primarily to low-status groups, and there are no effects on high-status groups, such as white people or businessmen (Miller et al. 1981; see also Sanchez and Vargas 2016).[4]

A second issue related to group status is the question of what, precisely, it refers to. Is the effect being examined the result of differences in symbolic group status or more concrete differences?[5] In social identity theory, concrete inequality, such as differences in income, might signal status, but it is not the direct cause nor is it necessary to affect behaviour. Group-consciousness theory is ambiguous on this point: it is unclear about symbolic versus material definitions of status. Of course, both might be at play, but there is little, if any, theorizing about status, and there has been no empirical investigation into which one matters (or if one matters more). Nonetheless, it should be noted that group-consciousness theory does not deny the existence of symbolic identity or status effects, even if it does emphasize more concrete interests. Since group-consciousness theory explicitly rejects the possibility of identity alone and does seem to include factors related to interest (income, discrimination, etc.), I consider it an interest-based theory.

Returning to the role of identity, since proponents of group-consciousness theory argue that identity is not enough to affect participation, should this argument apply to affinity voting?[6] Perhaps not. The first wave of group-consciousness research focused on political participation, and it was not obvious why identifying as black should lead to participation in an election dominated by white candidates. Rather, the crucial requirement is a *politicized* group identity in the sense that the relationship between the identity and politics needs to be established by some mechanism. This issue can be framed in various ways in different theoretical paradigms: in the terms of group-consciousness theory, identity needs to be politicized. In the framework used by the American Voter, identity needs to be relevant to the political question at hand (Campbell et al. 1960). In the terminology of social-identity theory (Tajfel 1981), there needs to be some reason why people identify as members of the relevant ethnic identity while making a political choice. These are all restatements of the same point: identity must be linked to politics to have an effect (Lee 2008).

When it comes to affinity voting, the link between identity and political behaviour is direct: if a candidate of that ethnic group is running in the election, the candidate links the identity to politics. Junn and Masuoka (2008), for example, found that showing Asian American respondents an Asian American candidate makes them more likely to say that being Asian American is important to their ideas about politics. In other words, the mere presence of the candidate makes the identity relevant to politics. Of course, there are multiple identities that a candidate could invoke and multiple routes by which that identity could affect behaviour. Nonetheless, the salience or politicization of an identity or its relevance to a political choice is no great mystery when one of the options is literally a candidate of that identity group. After all, no one is surprised when a Republican Party identity affects vote choice for a Republican candidate: the candidate's membership in the identity group is what links the identity to the behaviour. The result is that the various factors that group-consciousness theory proposes (system blame, dissatisfaction with group position, beliefs about collective action, and so on) might not be necessary for affinity voting. To be clear, it is certainly possible that these factors would lead to stronger effects of identity, but there is no reason that they should be a necessary condition. Arguments in group-consciousness research about the insufficiency of group identity alone may not apply to affinity voting because the presence of the candidates alone links identity to politics.

IDENTITY-BASED EXPLANATIONS

Contrary to interest-based motivations – which involve relatively conscious, rational, utility-maximizing behaviours – identity-based motivations are generally driven by in-group bias and the desire for positive group attributions.

The key theoretical framework to describe this type of motivation is social-identity theory, which posits that a need for self-esteem leads to positive in-group bias. This might affect candidate choice in a number of different ways, perhaps directly through in-group favouritism but also in other ways such as perception of candidate attributes, persuasion effects, and expressive voting.

Social identity theory provides an important account of how, and why, individuals react to attributions of social groups. It suggests that group relations are rooted in self-esteem and a desire for positive self-attribution. Henri Tajfel (1981) argued that group identities are incorporated into group members' self-concepts, meaning that the group becomes part of their self-identity. When the social group is salient, the result is depersonalization – a switch to a group level of self-categorization in which self and others are seen in terms of group identities. The status of the group then affects the status of the individual. As Tajfel (1981, 45) puts it, this shift affects our actions and opinions "based on the simple motivational assumption that individuals prefer a positive to a negative self-image." Because group attributes become attached to our self-identities, our desire for positive self-image leads to a demand for positive attributions for the group. A host of implications result from this simple mechanism but, for our purposes, in-group bias is the most important.

Simply put, in-group bias means we will have a positive bias toward our group and toward other members of our group. This was a central tenet of Tajfel's original work (Tajfel et al. 1971) and has since been widely confirmed (Mullen et al. 1992; Rubin and Hewstone 1998; Aberson et al. 2000). This bias can take many forms, including attribution of group traits, such as rating members of one's own group higher on measures such as trustworthiness, friendliness, and cooperativeness (Brewer and Silver 1978). In-group bias can also affect evaluations of particular circumstances, such as the performance of a task, or produce differential behaviour toward in-group and out-group targets, such as the distribution of rewards (Tajfel 1981).

One important explanation for in-group bias is the need for positive self-esteem – that is, our evaluations of members of our groups are biased because we desire positive evaluations of our own group (Hogg and Abrams 1990). The evidence for this mechanism is mixed (Long and Spears 1997). However, Stets and Burke (2000) point out that measuring self-esteem requires respondents to express it, such as answering questions about how they evaluate themselves. Yet these very questions fortify the respondents' level of self-esteem, leading to difficulties in manipulating it. This leads to a sort of Heisenberg uncertainty principle problem where we can't know a respondent's self-esteem without negating its effect on in-group bias. Thus, Burke and Stets (2009) suggest these null findings are simply an issue of measurement error. Alternative explanations have been suggested, such as identity verification (Burke and Stets 2009) and optimal distinctiveness theory (Brewer 2003). Optimal distinctiveness theory is rooted in evolutionary theory and suggests that people have competing drives for both inclusion and distinctiveness. As a result, people are motivated to differentiate their in-group from out-groups, but they also avoid being "too" different (Brewer 2003). These different mechanisms are important for potential measurements and treatments, such as self-esteem as a mediating or dependent variable or threats to self-esteem as a treatment. Nonetheless, the central insight – that group identification leads to in-group bias – remains intact.

Minorities tend to show especially large effects of in-group bias because the salience and relative size of groups influence the degree of in-group bias. The heightened salience of the group increases not only the level of in-group bias displayed but also the distance between perceived positions (Allen and Stephenson 1983). The literal relative size of the groups – that one group is simply smaller than the other – also increases in-group bias. Mullen and colleagues (1992) describe this as a salience effect, though it can also be conceptualized as a product of normalization: larger groups are normalized, and smaller groups tend to be noticed since they differ from the norm. In a sense, only the minority is recognized as being a distinct group. Since numerically smaller groups are more likely to be noticed by their members, and therefore to be salient in decision processes, they tend to exhibit more in-group bias. Therefore, in-group bias is particularly important among minority voters, and affinity effects may be higher for candidates of minority ethnicities. To be clear, in-group bias is not based on race or ethnicity – people of European origin are no less prone to it. Rather, any numerical minority, however defined, tends to be seen as unusual and noticed more and therefore shows greater in-group bias.

There are a number of different mechanisms through which in-group bias might lead to coethnic affinity voting. The most obvious is straightforward in-group favouritism. The link between group attributions and self-esteem means that victories are shared victories and losses are shared losses. For example, partisan identifiers are more likely to volunteer and donate when their party is threatened with losses (Huddy, Mason, and Aarøe 2015; Rogers and Moore 2015). Barreto (2010) also alludes to a similar phenomenon in suggesting that Latino voters will be especially excited about the election of a Latin candidate. A candidate winning or losing is a positive or negative attribution for their group. Simply put, voters support candidates of their own ethnic group because they want them to win (or not lose) because their success reflects on them as fellow in-group members.

A slightly different version of this mechanism may be desire for symbolic representation – that is, not just a desire to win the election but a desire for representation in government. The goal is not policy change or influence but rather the purely symbolic value of representation. This mechanism has been suggested by some theorists (Philips 1995; Mansbridge 1999), though empirical investigations of the influence of symbolic representation on participation reveal only mixed support (Wolbrecht and Campbell 2007; Gay 2001; Lawless 2004; Pantoja and Segura 2003; Rocha et al. 2010; Fraga 2016; Merolla, Sellers, and Fowler 2013). Interestingly, there is evidence that evaluation of the political system improves because of symbolic representation (Verge 2015). While there is little research on the effect of desire for symbolic representation on affinity voting, Bird (2015) does report it as a theme emerging from focus-group discussions. In any case, having group members hold positions of power and influence is a sign of achievement and success, which is a shared achievement, just like an electoral victory.

A second mechanism for identity-based affinity voting is bias in perceived candidate attributes. In-group bias makes it more likely that candidates of the same ethnic group will be evaluated more positively on their personal attributes, such as honesty or being hard-working. In part, this mechanism is a simple process of stereotyping by which perceived attributes of the group are applied to an individual (i.e., Taylor 1981). In-group bias leads to positive stereotyping of in-group candidates. Naturally, positive candidate attributes increase the likelihood of support (Stokes 1966; Bittner 2011). The causal route here could be complex: perhaps the desire for in-group candidates to win motivates both candidate support and bias in perceived candidate attributes, or perhaps they are mutually reinforcing. In either case, the basic cause is a desire for positive group attributions, which affect attitudes and behaviour toward the in-group candidate.

This mechanism raises some questions about categorization: is it an interest or an identity effect? Having an honest and hard-working candidate might be seen as a kind of interest, while identity shapes perceptions of which candidates are honest and hard-working. On the other hand, the voter would not necessarily have a rational, conscious opinion that all in-group members work harder (for example). Moreover, these candidates are in the voter's interest, but having a good candidate is in everyone's interest – that is, these are valence issues rather than group-related interests. While interests and identities could interact in complex ways, in my view, what is distinctively important about these identity effects from candidates is that they are rooted in ethnic self-identity.

A third identity-based motivation may be persuasion effects. In general, the source of a message affects its persuasiveness (Pornpitakpan 2004; Petty and Cacioppo 1986), which is a crucial point given the lack of credibility and trust in most politicians. The need to persuade is one reason why political advertisements often feature quotes from newspapers or third-party endorsements (Garramone 1985).

Since candidates of one's own ethnic group may have greater source credibility, their messages should therefore be more persuasive. Some research suggests that demographic matching – gender, age, or race similarity, for example – makes the source more convincing. Most of the research comes from consumer behaviour studies. For example, if the race or ethnicity of the source of an advertising message (e.g., the actor in a televised advertisement) is the same as the recipient's, the product is likely to be viewed more favourably than those with mismatching sources (Grier and Deshpandé 2001). Similarly, minority respondents are more likely to view a minority spokesperson in an ad as trustworthy, and this trustworthiness is transferred to the brand (Deshpandé and Stayman 1994).

A related, but slightly different, effect is that demographic matches function as cognitive filters: they cue that the information in a message is important, resulting in the message receiving greater attention and consideration by the consumer (Wheeler, Petty, and Bizer 2005). If voters pay more attention to campaign messages from candidates of their own ethnic group, they are more likely to be persuaded to vote for them. Given that politics is a relatively low-information environment, having voters pay more attention to campaign messages from candidates of their own ethnocultural group may lead to substantial effects on voter behaviour.

Finally, expressive voting mechanisms may lead to affinity voting because they transform vote choice into a way to express and confirm one's own identity. Schuessler (2000, 88) states that "for expressive voters, voting is a means to express political beliefs and preferences and, in doing so, to establish or reaffirm their own political identity." Expressing preferences, by supporting a candidate, for example, is a way to establish and affirm a person's identity. There is support for this idea in studies of expressive voting grounded in rational choice theory and in the literature on ethnic parties. Unlike in-group bias, expressive voting is motivated by the utility of expressing an identity (that is, voting) rather than a desire to influence the outcome of the election.

Perhaps surprisingly, the theory of expressive voting was developed by rational choice theorists, who proposed that expressing one's identity has value apart from more concrete interests (Buchanan 1954; Brennan and Buchanan 1984; Brennan and Lomasky 1997; for a recent review, see Hamlin and Jennings 2011). Voting is "booing and cheering," which leads citizens to participate in electoral politics even though they are unlikely to affect the outcome of the election. Thus, casting ballots for or against presidential candidates has utility beyond the duty to participate, despite the low likelihood of affecting the outcome (Kan and Yang 2001). Similarly, a citizen's desire to show solidarity with her community may mean that supporting community grants is worth more to her than the grants' monetary value (Jones and Soguel 2010). One experimental study investigated the conditions under which expressive voting is likely and found that expressive voting increases as the likelihood of being the pivotal voter decreases (Fischer 1996). Given the very small chance of being pivotal, expressive voting is highly likely. While the empirical evidence is limited, the theoretical contribution is clear: expressive voting may be a way of expressing identity, belonging, and membership, and it therefore may well have independent value to citizens.

Scholars of ethnic conflict have also investigated expressive voting as a way to register ethnic identities. The most prominent early study in this area, by Donald Horowitz, argues that expressive voting is especially prevalent in ethnically divided countries. He refers to it as a primordial product of an emotional attachment to the ethnic group. Voting is a way to express one's loyalty and membership to an ethnic group. Elections, therefore, are a kind of head-counting exercise (Horowitz 1985). Following Horowitz, there are a number of studies that focus on expressive voting in African elections (Ferree 2006; Ferree and Horowitz 2007; Mattes 1995).

These studies, unfortunately, do not observe expressive- or identity-based motivations directly; rather, these motivations are often assumed in the absence of plausible instrumental explanations. Moreover, the widespread presence of ethnic parties complicates comparisons with voting in Western democracies. While the evidence is certainly limited, this research suggests that expressing one's ethnic identity and group membership by voting for coethnic candidates is, at least, a theoretically plausible mechanism through which ethnicity influences vote choice.

To sum up the three identity-based mechanisms examined here, in-group bias may directly motivate voters to support candidates of the same group, or it may affect their perceptions of candidate attributes, since members of one's own ethnic group are perceived as more honest than others, to give one example. The campaign message of a candidate of the same ethnic group may also be more persuasive, since a member of the same ethnic group may be a more credible message source, and people pay more attention to demographically matching message sources. Finally, the concept of expressive voting suggests that citizens often vote not for policy reasons but as a way of expressing their identities and loyalties – in this case, their membership in the ethnic group.

However, there is little research that tests identity-based explanations for coethnic affinity voting. This is somewhat surprising, given the significant literature on in-group bias and persuasion effects in social psychology. Recall that the theory of group consciousness includes identity but holds that identity has no direct effect on its own. McConnaughy and colleagues (2010) do explicitly discuss and test the effect of identity on affinity voting, but argue instead that interests cause Latino affinity effects. Consistent with group-consciousness theory, they suggest that there will be "no direct connection between group membership and collective action" (McConnaughy et al. 2010, 1202), and they find that identification has no relationship to the likelihood of supporting a Latino candidate. However, the measure of identity they use is a scale that includes items such as speaking Spanish and having Latino friends. Thus, the scale includes a number of items describing a person's objective social position or behaviour rather than actual self-identification. Barreto (2010, especially 74) also argues that ethnic identity is responsible for affinity voting but uses questions that resemble Miller's (1981) group-consciousness factors: Latino underrepresentation, mentioning an ethnic theme as the most important issue, and feeling that Latinos have too little power. Fisher and colleagues (2015, 983, note 77) found coethnic voting in Britain, but no interaction with identity; however, they used a relative measure of identity (ethnic versus British) rather than direct ethnic self-identification. This is a problem because the question does not line up with the theory: not only might people have both strong British and ethnic identities, but the measure also conflates having a British identity with the white candidate. Still, it is striking that Fisher (2015) and McConnaughy and colleagues (2010) found no relationship between identity and affinity voting.

To conclude, identity-based motivations could produce coethnic affinity voting through a series of different mechanisms, including general group interest, ideological stereotyping, and policy attitudes. Nearly all the research to date uses theoretical explanations that are interest-based – but few test mechanisms directly. One variable often used is linked fate. While this measure is certainly a good predictor of coethnic affinity voting, it is unclear whether the measure is about interests or identity. Another interest-based explanation, ideological stereotyping, examined by McDermott (1998), is certainly plausible. However, the questions used to tap ideology could easily be interpreted as being about group interest. While policy-based heuristics are sometimes suggested, there is no research that actually tests this explanation. Finally, social-identity theory provides good theoretical reasons to expect voters to support candidates of the same ethnicity, including the direct effect of in-group favouritism, the role of credible sources in persuasion effects, and expressive voting. While a few studies explicitly examine the role of identity as a direct cause of affinity voting, they have found mixed results, and none use a direct measure of identity. Although coethnic affinity voting is well established, at least for black and Latino Americans, its causes need further investigation.

Racialized Affinity and Conflict

So far, most of the research discussed here has looked at coethnic affinity. But what about racialized affinity voting? For most racialized groups around the world, there is little solid information on inter-minority political relations. The little there is suggests, at least at first glance, that racialized affinity voting is unlikely. Most research in this area focuses on the United States, often in the study of urban politics, where researchers such as Browning, Marshall, and Tabb (1984) found little cooperation between blacks and Latinos. Meier and Stewart (1991) report similar findings in school district elections. The general finding is that black-Latino conflict, not cooperation, is the norm (Kaufmann 2003; Bobo et al. 1996; Johnson and Oliver 1989; Tedin and Murray 1994). On the other hand, this evidence of inter-minority conflict depends how we define groups – Latino and Asian Americans in particular are superordinate groups of a kind, composed of multiple nationalities (Junn and Masuoka 2008; Masuoka 2006), and there is certainly evidence of affinity voting among these groups.

In addition to political research, there is also sociological and attitudinal research on relationships among minority groups. In general, ethnic minorities tend to rate whites more highly than other ethnic-minority communities on positive attributes (honest, hard-working, etc.) and on closeness to their own group (Berry and Kalin 1979; Kalin and Berry 1996).[7] Similarly, minority groups prefer to maintain greater social distance (e.g., having members of a group as coworkers or neighbours) from one another than they do from the dominant majority (Hagendoorn et al. 1998; Poppe and Hagendoorn 2003). Given that we have good reason to think that generalized group affect will have an impact on political choices, this pattern of group preferences is important. Overall, the predominant finding of current research supports the presence of interminority conflict rather than cooperation.

Nonetheless, for a number of reasons, the prognosis of rainbow coalitions is not so grim as it might seem at first. The research on explicitly political interminority relations is essentially limited to the study of one pair of minorities: blacks and Latino Americans. Given the historical context and particular features of these two minority groups – particularity the unique black American experience and the potential differences between immigrant and nonimmigrant minorities – these dynamics may not be fully generalizable. Waters and Kasinitz (2012, 127), for example, argue that there are important differences between the experience of immigrant and nonimmigrant minorities. Moreover, even the children of immigrants do not bear the "scars and handicaps of a history of exclusion" the way that African Americans do.

In addition, there are at least some findings of cooperation between these and other ethnic groups in the United States (Browning et al. 1990; Saito 1998; Tedin and Murray 1994). There appears to be some cooperation between Asians and Latinos in Los Angeles (Saito 1998) and between blacks and Latinos in Denver (Kaufmann 2003) and Chicago (Torres 1988). One powerful, real-world demonstration of political cooperation between ethnic groups was the widespread support Barack Obama received from both Latino and Asian Americans (Minushkin and Lopez 2008; Pew Research Center 2009). While the cause of this support was not necessarily Obama's status as a fellow member of a minority group, his race was clearly not a serious barrier for many Latinos and Asian Americans. Thus, although racialized affinity voting is not the predominant finding, there are reasons to think that affinity voting for different racialized groups, and therefore rainbow coalitions, may emerge under the right circumstances.

Finally, we should consider the degree to which there is affinity voting between national groups. While not racialized affinity, as defined above, these panethnic groups are still superordinate groups. Junn and Masuoka (2008), for example, found that showing respondents an Asian American candidate leads to stronger Asian American identity among respondents with diverse (Asian) countries of origin. Similarly, Latino voters with different national identities are likely to support Latino candidates despite different national origins (Sanchez 2008). If superordinate group identities can be constructed at the ethnic group level to include multiple nationalities, the same process might occur at the more general racialized group level.

INTEREST-BASED THEORIES

While theoretical conclusions about coethnic affinity voting are relatively straightforward, the situation becomes considerably more complex when we consider ethnically diverse minority populations. The explanations for co-ethnic affinity require empirical testing, but the theoretical implications are simple: all of the mechanisms discussed above lead to coethnic affinity voting. Conversely, when the candidate and voter are racialized but of different ethnicities, the implications are less clear.

Two of the previously discussed interest-based explanations, ideological stereotyping and policy heuristics, ought to function in more or less the same way for racialized affinity voting as they do for coethnic affinity voting. If all racialized candidates are ideologically stereotyped as left-leaning, this would suggest racialized affinity rather than discrimination. While it is possible that some ethnic groups will be stereotyped differently on different issues. An Arab candidate, for example, might be stereotyped as being socially conservative and a Korean candidate socially liberal, but there is no evidence to suggest this is the case. More generally, on immigration and antiracism positions, policy heuristics are likely to be similar. Therefore, if racialized voters make use of specific policy heuristics or ideologically stereotype racialized candidates, the result may be racialized affinity voting.

Notably, a slightly different version of ideological stereotyping might produce different results. Racialized candidates might be ideologically stereotyped not as left-leaning but as ideologically closer, or more similar, to whatever ideological position the racialized voter takes. Fusing ideological stereotypes with a version of in-group bias; the racialized candidate is perceived as ideologically similar precisely because she or he is a member of the in-group. However, as discussed in Chapter 1, we should be careful about assuming that voters see candidates of other racialized ethnic groups as in-group members – they might well see those candidates and white candidates as out-group members. Even if there is a broader racialized identity, racial-ized affinity voting ought to show weaker effects than coethnic affinity voting. If the logic of demographic heuristics is that candidates that are demograph-ically similar are likely to have similar policies, then degrees of similarity ought to matter. Thus, the affinity effects for a candidate of the same ethni-city as the voter are likely to be stronger than for a racialized candidate who does not share the voter's ethnicity. Of course, this racialized affinity voting relies on the construction of racialized identity – but it is a construction that may well be prevalent.

A different type of interest-based explanation, generalized group interest, may depend on intergroup relations and, therefore, the economic and social context. Perhaps the most important theory of intergroup relations in this area is realistic conflict theory. This theory explains intergroup conflict as a result of the external situation and context rather than in terms of psycho-logical attitudes, group identities, or self-esteem. Specifically, intergroup conflict stems from competition (Sherif 1966). If ethnic groups compete for economic or government resources, then voters are likely to perceive candi-dates of other ethnic groups as not likely to act in their interests. Therefore, we could expect discrimination rather than racialized affinity voting.

In general, competition effects increase with lower income, residential proximity, greater inequality between groups, and competition over gov-ernment resources. Therefore, these factors should be associated with lower levels of racialized affinity, if not outright conflict. For example, Gay (2006) found that economic disparity is related to interminority conflict, which can be caused by two factors: a sense of competition (heightened by lack of re-sources) and a more general distrust and cynicism (linked to economic hard-ship). Bobo and Hutchings (1996) suggest that perceptions of zero-sum competition lead to greater conflict between minority groups. Similarly, Meier and colleagues (2004) found competition between blacks and Latinos in zero-sum political competitions but no competition when the situations were not zero-sum. Thus, they suggest that it is scarcity that drives competi-tion between these minority groups.

On the other hand, research shows that residential diversity actually re-duces interminority conflict and perceptions of threat (Oliver and Wong 2003). We might expect that local diversity means local competition, for jobs and other resources, among members of different ethnic groups, but this may not be the case. Alternatively, the effects of competition may simply be overridden by the effects of contact – this would be consistent with evidence that local racial diversity promotes tolerance and trust (e.g., Allport 1954; Marschall and Stolle 2004).

In sum, there are theoretical reasons and some evidence to expect that competition leads to increased conflict between ethnic minorities. Certainly, it is unlikely that competition leads to cooperation. Given this, racialized affinity voting is most likely to emerge when competition between minority groups is low, when there is residential diversity, when incomes are relatively high, and when inequality between groups is low.

IDENTITY-BASED THEORIES

If we shift the focus to identity motivations, there are two mechanisms that may impact racialized affinity voting. What I term *motivated social positioning* refers to the desire for positive group attributions among ethnic minorities, which may lead them to support white candidates and discriminate against other minority candidates. Conversely, identification with a more general racialized or ethnic-minority social group would lead to racialized affinity voting through the same mechanisms as coethnic affinity voting.

Motivated social positioning offers a novel psychological explanation for a lack of racialized affinity, or even conflict, between minority ethnic groups. Recall that Hagendoorn's studies in Europe and Berry and Kalin's studies in Canada found the same type of ranking of ethnic groups, with one's own minority group on top, followed by the white majority group, then other minority groups (Kalin and Berry 1996; Berry and Kalin 1979; Hagendoorn 1995; Minescu, Hagendoorn, and Poppe 2008). This ranking was consistent across a series of measures, including desired social distance and perceived similarity to the respondent. But the question remained: Why should *all* minority groups wish to associate themselves with the majority? As social-identity theory suggests, people are motivated by a desire for positive group attributions. I argue that this may extend to ethnic group position – that is, the positive attribution is the relative position of one's own group in the status hierarchy. Perceiving oneself as closer and more similar to the high-status majority and less similar to other lower-status minorities is itself a positive group attribution.

Moreover, this identification may be an instance of motivated reasoning: racialized minorities may want to be associated with the (white) majority for status reasons, so they conclude that they actually *are* more similar to the majority than to other minorities. There is considerable evidence that people are more likely to come to the conclusions they want when their motivations distort cognitive processes and perceptions (Kunda 1990). That is, people seek out, pay more attention to, and give more weight to information that fits with their own desires. This effect, however, only functions so long as people can construct apparently reasonable explanations – thus, motivated reasoning has greater effects when there is ambiguity and smaller effects when there are contradictory facts.

For example, Kalin and Berry (1996) report that Punjabi Canadians say they are closer and more similar to anglophones than to German-origin Canadians. Similarly, in the Netherlands, ethnically Surinamese respondents report that they would rather associate with native Dutch people than with residents of Turkish origin (Hagendoorn 1995). Both of these results, I suggest, are products of the social status hierarchy. Not only do people want to be associated with the high-status majority; they believe they actually *are* closer and more similar to the high-status majority and quite different from other low-status minority groups. Motivated reasoning bridges the gap between wanting to be closer and actually being closer. Thus, motivated reasoning links differences in social status to similarity-based heuristics. People want to be closer to a group, so they believe they actually are closer to that group and are therefore more likely to support candidates of that group. The end result, according to motivated social positioning theory, is that all minority groups are more likely to support candidates of the majority (white) ethnicity rather than candidates of other minority ethnic groups.

When is motivated social positioning likely to occur? Greater status differences between the majority and minority ethnic groups are likely to lead to more interminority discrimination. As noted earlier, a desire for positive self-attribution is the root cause of the desire for association with the high-status majority group and, by extension, distancing from other low-status minority groups. Clearly, if the difference in status is not great, then the need for motivated social positioning will diminish. If minority groups are not seen as lower status, then there is no reason for citizens to want to distance themselves. As a result, according to motivated social positioning, racialized discrimination is more likely to occur in contexts or societies where there is a considerable difference in status between the majority and minority ethnic groups.

The second type of identity-based mechanism has the opposite implication: identity may drive cooperation rather than conflict between racialized ethnic groups. Cooperation might occur if citizens draw on a more general identity as a racialized person rather than a more specific ethnocultural identity. The motivated-social-positioning and realistic-conflict models assume that citizens will draw on their ethnic identity defined in a relatively narrow way, and therefore that the relations of different ethnic groups, determined by status difference or competition, are crucial to determining if there is interminority discrimination or affinity. However, it is also possible that citizens might identify with a broader social group of racialized people, depending on the context under which they are making their decision. Specifically, a choice between a white and a racialized candidate might lead to voters conceptualizing themselves in one of those two categories.

This kind of context-driven social-group construction is based on categorization theory (Turner et al. 1987; Hornsey 2008). While social-identity theory focuses on the effects of social identity, categorization theory explains how people categorize themselves and others into social groups. The key insight is that identification with a social group (that is, categorization) depends in part on the relationship of the perceiver to the social context. As Turner and colleagues (1994, 458) put it: "Self-categories are reflexive judgements in which the perceiver is defined in terms of his or her changing relationship to others within the frame of references." Identities vary but not in a meaningless or random way. Rather, these categories are negotiated between a person's long-term knowledge and opinions and the circumstances in which they are making a judgment at any particular time. Thus, a given context interacts with a person's long-term knowledge about groups, resulting in his or her identification with a particular social category in a particular circumstance or time.

The key contexts for affinity voting are those related to the election and voting. As noted earlier in this chapter, the presence of a candidate is likely to increase the salience of the relevant identity. The contexts we are most interested in are those where a racialized voter chooses either between a) a white candidate and a racialized candidate of the same ethnicity as the voter or b) a white candidate and a racialized candidate of a different ethnicity than the voter.[8] Where there is a candidate of the same ethnicity, the voter would categorize himself or herself and that candidate in one ethnic group (e.g., Chinese Canadians) and the white candidate in another group. Where there is a candidate of a different ethnicity, the voter may – I argue – similarly categorize him or herself and the candidate as part of a more general social group of racialized people or ethnic minorities.

This supposition is supported by research using the common-intergroup-identity model, which suggests that intergroup discrimination can be mitigated by recategorization – that is, by broadening the definition of the in-group to include others. Gaertner and colleagues suggest this can occur for a number of reasons – and they use context to successfully manipulate group identities. Notably, they apply their theory to ethnic group boundaries (Gaertner and Dovidio 2000; Gaertner et al. 1993), and there is a range of research applying superordinate identities in politics (e.g., Transue 2007, Berinsky et al. 2018, Breton 2015). It might well be that framing a choice between a white and a racialized candidate would result in voters recategorizing themselves as Gaertner and colleagues suggest and that, in this setting, the reference group for in-group bias would be racialized people.

While there is little research that examines the construction of racialized or minority group identities, there is some evidence for intermediate-level ethnic identities. One crucial study, Junn and Masuoka (2008), examines Asian American identity. The "Asian American" category covers people of diverse origins, including Chinese, Japanese, Thai, Pakistani, and Pacific Islanders. Junn and Masuoka (2008) demonstrate that being shown information about an Asian American politician strengthens voters' identification as Asian American. Latino Americans are also diverse in terms of their national origins, and Stokes (2003) argues that a broader Latino identity increases with time spent in the United States. First-generation immigrants identify with their nationality – Mexican, Dominican, or Cuban – but second-generation immigrants are much more likely to identify as Latino.

Social categorization is not entirely context-driven; context interacts with a person's long-term knowledge, including substantive knowledge about ethnic groups, history, and the opinions of others. One factor may be broad social definitions of race and ethnicity. That is, presenting a racialized voter with a slate of white and racialized candidates will induce a broader racialized identification *only* if there is already a belief that identification with this social group has some plausible basis. For example, faced with a choice between a white candidate and a Chinese one, why should a South Asian voter view the Chinese candidate as a fellow racialized group member rather than viewing the white candidate as a fellow "non-Chinese group" member? The answer is that the idea of a racialized or minority group appears more plausible or correct depending on how race and ethnicity are understood in society. Since both Chinese and South Asian candidates are racialized while white candidates are not, racialized status could be the basis of a common in-group identity. This is, of course, not a necessary configuration of identities; rather, it is a point to be empirically investigated.

Research suggests that "real" social identities have stronger effects than so-called minimal groups, which are experimentally induced. If racialized identity is a group identity created by relatively uncommon circumstances, such as a particular candidate choice set, it may have weaker effects than a deeply rooted identity that structures social and cultural life, implying that racialized-affinity effects might be weaker than ethnic-affinity effects. Research suggests that experimentally induced minimal-group effects are weaker than effects caused by relatively permanent, real groups, with which an individual may identify for many years or even a whole lifetime (Goette, Huffman, and Meier 2006). An in-group defined as a racialized people would be less socially real in the sense that this identity does not shape the daily lives of Canadians. There are, for instance, no racialized malls, whereas the Pacific Mall near Toronto is marketed as the largest indoor Chinese mall in North America. Nor are there holidays or family traditions that identify racialized people as such. Of course, it is true that racialized Canadians may be portrayed as a homogeneous group (often as immigrants) in the media, and white Canadians may see them that way. The state itself also administers these categories, defining "visible minority" as an important administrative category. Yet there is no evidence that these are persistent ways of self-identifying, and so the effects on behaviour may well be weaker.

Unfortunately, as with coethnic affinity, there is little research on identity motivations for racialized affinity voting. In fact, the only research may be a study that examines how Latinos' believing they have "a lot in common" with other Latinos affects their opinions of African Americans. The study concludes that Latinos who say they have a lot (or a fair amount) in common with other Latinos also have more positive attitudes toward African Americans (Kaufmann 2003). This study provides at least some support for explanations based on general minority identity, since it relates a strong ethnic identity to more positive attitudes toward another racialized group.

In sum, there is a good deal of research demonstrating ethnic-affinity effects. While the evidence regarding causal mechanisms is limited, there are good theoretical reasons to explore both interest- and identity-based explanations. On the other hand, there is little evidence of racialized affinity; in fact, most research finds conflict rather than affinity. While the theories about coethnic affinity are relatively straightforward, theoretical accounts relevant to racialized affinity are more complex. For interest-based explanations, ideological stereotyping and specific policy heuristics are both likely to lead to racialized affinity. The effects of general group interest, on the other hand, depend on the context: realistic conflict theory suggests that racialized affinity should be contingent on the competitive relationships among ethnic groups. For identity-based explanations, there are also conflicting expectations. Motivated social positioning suggests that when the racialized candidate is of a different ethnicity, racialized people might use their vote choice to position themselves as closer to the white candidate. On the other hand, if a broader identification as a racialized person is salient, racialized affinity voting may result.

Potential for Rainbow Coalitions in Canada

What are the prospects of racialized political coalitions in Canada? The comparative literature, dominated by research from the United States, shows quite limited evidence of racialized affinity – in fact, interminority conflict is more common. This dynamic is particularly important in Canada because not only are the numbers of racialized Canadians growing, racialized Canadians are also diverse in terms of ethnicity: while nearly one in five Canadians is classified as a visible minority, the largest subgroup, South Asians, comprises only 25 percent of the total visible-minority population (Statistics Canada 2011). Facilitating conditions, such as experiences of prejudice or economic circumstances, are quite likely to vary between countries. Given this, what should we expect for racialized-affinity effects in Canada?

In multiple-group situations, the competitive situation between groups is an important determinant of whether people view members of a different racialized ethnicity as a threat to their interests (Gay 2004; Meier and Stewart 1991). Realistic conflict theory provides a robust theoretical explanation for this – when structural circumstances put groups in competition, members will adopt negative attitudes toward the other group (Sherif 1966). There are a number of factors that could contribute to this pattern: low income (and hence greater sensitivity toward competition), income inequality between minorities, and competition for jobs or for government resources.

A second possible category of factors includes general levels of prejudice in society and overall perceptions of discrimination. Some, such as Gay (2006), argue that perceived discrimination leads to a general hardening and suspiciousness of all other groups, thus leading to interminority conflict. Similarly, this chapter has already suggested that discrimination might lead to motivated social positioning – that is, distancing oneself from ethnic groups lower down in the social hierarchy. In that case, higher levels of prejudice in society would promote conflict between racialized ethnic groups, not decrease it. Thus, the effects of prejudice might be conditional on status difference between ethnocultural groups.

On the other hand, research on linked fate has found that a sense of common fate among group members leads to greater ethnic-affinity effects (Dawson 1994; McConnaughy et al. 2010). Since linked fate is both conceptually and empirically linked to discrimination, high levels of discrimination in society should be linked to higher levels of coethnic affinity voting.

How is Canada positioned on these dimensions relative to other countries? Good cross-national comparisons are surprisingly difficult to find, especially for differences between ethnic minorities. For example, there are no cross-national studies of differences in income between racialized ethnic groups. In good part this stems from how the category "racial minority" is defined in different countries. The data on economic outcomes and levels of discrimination that do exist, though, suggest that racialized affinity is more likely in Canada than in the United States, where most of the research has been conducted.

One important source of data is the Organisation for Economic Cooperation and Development's (OECD) cross-national analysis of immigrant outcomes (OECD 2012). Of course, not all racialized citizens are immigrants, but in developed countries a large proportion are, so these data should give us at least some comparative insights. The OECD data include Canada, the United States, most European countries, and other countries such as Japan, Israel, and Australia. In general, immigrants in Canada are better off than the OECD average on most indicators, particularly as compared to immigrants in the United States. For example, 90 percent of Canadian immigrants live in suitably sized housing, as opposed to an OECD average of 80 percent and 72 percent in the United States. Average disposable income levels are slightly higher in Canada ($21,600) than in the United States ($20,300) and considerably higher than the OECD average ($18,372).[9] Employment rates follow a similar pattern; 68 percent of foreign-born Canadians are employed compared to 67 percent in the United States and 65 percent across the OECD. Finally, poverty rates may have a particularly important effect, separate from income-level effects. On this measure,

Canadian immigrant households are somewhat higher than the OECD average with a poverty rate of 22.3 percent compared to an OECD average of 17.3 percent. Immigrant households in the United States, however, fare considerably worse than Canadian immigrant households: they have a poverty rate of 31.2 percent. The same pattern seems to be emerging in education: an analysis of standardized test scores (PISA) shows that Canadian immigrants actually fare better than native-born Canadians, whereas immigrant scores in the United States and in the OECD on average are somewhat worse (Schleicher 2006).

It is not clear what magnitude of objective social differences is required to create the conditions for interest- or identity-based interminority conflict. Still, the pattern is clear: Canadian immigrants are significantly better off in terms of economic outcomes than immigrants in the United States and somewhat better than the OECD average. Importantly, these figures are for immigrants; they exclude most African Americans, suggesting that the difference in economic outcomes in Canada and the United States for racialized citizens as a whole is likely to be greater than these statistics show. If conflict is generated or increased by economic marginalization, it appears that the United States should be at the high end, Canada should experience considerably less conflict, and many OECD countries may fall in between.

Residential integration also contributes to interminority affinity, as residential diversity reduces conflict between black and Latino Americans. In general, in Canada, the residential patterns of ethnic minorities are characterized by fragmentation and dispersal rather than concentration or segregation (Bauder and Sharpe 2002). Moreover, occupational segregation is (or at least was) on a downward trend (Balakrishnan and Feng Hou 1999), suggesting that ethnic minorities both live and work in relatively diverse environments. Comparatively, racial and ethnic segregation in the United States has long been considered quite high (Massey and Denton 1988). Despite some evidence of decline, in part stemming from increasing numbers of Hispanic and other immigrants, residential segregation continues to be a significant issue (Charles 2003; Farley and Frey 1994). Although there is no direct international comparison, residential segregation is likely to contribute to higher levels of interethnic conflict in the United States than in Canada.

Finally, one of the identity-based explanations for interminority conflict, motivated social positioning, is conditional on status differences. While there is no direct data to support this, it seems reasonable to expect perceived status differences to be related to prejudice and discrimination. In societies where there is a great deal of discrimination against minorities, those minorities will likely have low perceived social status. However, levels of discrimination are difficult to evaluate. Many surveys do not have a large sample of immigrants or of the racialized population, and there are often differences in both the wording of questions and the meaning of terminology that make cross-national comparisons difficult. That said, there are two useful sources of evidence: 1) perceptions of discrimination expressed by racialized minorities and immigrants in a number of similarly worded surveys and 2) the general public's attitude toward racial minorities and immigrants in the World Values Survey.

Data from the European Social Survey (ESS) measure "belonging to a group that is discriminated against on the grounds of race, ethnicity or nationality." The Canadian question asks if "in the past five years, you have experienced discrimination or [been] treated unfairly by others in Canada because of your ethnicity or culture, race or colour?" (OECD 2012, 148). While these questions are different, in that the European question asks about discrimination against a group rather than an individual, they should still be comparable in broad terms. These data are for immigrants but are separated into low-income and high-income countries, and most racialized immigrants come from low-income countries. On these measures, it appears that Canada is average: 18.4 percent of respondents said they had experienced discrimination, compared to 18.6 percent of European respondents who said the same (OECD 2012). In the United States, however, perceived discrimination appears to be considerably higher: 35 percent of African Americans say they have "personally experienced discrimination or been treated unfairly because of their race or ethnicity over the past year" (Pew Research Center 2013). Similarly, 34 percent of Hispanics say they, a member of their family, or a close friend has experienced discrimination in the past five years (Heimlich 2010). Perceived discrimination in the United States appears to be significantly higher than in Canada or Europe.

Attitudes toward racialized minorities and immigrants among the general population are also useful measures of prejudice or hostility toward minority groups. According to the World Values Survey, Canada ranks very low on questions about hostility toward immigrants or racial minorities – certainly lower than the United States and also lower than most European countries. Table 2.2 includes a comparison of selected countries: only 3.8 percent of Canadians said they would not want to have racial minorities as neighbours, compared with 8 percent of Americans and, for example, 8.9

TABLE 2.2

"Would not like to have as neighbours"

	Different race (%)	Immigrant (%)
Belgium	16.5	18.2
Canada	3.4	4.2
Czech Republic	9.8	19.4
France	8.9	12.0
Italy	15.6	16.5
Sweden	2.5	2.8
Great Britain	8.6	15.5
United States	8.0	10.1

NOTE: All respondents are included.
SOURCE: World Values Survey, 1999–2000.

percent of French respondents. Negative responses to immigrants are higher across the board, but only 4.2 percent of Canadians said they would not want to have immigrants as neighbours, compared to 10.1 percent of respondents from the United States and 12 percent of those from France. Of course, these questions are probably low estimates, given the likelihood of social desirability effects. Still, these data provide more evidence that discrimination and racial tension in Canada are lower than in the United States as well as some, though not all, European countries.

Clearly, this analysis provides only a limited picture of the factors that might influence interminority relations. Still, it may give some indication of what we should expect. One key factor in interminority conflict is economic marginalization. On most measures – including income, housing, employment, and poverty rates – Canadian immigrants score higher than those in the United States and in some, but not all, European countries. Moreover, residential diversity, which should reduce interminority conflict, appears to be higher in Canada than in the United States. The other major factor is perceived discrimination and prejudice. Canadian immigrants from low income-countries, who are most likely to be racialized, report considerably less discrimination than Hispanic and African Americans. European data are more difficult to compare, but rates of reported discrimination may be similar to those in Canada. Finally, Canadians are more likely to say they are accepting of racial minorities and immigrants as neighbours than respondents in both the United States and most European countries.

These data strongly suggest that, compared to the United States, both the economic marginalization of immigrants and discrimination against racial minorities are lower in Canada. On the other hand, compared to European countries, Canada tends to be higher than average but is not an outlier. All of these factors suggest that Canada is a relatively favourable environment for racialized affinity and certainly more favourable than the environment for blacks and Latinos in the United States. Therefore, findings of inter-minority conflict in the United States may not apply to Canada. At the same time, if there is cooperation and affinity between ethnic-minority groups in Canada, it may nót be unique – the same circumstances may well occur in a number of other countries.

The Likelihood of Candidate Effects

Even if there is racialized affinity at an attitudinal level, is it likely to manifest itself in votes for candidates? The focus in the present research is on local candidates simply because there have only been three visible-minority pre-miers.[10] In addition, the first visible-minority leader of a major federal party, Jagmeet Singh, has yet to run in an election. Much of the research cited so far has been conducted in the United States. Given loose party discipline and a candidate-centred electoral system, it is not surprising that much of that research suggests that candidates are more influential in the United States than elsewhere. Nonetheless, there is reason to think that there may still be important candidate effects in Canada.

In Westminster systems, findings suggest that local candidate influence is smaller because of party discipline and stricter spending rules. The magni-tude of Canadian estimates is similar to international findings: in an early study, Cunningham (1971) reported that 10 percent of voters had stated that the local candidate was a decisive factor (not including the candidate's own party identifiers). Krashinsky and Milne (1983, 1986) found that in-cumbents get a greater share of the total vote than nonincumbents – 6 to 12 percentage points more in Ontario provincial elections, and 3 to 4 percent-age points more in federal elections. More recently, Blais and colleagues (2003) have suggested that the local candidate was decisive for 5 percent of Canadian voters and influential for 44 percent of voters, even controlling for feelings about parties and leaders.

If we put the size of these candidate effects in context, there are a number of reasons to consider them important factors. A difference of 5 percentage points – the percentage for whom the local candidate was "decisive" according to Blais and colleagues (2003) – would certainly have decided many ridings across the country and may well have changed the winner in recent Canadian federal elections. In fact, fifty-one seats were decided with a margin of less than 5 percentage points in the 2011 federal election (analysis by author). Moreover, uniform change among 5 percent of voters could actually produce a 10 percent swing as one party gains and another party loses. In addition, racialized Canadians are concentrated in a swath of battleground ridings in the Greater Toronto area (GTA), Vancouver, and urban ridings on the Prairies (Marwah, Triadafilopoulos, and White 2013). In other words, the citizens who are subject to the dynamics being investigated in this research tend to live in highly contested seats, magnifying the effect of even modest shifts in support.

Finally, even if affinity effects are not very large, Canada is still a least-likely case (Eckstein 1975) in that the Canadian electoral and party systems make candidate effects relatively unlikely. Least-likely cases are especially important for theory testing because, if a theory is confirmed in such a setting, it implies the phenomenon is likely to occur elsewhere – that is, in more propitious settings. In Carey and Shugart's (1995) systematic classification of electoral systems according to incentives for developing a personal vote (support based on the individual candidate rather than the party), Canada ranks at the bottom. In other words, candidates are likely to be more influential in other countries. Moreover, not only is Canada a least-likely case cross-nationally, local candidates are the least-likely case among political office-holders: the characteristics of local candidates are less influential than those of provincial and federal party leaders. If we find affinity effects of relatively small magnitudes at the local candidate level, it seems very likely there will be much larger effects from party leaders.

In sum, candidate effects are probably modest but still important. Racialized citizens are a key battleground geographically, in hotly contested ridings around Vancouver and the GTA, and demographically, as the Conservative Party mounts a concerted campaign to sway their support. In addition, the impact of local candidates varies based on structural factors such as the electoral system, and Canada is likely to be at the low end on this dimension, suggesting that analogous effects are likely to be larger in other countries. Thus, while the expectation of effects from candidate ethnicity should be modest, there are reasons to think they may not only affect electoral results but also have major implications for more candidate-centric electoral contexts, such as party leader selection.

Summary of the Theoretical Framework

Political coalitions of racialized voters may well become increasingly important in Canada and elsewhere. Even without dominating national discourse, the ethnicity of candidates and voters may affect political decisions in important ways. Current research suggests that coethnic affinity is common and that its effect on voting can be quite large (Barreto 2007). Racialized affinity, on the other hand, is much less common. Most research finds conflict and discrimination rather than affinity (Meier and Stewart 1991; McClain et al. 2006). However, this research is largely focused on blacks and Latinos in the United States and often looks at more general attitudes and behaviour than vote choice. Moreover, there is at least some evidence of political coalitions among ethnic minorities (Tedin and Murray 1994; Browning et al. 1990), suggesting that racialized affinity can occur under some conditions.

There are a number of ways that interest- and identity-based motivations can produce coethnic affinity. Interest-based motivations include general group interest, specific policy heuristics, and ideological stereotyping, while identity-based motivations include direct in-group bias, persuasion effects, and expressive voting. Previous research has focused almost entirely on interests and often theorized, but failed to test, a heuristic mechanism motivated by general group interest. Those studies that do test explanations for affinity effects often use ambiguous measures of ideology (McDermott 1998), identity (McConnaughy et al. 2010), or linked fate (Dawson 1994).

Interest- and identity-based explanations for racialized affinity are more complex. Identities could affect the likelihood of racialized affinity in two ways. First, a general racialized identity could lead to affinity for candidates of different racialized ethnic groups by including them as members of the in-group. This broader identity might be induced by the context – specifically, a choice between a white candidate and a candidate of a racialized ethnic group different from the voter. However, it would also be contingent on a more general belief that racialized people are a plausible social group, reflecting generally accepted social definitions of race and ethnicity. Indeed, the little research that exists suggests that, in the United States, identifying with other Latinos is related to also identifying with blacks (Kaufmann 2003; Sanchez 2008). This finding is consistent with the general-racialized-identity explanation in that identifying with a specific racialized ethnic group is correlated with feeling close to other racialized groups. Second, motivated social positioning, dependent on differences in status between majority and minority ethnic groups, could motivate racialized citizens to position their group as similar to the (white) majority and to socially distance themselves from other racialized ethnic groups. Therefore, ethnic-group identity combined with status differences might lead to discrimination against candidates of a different racialized ethnicity.

Interest-based motivations for racialized affinity might be influenced by identity or by intergroup competition. Ideological stereotyping being left-leaning or having specific policy positions might emerge even in the absence of racialized identity. On the other hand, if ideological stereotyping is produced when in-group members are perceived as being ideologically closer, then racialized affinity depends on racialized identity. Finally, perceptions of generalized group interests might depend on intergroup competition – thus lower levels of discrimination, inequality, or other factors related to competition would increase racialized affinity.

Finally, racialized affinity voting appears more likely in Canada than in the United States. Economic outcomes – including income, education, and housing – are better for Canadian immigrants, most of whom are racialized. Similarly, levels of perceived prejudice and discrimination are lower in Canada. Given that research into interminority conflict shows that economic marginalization and discrimination are important causes (Gay 2006), racialized affinity is more likely in Canada than in the United States and in some, though not all, European countries.

When it comes to the possibility of multicultural coalitions, there are three clear gaps in the research on affinity voting. First, there are few studies of ethnic and racialized affinity voting outside the United States or among groups other than blacks and Latinos. Second, little research focuses on identity-based motivations. Third, the interest-based measures have been ambiguous; for instance, linked fate is interpreted as being about interests (e.g., McConnaughy et al. 2010), but I argue that it may actually be strongly influenced by group identity. Similarly, measures of ideological stereotyping may actually measure group interests (e.g., McDermott 1998). This study addresses these gaps by testing affinity effects with multiple ethnic groups, focusing on the influence of identity and using better measures of self-interest and ideological stereotyping.

3
Coethnic and Racialized
...... Affinity in Canada

What effect does candidate ethnicity have on the electoral choices of racialized voters in Canada? This question involves two related issues: 1) whether voters do, indeed, see candidates' ethnicity as a relevant consideration when casting ballots, and 2) how voters view racialized ethnic groups. This chapter establishes the existence and reveals the structure of affinity voting in Canada, drawing on evidence from a national survey with a large overrepresentation of racialized respondents. The centrepiece of the survey, and the focus of the analysis here, is a voting experiment that manipulated the apparent ethnicity of a candidate in a hypothetical election. I begin by discussing methodological issues, focusing on causal inference and the effects of race and ethnicity. I then discuss similar affinity experiments and set out, in some detail, the national survey and its manipulations. Finally, I present the results of the experiment.

Causality and Candidate Ethnicity
In the social sciences, establishing causality is difficult in general but even more so when studying the effects of race and ethnicity. One problem is spurious correlation – often referred to as the third-variable problem. Observational studies may find correlations, but it is always uncertain whether they reflect causal relationships or some other variable not incorporated in the analysis. Spurious correlation is a particular issue in the study of candidate effects because there are many factors that vary systematically with candidate characteristics. For example, because each candidate runs in only one riding, we must compare results for different candidates, who may be different in ways other than their ethnicity; indeed, there is a good deal of research on how women candidates tend to be overqualified to compensate for their gender (e.g., Black and Erikson 2006; Carroll and Strimling 1983), implying that gender and candidate quality are confounded, a problem that

could apply to candidate ethnicity. In addition, the fact that political scientists cannot randomly assign candidates to electoral districts has repercussions for establishing causality. For example, it is plausible that racialized candidates are more likely to run in urban areas, perhaps because they believe they will have a better chance of winning, or simply because they are more likely to live there (Black 2008). This means that ridings with racialized candidates could differ in many ways, such as greater numbers of racialized voters, different educational profiles, and a different partisan mix from rural areas.

At a more practical level, the easiest way to test affinity effects is to combine candidate data either with aggregate election results or survey data. Unfortunately, either method is likely to fail. The first option suggests that the higher the percentage of racialized voters, the more votes a racialized candidate should get. The problem with this approach is that almost all electoral districts are dominated by white voters – only 8 percent (24 of 308) of federal electoral districts in Canada have a population that is more than 50 percent visible minorities. In fact, most have quite small percentages of minorities; in 75 percent of electoral districts, minority populations constitute less than 20 percent of the population (2006 census data). Consequently, the attitudes of white voters, rather than racialized voters, are likely to dominate the results. We can hardly assume that white voters are neutral – in fact, V.O. Key's (1949) classic theory of racial threat suggests that as the size of the minority increases, the majority becomes more hostile. As a result, an analysis of aggregate election data that seeks a correlation between the racialized percentage of the population and support for racialized candidates might produce a conclusion that is not simply false but rather the polar opposite of the correct conclusion to be drawn about racial affinity.

The second option is to link surveys of vote choice, such as the Canadian Election Study, to data on candidate ethnicity. In this case, the problem is simply sample size – remember, the population of interest is racialized voters who live in an electoral district with a racialized candidate, which would likely amount to only sixty respondents in each Canadian Election Study – not nearly enough to analyze even if multiple surveys are pooled.[1] The method of linking survey results to vote choice could work with a major survey focused on racialized voters, and in fact Fisher and colleagues (2015) and Bird and colleagues (2015) have done precisely that in the United Kingdom and Toronto, respectively – but the potential for unobserved confounders related to candidates and districts noted above remain.

By randomly assigning candidate ethnicity in an experiment, we can ensure that differences in support indeed stem from the treatment and not a spurious third variable. This is true for both candidates and respondents. That is, unlike in real elections, we can have candidates who are completely identical, except for their ethnicity. In addition, respondents can be randomly assigned to treatment groups so the distribution of demographics and attitudes are the same, unlike in real ridings. Of course, questions remain about *why* the treatment has the effect it does – but experimental methodologies still provide a great advantage over traditional observational survey methods and aggregate election data.

The experiment used here (offering a choice between fictional candidates) is also more similar to the behaviour we hope to study (voting for real candidates) than a survey about attitudes would be. Asking respondents if they like or dislike a particular ethnic group may not produce the same results as observing their actual behaviour, because people often respond differently to abstract groups and individuals (Sears 1983). This tendency poses a problem when examining voters' general attitudes toward groups or their willingness to support an abstract candidate, for example, "a woman for president" (Sigelman and Sigelman 1982). Of course, an experiment is not identical to actual behaviour – it still constitutes a question on a survey, and the conditions under which the respondents are "voting" for candidates are considerably different than in an actual election. Nonetheless, the campaign experiment is more similar to actual electoral decision making than, for example, survey questions about how people feel about certain ethnic groups. Therefore, the experiment should give us a better idea of how candidate and voter ethnicity interact in elections.

The Candidate Survey Experiment

The candidate survey experiment used here was based on a national sample that included respondents in all provinces except Quebec (see Appendix A for details). The sample was drawn from a web panel and included a large oversample of racialized respondents – 1,518 out of a total of 2,502 respondents. While there has been some criticism of such panels (Malhotra and Krosnik 2007), recent comparisons have found that different modes have similar rates of total survey error (Stephenson and Crête 2011; Ansolabehere and Schaffner 2014). While tests suggested that the sample was generally representative (see Appendix A), as is usual for web samples respondents did have a higher level of political interest and education than the general population (Chang and Krosnick 2010). Since the key issue being studied is vote choice, this sample issue might actually be a benefit, because the sample would represent the voting population better than census figures do. Put simply, the same variables that predict participation in internet surveys (e.g., political interest) also predict real political participation. If we are interested in the effect that ethnocultural identities have on vote choice, then a sampling bias toward likely voters makes the analysis more realistic.

The central experiment consisted of presenting respondents with short biographies of two candidates and asking them who they would vote for. Several items were manipulated, most importantly the apparent ethnicity of one of the two candidates. This design followed an increasingly common approach, but it improved on many previous studies by presenting two candidates and including a manipulation of party labels. Experiments that examine the influence of race on candidate choice have been used for a number of years and generally show a biography of one or more candidates, vary the race of the candidates, and ask respondents whom they would be likely to support (e.g., Bird 2015; Jones 2014; Kam 2007; McDermott 1998; Philpot and Walton 2007; Reeves 1997; Sigelman and Sigelman 1982; Sigelman et al. 1995; Weaver 2012). These experiments have two major issues. First, many ask about only one candidate (e.g., Bird 2016; Jones 2014; Kam 2007). One benefit of offering a choice between two candidates is that it provides a more realistic test of the question at hand. The two-candidate design replicates the structure of a real election, where citizens are asked to choose among multiple options rather than to evaluate a single candidate. Asking respondents to "disapprove" of a single person may actually be setting a higher bar for discriminatory behaviour than simply requiring an expression of preference for one option over another. Most importantly, as noted in Chapter 2, the two-candidate design may be crucial in the self-identity categorization process. The presence of a racialized candidate may influence how the voter identifies at that moment in time, so presenting a choice between white and racialized candidates may be quite different than offering voters a single racialized candidate.

The treatment and candidate-preference question read as follows (manipulated sections are italicized):

Candidate 1
John Hawkes is an entrepreneur, and after being laid off twice he started the successful company Allsort Inc. Despite a busy schedule,

Mr. Hawkes works with a number of organizations, including Kids Help Phone, and served as vice chair of the Municipal Safety Committee. John Hawkes is an independent candidate.

Candidate 2
Arthur Dorre/Jun Zhang/Satveer Chaudhary is an active local businessman who was recently honoured as "Businessman of the Year" for his many contributions. Mr. *Dorre/Zhang/Chaudhary* helps at the local community centre and is the fundraising chair for the Hospital Foundation. A former provincial candidate, he lost in the most recent election. *Arthur Dorre/Jun Zhang/Satveer Chaudhary* is an independent candidate.

Which candidate would you vote for?

The biographies were written to present more or less equally qualified candidates to represent them in Parliament, balancing the need to have plausibly different candidates while not introducing factors that might interact with the treatments. Each candidate was described as having a career in business and noncontroversial community involvement.[2] Unlike some studies, pictures of the candidates were not shown to avoid confounding the effects of candidate attractiveness with candidate ethnicity. In addition, the omission of pictures reflects the reality of Canadian elections at the electoral district level, where most voters see signs that feature the local candidate's name but no picture.[3]

One notable feature of the biographies was that each contained a fault; that is, some less-than-ideal (from the perspective of electoral politics) personal feature was attributed to each candidate. Candidate 1 is described as having been laid off twice before going on to found his own company. Candidate 2 is described as having run and lost in a previous election. Past research demonstrates that discrimination is often evident only when there is an excuse for such behaviour, also called covering (see Crandall and Eshleman 2003). When evaluating a "perfect" candidate, even highly prejudiced people might not discriminate because there is no socially acceptable justification for doing so. They may want to avoid social censure. Likewise, a similar situation is possible among those who hold unconsciously prejudiced attitudes. They may see themselves as tolerant but may (unconsciously) exaggerate and overemphasize a fault in a racialized candidate more than they would if the candidate were white. Thus, the faults in the biographies provide both an external social justification and an internal psychological justification for respondents who might have discriminatory tendencies.

The candidates were manipulated along two factors: candidate ethnicity and biography version (see Appendix A for assignment details). The central factor is candidate ethnicity, which manipulates the candidates' names and, thus, their apparent ethnocultural origin. The second factor includes two theoretically distinct conditions – party labels and a self-interest prime, which are used in later chapters to examine the moderators of, and explanations, for affinity voting.

The key experimental treatment was a manipulation of candidate ethnicity. The control group was presented with two candidates both of whom had stereotypically European names: John Hawkes (Candidate 1) and Arthur Dorre (Candidate 2). The two treatment groups were presented with the same two candidate biographies, but Candidate 2 was given either a traditionally Chinese (Jun Zhang) or South Asian (Satveer Chaudhary) name. While names themselves are not necessarily a reliable signifier of ethnocultural background, pretesting indicated that respondents accepted the implied ethnicities. The names were chosen from a list of common Chinese and South Asian names in Ontario drawn from health care records (Shah et al. 2010). Several names were selected and discussed with members of the respective communities, as well as with researchers with relevant experience. Names that were the same as recent federal Canadian politicians or candidates were excluded. The names were compared to a list of federal election candidates from major parties from 2004 to 2011 (discussed in more detail in Chapter 7). In addition, an extensive internet search was conducted, and no Canadian provincial or municipal politicians with these names were discovered. Names that had highly specific religious associations (e.g., Singh) or that might also be European (e.g., Lee) were avoided.

Hypotheses and Candidate Experiment Results

Drawing on the theory and research discussed in Chapter 2, two hypotheses were considered for affinity voting among racialized voters: ethnicity affinity and racialized affinity. The first hypothesis proposes affinity effects on the basis of ethnicity: are racialized voters more likely to support candidates who share their ethnocultural background? Given positive findings for black and Latino affinity in the United States, we expected affinity effects for ethnocultural minorities in Canada as well:

H3.1: Racialized respondents will be more likely to choose a candidate of their own ethnocultural background than a white candidate.

The second hypothesis was based on interminority relations research, which has mixed findings. If racialized citizens see other racialized citizens as part of a common group (per the identity account) or as in their interest in relevant ways (per the interest-based heuristic account), then there should be affinity effects for racialized candidates in general. Given relatively positive conditions in Canada, on balance it seems likely that there will be different-ethnicity affinity. However, these racialized-affinity effects may be less reliable, or smaller, than ethnicity affinity.

H3.2: Racialized respondents will be more likely to choose a candidate with a different racialized ethnocultural background than a white candidate.

The results are presented in two stages. In the first stage, to convey an intuitive sense of the findings, simple comparisons of percentages across experimental conditions for specific groups of respondents are shown. In the second stage, in order to control for a range of observed covariates to enhance estimation precision and present the formal hypothesis tests, a set of logistic regression models is presented. Throughout the analysis, the primary measure reported is support for Candidate 2 – that is, support for the candidate whose name (and, hence, perceived ethnicity) was manipulated. Because the key comparisons are across experimental conditions, we are interested in different levels of support for the different versions of Candidate 2. I collapsed the independent and party versions since, as Chapter 7 explores in detail, this treatment has little effect on the role of ethnicity; this improved the precision of the estimates but did not substantially change the findings (see Besco 2015). A number of respondent ethnic categories were also collapsed into the categories "Chinese," "South Asian," and "other racialized respondents." In part, this decision stemmed from the small numbers, but other racialized respondents (e.g., Arab, black, West-Asian) all have the same relationship to the candidates in that they are all of different ethnicity than the candidates (Chinese and South Asian) and therefore all represent cases of racialized affinity.

TABLE 3.1

Support for Candidate 2

	Version (%)		
	White	Chinese	South Asian
Chinese respondents	52	53	56
South Asian respondents	41	50	51
Other racialized respondents	36	38	44

The vote percentages for Candidate 2, whose ethnicity was experimentally manipulated, are shown in Table 3.1. The key comparison is between the support for the white version of Candidate 2 and support for the various racialized versions of Candidate 2. Looking at the coethnic affinity pairs – that is, when a respondent saw a candidate of their own ethnic group – support is higher than for the white version of the candidate. For South Asian respondents, the results are consistent with coethnic affinity: respondents are more likely to support a candidate who belongs to their own ethnocultural group. The South Asian version of Candidate 2 gets 9 percentage points more support than the white version of Candidate 2. On the other hand, Chinese-origin respondents are only 1 percentage point more likely to support the Chinese candidate.

Racialized affinity voting suggests that respondents will be more likely to support a candidate of a different racialized ethnocultural group than a white candidate, and there are four candidate-voter combinations of this kind. For example, we would expect that more respondents who identify as Chinese would support the South Asian version of Candidate 2 then the white version of Candidate 2. All combinations of groups show racial-affinity effects – that is, all racialized ethnic groups are more likely to support a racialized candidate, even when they are of a different ethnic background, a finding that provides some initial evidence for the plausibility of rainbow coalitions. Again, while the pattern is the same for all groups, there are clear differences in the size of the effect between ethnic groups. For instance, South Asian respondents show the largest effect at 10 percentage points, while Chinese respondents are only 4 percentage points more likely to support the South Asian candidate than the white candidate.

LOGISTIC REGRESSION MODELS

To provide a more rigorous analysis of the experiment and formal hypothesis tests, logistic regression models are estimated. In the first model, the independent variable merges the candidate-voter combinations into co-ethnic affinity and racialized affinity groups. The second model examines each ethnic group in detail. The dependent variable is vote choice: 1 is support for Candidate 2, and 0 is support for Candidate 1. For Model 3.1, the independent variable is a three-category nominal variable: if the respondent saw a white candidate, a candidate of his or her own ethnicity, or a candidate of a different racialized ethnicity. Only racialized respondents are included in the model.

The regression models discussed here, and in the following chapters, include covariates (age, education, gender, immigrant status, income, and religion [Christian, non-Christian, nonreligious]). While not strictly necessary given random assignment, they reduce the total unexplained variation and therefore increase the precision with which the effect of the experimental treatment can be estimated (Mutz 2011).[4] Covariates are sometimes referred to as control variables, but it should be noted they are not controls in the sense often used in observational data – they are not required since treatments are randomly assigned. That said, comparisons across non-randomly assigned variables (i.e., between South Asian respondents and Chinese respondents) should be treated with caution because groups defined by observed characteristics, such as ethnicity, might differ systematically on some unknown variable. However, none of the formal hypothesis tests rely on this kind of comparison between groups.

To provide a formal test of Hypothesis 3.1, I compared the predicted probability of racialized respondents voting for Candidate 2 under two conditions: seeing a white Candidate 2 and seeing a Candidate 2 of their own ethnicity. Similar to the results in Table 3.1, the predicted probabilities in Figure 3.1 show that racialized respondents are 8 percentage points more likely to support a candidate of their own ethnic group than an identical white candidate, and the difference between the predicted probabilities is statistically significant ($p = .05$). This confirms that the ethnic-affinity effects reported by research on black and Latino Americans apply to racialized Canadians.

A second set of predicted probabilities tested Hypothesis 3.2. As 3.1 shows, the predicted probability of supporting racialized candidates of a different ethnic group is also higher than that of supporting white candidates. The

FIGURE 3.1

Coethnic and racialized affinity voting

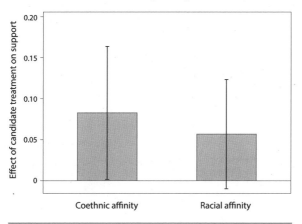

NOTES: Difference in predicted probability of choosing
Candidate 2, between white and racialized candidate versions;
$n = 1,125$.

size of the effect is smaller: 6 percentage points ($p = .09$). There is at least
some evidence of affinity among racialized respondents in general – in other
words, evidence for the plausibility of rainbow coalitions.

Having established evidence for ethnic and racialized affinity in Model
3.1, we then examined more specific categories of ethnicity. In Model 3.2,
candidate and participant ethnicity are broken down into dummy variables
for specific ethnicities. For candidate ethnicity, the categories are "white,"
"Chinese" and "South Asian"; for participant ethnicity, the categories are
"Chinese," "South Asian," and "other racialized respondents." Interactions
for each combination of candidate and respondent ethnicity are included.[5]
The dependent variable remains voting for Candidate 2. Predicted probabilities were generated for each combination of participant-candidate ethnicity, and the first difference of the experimental manipulation was taken.
This is the treatment effect – that is, difference in support for white and
racialized versions of the candidates.

As Figure 3.2 shows, all six candidate-respondent ethnic pairs have positive point estimates. These effects are not estimated with much precision – the
confidence intervals are wide and not statistically significant. Nonetheless,
they show that the point estimates are positive across all ethnic groups,

FIGURE 3.2

Affinity for ethnic groups

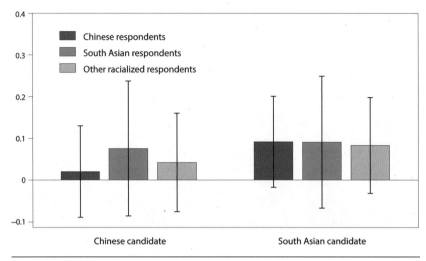

NOTES: Difference in predicted probability of choosing Candidate 2, between white and minority candidate versions; n = 1,125.

rather than negative for some, but with a positive average effect driven by some particular group.

Taken as a whole, these data show evidence for both ethnic and racialized affinity voting. Figure 3.1 shows that when the groups are pooled, on average racialized respondents are 8 percentage points more likely to support a candidate of the same ethnic group (p = .05) and 6 percentage points more likely to support a candidate of a different racialized ethnicity than a white candidate (p = .09). While most of the results in Figure 3.2 are not statistically significant, the point estimates for each combination of ethnocultural group are positive, providing at least some evidence that these effects apply to all groups.

Patterns of Coethnic and Racialized Affinity Voting

The data confirmed the existence of coethnic affinity and, contrary to some previous research, provided no evidence of discrimination between racialized ethnicities. In fact, affinity effects seem to extend to racialized candidates in general. These findings suggest four broad conclusions. First, there are affinity effects for candidates of the same ethnocultural group. Second, there appears to be some affinity across ethnocultural lines: racialized respondents are more likely to support candidates from a different racialized ethnocultural group than white candidates. Third, racialized-affinity effects are weaker than ethnicity affinity effects. Fourth, there may be some variation in strength of affinity between the different racialized respondent groups.

Looking at coethnic affinity along specific ethnocultural lines, Hypothesis 3.1 was confirmed – respondents were 8 percentage points more likely to support a candidate of the same ethnic group ($p = .05$). On this point, the evidence is consistent with previous research, confirming that ethnic-affinity effects apply broadly, not just to black and Latino Americans. There appears to be no reason these effects will not apply to established democracies generally and perhaps globally.

Hypothesis 3.2 was also confirmed and showed racialized-affinity effects. As suggested in Chapter 2, the conditions for rainbow coalitions are better in Canada than in the United States, and the evidences so far bears this out. Combining all ethnic groups together, racialized respondents are 6 percentage points more likely to support a racialized candidate of a different ethnicity than a white candidate ($p = .09$). Looking specifically at the voters' willingness to support candidates of different racialized ethnic groups from their own, the first differences are not statistically significant for individual ethnic groups, but there are positive point estimates for all groups. However, given the results of pooling the categories, it seems likely that the issues with statistical significance may simply be the result of small cell size rather than a real null effect. Certainly, there is no evidence of discrimination against other ethnic minorities or preference for white candidates. While the evidence for racialized-affinity effects for individual ethnic groups is weak, it does seem to suggest that they apply to all ethnic groups, rendering rainbow coalitions plausible.

There was considerable variation in the size of effects for different ethnic groups, although the wide confidence intervals make this difficult to evaluate. Why should ethnic-affinity effects vary so greatly between ethnic groups? One possible explanation is rooted in ethnicity and cultural factors: different ethnic groups are distinct, perhaps because of cultural values or experience with democracy in their countries of origin (Bilodeau 2008). Alternatively, the difference in affinity effects might be due to historical and structural factors that affect identification. Notably, Chinese immigrants were by far the earliest non-Europeans to arrive in Canada in significant numbers – they began to immigrate during the late 1800s. Some Chinese

Canadians are many generations removed from immigration, whereas immigration from most other non-European countries did not begin until the 1970s (Kelley and Trebilcock 1998). The first explanation relies on attributes of specific ethnocultural groups and the second on a more general concept of self-identification, which will be explored further in Chapters 5 and 6.

These results for different-ethnicity affinity, however, contradict many studies that found conflict among minorities (e.g., Kaufmann 2003). Are relations between racialized ethnic groups in Canada systematically different than those in the United States? As discussed in Chapter 2, we do have some reasons to expect that they are, perhaps because of the greater economic success of racialized Canadians and lower levels of prejudice and discrimination. However, a mere lack of causes for interminority conflict is not sufficient to explain a positive effect of racialized affinity. Perhaps the non-white ethnic groups are seen as being linked by a common identity. If respondents see themselves as part of a broader racialized group, this self-identification might lead to racialized affinity. A more detailed examination of these issues, however, requires better measures of identity.

4
The Importance
of Self-Identification

The race and ethnicity of both candidates and voters clearly matters, but we know little about the reasons why. This chapter makes an argument for the importance of self-identity, rather than ethnic group membership, as the key causal mechanism, and it examines the measure of self-identification used in this study: the Identification with a Psychological Group (IDPG) scale. There are two reasons that using a measure of ethnic self-identification is better than simply relying on ethnic group membership (as in the previous chapter's analysis): it can be measured more precisely, and it provides insights into the mechanism of affinity. Group membership is, generally speaking, a binary state, but political science has long recognized that we can gain better estimates of social-group effects by using a scale measure that rests on the strength of identification with that group. In addition, many of the identity-based mechanisms for affinity effects, such as in-group bias, rest on self-identification. Conversely, interest-based mechanisms are more likely to be mediators of simple group membership rather than self-identification.

This chapter is divided into three parts. The first presents a general discussion of the importance of measuring self-identification with a group. The second examines the IDPG scale, and the third presents details of the scale along with some basic analysis. Two levels of identity are measured: a specific, lower-order cultural or national identity and a broader, higher-order ethnic identity, as defined by Statistics Canada. As predicted by nested-identity theory, the lower-order identity is stronger, but the difference is small. The demographic correlates are quite similar to both IDPG scales, including age at immigration but not time in Canada. This suggests that socialization in the country of origin is an important factor and that identity does not fade even over multiple decades.

Degrees and Dimensions of Social-Group Identification

A wide array of group identities has been shown to be related to political action (Huddy 2001). Identities can drive both behaviour and attitudes, including, of course, partisan identities (Green et al. 2004; Iyengar et al. 2012; Mason 2013) but also ideological identities such as "small-c conservative" (Malka and Lelkes 2010), issue identities such as environmentalism (McGarty et al. 2009), and national identities (Huddy and Khatib 2007; Theiss-Morse 2009). There is good evidence that it really can be self-identity, rather than related instrumental factors, that motivates political action (Huddy et al. 2015).

There seems to be something of a conflict between the idea of emphasizing identity as a fluid process rather than a fixed state and the notion of measuring it as a relatively permanent trait at an individual level. If people identify in a certain way in a certain moment, rather than have identities in a relatively permanent fashion, as is described in Chapter 2, what would it mean to measure the strength of a person's ethnic identity? Recall that active identification in the moment is a product of the context and the centrality of the identity to a person, which is relatively stable over time. Among other things, centrality affects the accessibility, or readiness, of the identity, which interacts with the context to produce identification at a given time (Cameron 2004; Rosenberg 1979). This centrality is a product, among other things, of knowledge about expectations of others, personal experience, social history, and repeated self-categorization in the past (Oakes 1987, 1996). The relative emphasis on identities constructed "on the fly" or permanent identification is a matter of some debate (Huddy 2002; Oakes 2002), but it is largely a matter of degree rather than a theoretical disagreement. The best way to understand measures of identification with a group, I suggest, is that they capture variation between individuals in centrality of the group to the person's self-concept. In the following chapters this is referred to as the centrality of identity, or high/low identifiers.[1]

Group self-identification measures are the focus of considerable current research, but they are also prominent in some of the earliest behavioural studies. Along with the development of partisanship as a form of social identification, Campbell and colleagues (1960), in *The American Voter*, examined the influence of race, ethnicity, religion, unions, and other social groups. Their analysis began with simple group membership but acknowledged that there would be important differences between those who identified with that membership and those who did not. While age, income, or other characteristics might distinguish subsets of the population behaving in distinctive ways, these categories are different from real social groups. The key attribute is that rather than simply being defined as a set of individuals who are distinct, real social groups exert causal influence.

Self-identification is portrayed in *The American Voter* as a kind of degree of membership. In fact, the first hypothesis that Campbell and colleagues (1960, 307) set out is that "the higher the identification of the individual with the group, the higher the probability that he will think and behave in ways that distinguish the members of the group from non-members." This is a crucial point: nominal members, who belong to the group but do not identify psychologically with it, are less likely to be influenced by group membership. Though the authors do not examine this concept of identification in detail, the sense seems to be that strength of identification is membership by degree – strong identifiers are "more" of a member of the group and nominal identifiers are "less." As a result, the authors discuss their findings in these terms and ask the so-called commonality question: "Would you say you feel pretty close to [group] people in general?" Versions of this question have been asked in many other studies and for a number of social groups.[2] For the authors of *The American Voter*, the "degree of psychological membership" (Campbell et al. 1960, 306) is a key way of understanding and, more precisely, predicting the effect of social groups.

Yet, self-identity is more than simply a degree of membership. It also involves a distinction between an internal and external self. Verkuyten (2005, 61) points out that "identity as a social fact" should not be confused with a subjective sense of identity. That is, the sense that one is a member of a group as defined in a certain way is distinct from feeling a sense of attachment and connection to it. These two concepts are what I call group membership and group identification. They are likely to be associated in practice simply because identity is social in the sense that it is influenced by other people. Nonetheless, group membership and group identification are both conceptually distinct, separate in the mind of the individual and with different behavioural implications.

The difference between membership and identification is discussed explicitly in social-identity theory. As Turner (1978, 138) puts it: "Social categorization per se ... is not sufficient for in-group favouritism ... The distinction between [experiments] classification of [subjects] into two groups and the identification with these categories by [subjects] needs to be firmly made." Of course, as is discussed in Chapter 2, people are not purely free to choose how they identify, because society, the media, and the state restrict their external ability to do so. The degree of variation between internal and external identity, between "objective" group membership and group identification depends on many factors, but the difference is important because of its relationship to the mechanisms of affinity voting. Of course, categorization as a member of a group often leads to identification, as is also discussed in Chapter 2. But this is not necessarily the case; where identification is lacking, behaviour effects will not materialize (Oakes 2002).

Research in social psychology suggests that there are three dimensions of attitudes toward social groups: cognitive, evaluative, and affective (Cameron 2004; Ellemers, Kortekaas, and Ouwerkerk 1999; see also Ashmore, Deaux, and McLaughlin 2004; Bergami and Bagozzi 2000; Jackson 2002). Distinguishing these three dimensions is actually quite natural. It is certainly possible to recognize that one is categorized as belonging to an ethnic group (cognitive) without necessarily having a positive view of that group in general (evaluative). Similarly, someone might say they are a racialized person, not because they strongly self-identify as such (affective) but because they know they fit the government-determined rules for the category (cognitive).

Cognitive group membership and affective self-identification with the group probably go together often – but that need not always be the case, and not always to the same degree. Specifically, for "chosen" social groups, self-identification and membership will likely go together, but this will be less true in the case of imposed group membership. If a person ceases to self-identify as a partisan, they can also choose to cease being a member of that party. Exiting the group is much more difficult with demographic categories such as gender or race, which are reinforced by the expectations and opinions of others. If group memberships are not chosen, then leaving the group is difficult, if not impossible. This characteristic is sometimes defined as the permeability of the group (Tajfel 1981; Jackson et al. 1996).

Since, to a substantial extent, race and ethnicity are imposed rather than chosen, cognitive understanding of membership and affective sense of identification for these groups might be quite different. The state also enforces and reproduces these categories (Thompson 2012) – including the Statistics Canada ethnic categories question used in this study. Clearly, visible-minority status is a bureaucratic category with a notionally objective definition based on family heritage and physical features. Even if people do not identify with those characteristics, they will likely accept that the category, as defined by society and the state, still applies to them. A woman might easily recognize that she meets the bureaucratic criteria of being Chinese Canadian, even if that is not an important part of her self-identity. As a result, there is probably more "slippage" between self-identification and group membership for imposed groups based on ethnicity than for choice groups such as political parties. Self-identification and group membership are more likely to be noncongruent for groups with low permeability, such as racial and ethnic groups, and therefore the importance of measuring the correct concept is all the greater.

A number of the mechanisms for affinity effects depend on self-identification. Ellemers, Kortekaas, and Ouwerkerk (1999, 375) argue that the affective dimension is about emotional involvement with the group, and that it is this dimension that leads to in-group favouritism. As discussed in Chapter 2, affective self-identification with a group, along with desire for positive self-attributions, leads to in-group bias. If a person's ethnicity is not an important part of his or her self-identity, then the link between group status and the self will be weak, and the person is unlikely to be impacted by the performance of other members of that ethnic group. In-group bias, I argue, underlies a number of the identity-based mechanisms for affinity voting, including direct effects from simply wanting a member of one's own group to win the election, indirect effects from seeing candidates from one's own group as more honest or hard-working, and persuasion effects from being more likely to believe the campaign messages of candidates belonging to one's group. This is a key point: it is affective self-identification with a group that leads to in-group bias and, therefore, the other identity-based mechanisms discussed in Chapter 2. Cognitive group membership on its own will not produce in-group bias.

On the other hand, many of the interest-based explanations only require cognitive membership in the group because group interests are generally related to group membership and not subjective self-identification. That is, people who recognize they are a member of a group, because of how the government classifies them, or how others perceive them, will also recognize they have interests in common with that group. Discrimination, for example, is caused by the perceived (socially imposed) membership in a group, not an individual's subjective self-identification. If coethnic affinity voting is caused by a policy heuristic about antidiscrimination policy, then it ought to be correlated with membership in the ethnic group rather than the degree of self-identification. Therefore, the interest-based mechanisms discussed in Chapter 2, such as policy heuristics or general group interest, should be contingent on group membership, but identity-based mechanisms should require identification with the group, not just membership. As a result, the different dimensions of group membership are probably linked to different mechanisms for affinity effects. Considering the relative effects of group membership and self-identification should therefore give us at least some purchase on motivations for affinity voting.

Measures of Ethnic and Racial Group Identity

Studies of affinity voting have not tended to include measures of ethnic or racial self-identity; instead, they often simply use group membership (e.g., Bird 2015; Barreto 2007; Philpot and Walton 2007; McDermott 1998). Sometimes, measures of behaviours that are plausibly correlated with identity are used, such as associating with members of the group or speaking the language (McConnaughy et al. 2010) or mentioning issues related to ethnicity (Barreto 2010) but these behaviours might be correlated with other important variables. Fisher and colleagues (2015) use a measure of relative ethnic versus British identity, but this measure might also capture a variety of other factors; furthermore, ethnic and national identities are not necessarily at odds (Breton 2015).

There are a number of other ethnic self-identification measures used in psychology and political science. The American National Election Study (ANES) has included questions about feeling "close to" various groups for years, and these questions have been adopted by other surveys. Sanchez (2008), for example, uses a measure of Latino commonality by asking about national groups such as Mexicans and Cubans: "Do you feel [national group] have a lot, a fair amount, or nothing in common with the following groups [other groups]." Unfortunately, measures that ask about "feeling close to" or "having much in common" with another group are imprecise: using Ellemers, Kortekaas, and Ouwerkerk (1999) schema, as discussed above, it is not clear if they are cognitive or affective measures. The question could easily be interpreted as being about objective similarities (speaking the same language, being an immigrant), and the measures are not discussed or evaluated specifically as measures of self-identity, as distinct from group membership.

The related concept of linked fate has been highly influential in research on African Americans and to a lesser extent on Latinos and Asian Americans (Dawson 1994; Herring, Jankowski, and Brown 1999; Tate 1994; McConnaughy et al. 2010). The strength of the sense of linked fate has been used to explain relative unity in policy preferences (Herring, Jankowski, and Brown 1999) and voting behaviour (Tate 1994). Linked fate has been so influential that Simien (2005, 530) notes that "political scientists have relied almost exclusively on one single indicator – the linked fate item – to measure race identification among African Americans."

The classic linked-fate measure, used in many studies, including the American National Election Study and the Black National Election Study, is as follows: "Do you think what happens to Black people in this country will have something to do with what happens in your life?" There are different variations, as well as multi-item scales, but this wording embodies the central focus of the concept. While most research on linked fate looks at black Americans, the measure has also been applied to Latinos. Sanchez and Masuoka (2010) asked a version of the linked fate question: "How much does your 'doing well' depend on other Latinos/Hispanics also doing well?" Some studies have also looked at linked fate among Asian Americans with limited success (Sanchez and Vargas 2016), although there seems to be considerable differences between national subgroups (Lien, Conway, and Wong 2004).

The difficulty is that the linked-fate question appears to capture a number of different dimensions, including respondent group membership, the structure of society, and perceived discrimination. The fate of the individual is linked to the group because generalized prejudice stops the individual from succeeding on his or her own merits. As a result, self-interest is unified with group-interest. As Sanchez and Masuoka (2010, 520) put it: "Resolving the problems facing their group will directly affect his or her individual life chances." While important, this is different from a sense of self-identification with a group. In fact, this interpretation of linked fate points toward the importance of the distinction between group membership and self-identification – a high sense of linked fate suggests that the respondent believes his or her own self-identification is irrelevant and that it is the socially imposed racial identity that will determine his or her place in the world. In other words, linked fate is not a measure of group identity but rather captures perceptions of interests in a social situation where self-identity is irrelevant. In some sense, linked fate is a belief about the individual but not the self.

Herring, Jankowski, and Brown (1999) grapple with these multiple dimensions and attempt to evaluate the different aspects of closeness, group salience, and common fate using a type of factor analysis and a set of twelve questions from the Black National Election Study. They conclude that these factors seem to be distinct dimensions, but the closeness measure might tap both cognitive and affective dimensions. Thus, while the linked-fate and "close to" measures have proven both informative and influential, they also have drawbacks: the nature of the psychological construct they draw on is not clear (affective, cognitive, evaluative) and the implied target of the question might vary (self-identification, structure of society).

Finally, there are some multi-item scales that are explicit measures of self-identity, and they include questions that aim to tap a connection to the group. Sidanius and colleagues (2008), for example, use a three-question scale, asking "How important is your ethnicity to your identity?," "How often do you think of yourself as a member of your ethnic group?," and "How close do you feel to members of your ethnic group?" Sniderman, Hagendoorn, and Prior (2004) include a similar set of statements – "I often think of myself as Dutch," "I consider myself a typical Dutchman," and "I'm proud that I'm Dutch" – though they do not mention identity quite so explicitly. The major benefit of these kind of measures is that they are focused on self-identity rather than behaviour; they are therefore less likely to capture things such opinions about society rather than the self. As multi-item scales, they are more accurate measures. While there is political-science research that uses these kinds of measures of self-identity, they have not been applied to affinity voting. Using a measure that directly measures self-identification with a group should produce much better estimates of the effect of self-identity on affinity voting.

Identification with a Psychological Group

The IDPG scale measures "feeling of oneness with a defined aggregate of persons, involving the perceived experience of its successes and failures" (Mael and Tetrick 1992, 851). As noted above, the scale has three key aspects: it focuses on self-identity rather than membership, it avoids measuring nonidentity factors such as behaviour, and it includes multiple items. It is symbolic rather than evaluative and describes a perception of oneness with the group rather than positive or negative attitudes toward that group (Ashforth and Mael 1989). The IDPG scale is symbolic in the sense that it asks hypothetical questions about how a person might react or how they typically express themselves. It does not, by contrast, ask how often an individual actually socializes with members of a group, making it quite different from, for example, measures of bonding social capital, which focus on substantive social relationships (Kay and Johnston 2011), or the behavioural measures used in some affinity-voting studies (e.g., McConnaughy et al. 2010). Finally, Mael and Ashforth (1992) argue that IDPG is different from measures such as organizational commitment, which also include questions on acceptance of values, willingness to exert effort, and desire to achieve the same goals (e.g., Wiener 1982). In other words, people with high levels of IDPG may behave in ways that are typical of the group, but this behaviour – or intention to behave in certain ways – is not part of the measure. Since this scale is intended to predict behaviour, keeping the measure focused strictly on identification, not behavioural intentions, is crucial.

Numerous studies in multiple research areas have applied versions of the IDPG scale. Since the original intent of the scale was to measure identification with organizations, it is not surprising that a substantial number of the studies are in management and organizational behaviour research (for a meta-analysis, see Riketta 2005). Nonetheless, the IDPG scale has also been applied to a number of other identity groups, such as gender (Walsh and Smith 2007), military units (Mael and Alderks 1993), friendship groups (Tong and Chang 2008), and religious organizations (Patrikios 2013). One study has validated the IDPG's use with ethnicity. Kester and Marshall (2003) apply the IDPG scale to Chinese Canadian immigrants to determine whether they identify ethnically as Chinese. While this study focuses on gender and the intergenerational transmission of ethnicity, the scale seems to work quite well to measure identification with a minority ethnicity in an immigrant population.

The IDPG scale has also been adopted by political-science studies in party identification research (Greene 1999, 2002, 2004; Huddy, Mason, and Aarøe 2015). Greene (1999) argues that the early characterization of partisan identification in *The American Voter* describes a social-group membership similar to ethnicity or religion. That is, partisanship is not just an attitude toward a party; it is a social-group membership. Therefore, the instinctive categorization of the world into "us" versus "them," and the in-group/out-group bias that results, apply to parties. Greene used the IDPG scale, with partisans as its target group, to develop a theoretically richer understanding of partisanship and the motivations for perceptual bias, dislike of other parties, and behaviour of "leaning" independents. In fact, one of his findings is that "independent" is itself a social identity, which helps explain why independents who lean Democrat or Republican are just as likely (and sometimes more likely) to vote for their party, as are weak partisans (Greene 1999). Although Greene does not describe it in this way, we can understand this phenomenon as the separation of evaluative and affective dimensions, discussed by Ellemers, Kortekaas, and Ouwerkerk (1999). Identifying with a group is not the same as having positive evaluations of that group – in this case, a person might like the Republican Party yet identify as independent. In this way, the distinctions between different dimensions of group identity help us better understand this puzzling partisanship dynamic, and they also shed light on other political phenomena.

The substantial amount of testing and validation of the IDPG and the scale's focus on self-identification as an affective attitude toward a social group suggests that using it would be an improvement on other group-identity measures used in political science. In addition, the scale has been applied to political constructs such as partisanship (Greene 1999) and ethnicity among Chinese immigrants to Canada (Kester and Marshall 2003) with success. While measures such as linked fate and group commonality may continue to be informative, IDPG offers a good option for examining social identity–based explanations for affinity effects.

THE IDPG SCALE

The original IDPG scale has ten statements focused on organizational identification and several reversed statements (Mael and Tetrick 1992). Given constraints pertaining to the length of the survey, a shorter version of the scale was adopted for this research (Patrikios 2013). Following pretesting feedback, one question was dropped because it did not fit well with ethnicity.[3] The following three statements were administered to the web-panel:

- When someone criticizes [group], it feels like a personal insult.
- When I talk about [group], I usually say "we" rather than "they."
- When someone praises [group], it feels like a personal compliment.

The response categories were on a five-point scale, ranging from "strongly agree" to "strongly disagree"; "neither agree nor disagree" was the middle category.

The statements were put forward in a two-step sequence. As part of the screening survey, respondents were asked if they belonged to a racialized group, and they were provided with the Statistics Canada categories (Arab, black, Chinese, Filipino, Japanese, Korean, Latin American, South Asian [e.g., East Indian, Pakistani, Sri Lankan], Southeast Asian [e.g., Vietnamese, Cambodian, Malaysian, Laotian], and West Asian [e.g., Iranian, Afghan]). The category selected defined what was inserted into "[group]" in the statement. For instance, the participant might read: "When someone criticizes South Asian people, it feels like a personal insult." However, since the question included both national terms (Chinese, Korean) and broader ethnic identifications (South Asian, Arab), comparisons across groups might be problematic. Therefore, for the applicable categories, broader ethnic identifications were substituted for national identifications. Specifically, Japanese, Chinese, and Korean respondents were asked about "Asian"[4] people, and Filipino respondents were asked about "Southeast Asian" people. The other categories provided by Statistics Canada could be used without modification. There was no hypothesis for the identification of white respondents, so the social-identity questions were not administered to those respondents.

IDPG DESCRIPTIVE STATISTICS

Responses to the three statements were combined into a fifteen-point additive index and scaled to the (0, 1) interval. The Cronbach's alpha score was 0.68, which is well within the acceptable range (Nunnally and Bernstein 1967). Notably, this is higher than scores for scales used in past analyses of Canadian Election Studies data (Gidengil et al. 2005; Soroka et al. 2013). Combined with the fact that the IDPG scale has been extensively tested elsewhere, this gives us good reason to be confident in the scale.

As Figure 4.1 makes clear, the mean scores are relatively similar across ethnicities and statements. The means range from 0.54 to 0.65, and there do not seem to be interactions between the questions and the ethnicity of respondents, nor are there obvious outliers. One methodological concern might be that seeing a racialized candidate would affect the strength of the identity statements, but in this case, the difference in the mean value of the strength-of-identity scale between treatment groups is very small (0.011) and statistically insignificant. Table 4.1 provides the standard deviation and 25th and 75th percentiles – an intuitive measure of what a person located moderately high or low on the scale might score.

An examination of histograms of the IDPG scale by ethnicity (Figure 4.2) suggests two points. First, there seem to be a significant number of South Asian respondents at the high end of the scale – above 0.8. By contrast, the Chinese or other racialized respondents have fewer high scores. This result is reflected in the percentiles in Table 4.1 – for South Asians, the 75 percent

FIGURE 4.1

Mean IDPG scores

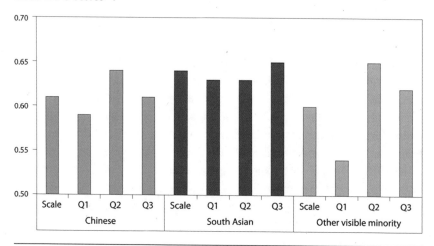

NOTES: Racialized respondents only; scale and individual questions; $n = 1,518$.

TABLE 4.1

Descriptive statistics for ethnicity and IDPG

	Mean	25th	75th	Standard deviation
Chinese	0.61	0.50	0.75	0.18
South Asian	0.64	0.50	0.83	0.23
Other racialized	0.60	0.50	0.75	0.21

percentile is 0.83, as opposed to 0.75 for the other groups. In addition, for all three groups there are a large number of respondents around 0.5 – but few lower, suggesting that there were a considerable number of respondents who were somewhat indifferent toward the ethnic group in question. However, it also suggests that there were very few who actively distanced themselves from their ethnic group or saw themselves as very unlike other members of the group. When asked whether they say "we" instead of "they" when speaking about their ethnic group, very few (4 percent of all racialized respondents) reported that they "strongly disagree." It seems that some racialized Canadians are indifferent toward their ethnic group, but they rarely reject or distance themselves from it.

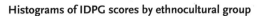

FIGURE 4.2

Histograms of IDPG scores by ethnocultural group

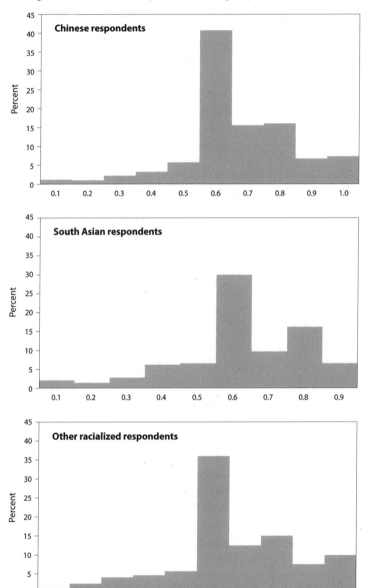

Demographic Predictors of IDPG

Given the importance of the IDPG variable, it is useful to know who identifies strongly with their ethnic group. In addition, knowing this sheds some light on moderators of these effects; the socializing effect of education, for example, might reduce the distinctness of a person's ethnic identity. Similarly, income could affect identity either because it indicates residential and economic segregation or because it is connected to a sense of exclusion and prejudice from the host society (Rumbaut 2005). In addition, immigration-related variables are of particular interest since they can give some indication of the long-term implications of ethnic identities, whether these identities are likely to have increasing effects in Canada as the proportion of ethnic minorities continues to increase or whether they will fade relatively quickly after immigration.

To examine demographic predictors, two models were estimated: one with standard demographic predictors and one focused on immigration-related variables. Model 4.1 uses ordinary least squares (OLS) regression and the IDPG scale as the dependent variable. Demographic indicators are independent variables and include income, education, gender, age, and immigration status. Since its impact may be nonlinear, age is constructed as a series of dummy variables. Since education received in Canada might have quite a different effect on ethnic identity than education completed outside Canada, this variable is also included in the model. Respondents were asked if their highest level of education was from an institution in Canada or outside Canada – the responses to this item were interacted with the level of education. The results are shown in Table 4.2. Surprisingly, very few of the demographic variables seem to be related to the strength-of-identity scale. Only two of the independent variables are significant: age and immigration status. Immigration has a positive and statistically significant coefficient, meaning that, on average, immigrants have a higher IDPG score than Canadian-born respondents. Age is negatively related to strength of identity; older respondents have lower IDPG scores. However, the difference is relatively small. The coefficient for the highest and lowest age categories ("60+" compared to the reference category "under 30") is only 0.042. While statistically significant ($p = .04$), it appears that the effect of age on strength of identity is modest.

Since interactions can be difficult to interpret, Figure 4.3 shows predicted values for the difference between Canadian and foreign education and for different levels of education (generated using Model 4.1). The predicted

TABLE 4.2

Demographic predictors of IDPG

Variables		Model 4.1	
Education		0.00	(0.00)
Foreign education		0.04	(0.04)
Foreign education* Education		0.00	(0.01)
Age:	30–39	0.01	(0.02)
	40–49	−0.03*	(0.02)
	50–59	−0.03	(0.02)
	60+	−0.04**	(0.02)
Income		0.01	(0.02)
Gender (male)		−0.01	(0.01)
Immigrant		0.04***	(0.01)
Constant		0.58***	(0.03)
Observations		1,355	
R-squared		0.03	

NOTES: OLS regression, with IDPG as dependent variable. Standard errors are in parentheses.

$* \, p < .1.$ $** \, p < .05.$ $*** \, p < .01.$

FIGURE 4.3

Effect of foreign education on IDPG scores, for different levels of education

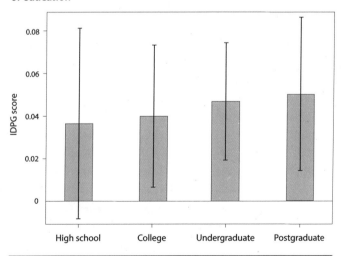

NOTES: Predicted values for racialized immigrant respondents only; $n = 979$.

values are for immigrants, since few nonimmigrants are educated outside Canada. Other demographic variables are set to their means. The effect of receiving an education outside of Canada appears to be conditional on the level of education. For those educated outside Canada who only have high school or some university or college education, the effect is not significant. However, the difference between being educated in Canada and education received elsewhere is not very large. For those with an undergraduate degree (the median category), those with a degree from a Canadian university scored, on average, 0.03 points lower on the IDPG than those with an undergraduate degree from outside Canada; those with a graduate or professional degree scored 0.04 lower. As with age, education in a foreign country does appear to have a significant effect, but the increase in IDPG scores is not very large.

Three of the variables discussed above – age, place of education, and immigration status – are closely related. One reason is that non-European immigration, for the most part, only began in the 1970s, therefore, most nonimmigrant, racialized respondents tend to be younger. In addition, the time in Canada and the time in the country of origin are very likely to be correlated. The relationship between identification with an ethnic group and these four variables – age, time resident in Canada, education in Canada, and age at time of immigration – is examined in Model 4.2 (see Table 4.3). In this model, the IDPG scale is again the dependent variable, and the four immigration-related variables – age, time as a resident in Canada, education in Canada, and age at time of immigration – are the independent variables, along with the variables from the previous model (age, income, gender, and education). Since multicollinearity is likely between age, years in Canada, and age at immigration, logged versions of these variables are used (following White et al. 2008).

Age at immigration is the only statistically significant predictor of strength of ethnic identification ($p = .01$) in Model 4.2. While the logged variable is difficult to interpret directly, respondents who immigrated to Canada when they were younger had a weaker identification with their ethnic group, while those who spent more time in their country of origin had stronger ethnic identities. Logged age was not too far from significance ($p = .09$), and the coefficient was negative, as in the previous model: older people have weaker ethnic identities. Income was nearly significant ($p = .08$), but gender was not ($p = .59$). The education variables were also insignificant; it is therefore

TABLE 4.3

Immigration-related predictors of IDPG

Variables	Model 4.2 Ethnic IDPG		Model 4.3 Specific cultural IDPG	
Education	−0.03	(0.04)	0.06	(0.06)
Foreign education	−0.02	(0.05)	0.08	(0.07)
Foreign education*	0.07	(0.06)	−0.06	(0.09)
Income	0.04*	(0.02)	0.06**	(0.03)
Gender (male)	0.01	(0.01)	0.01	(0.02)
Logged age	−0.07*	(0.04)	−0.12**	(0.05)
Logged age at immigration	0.03**	(0.01)	0.04**	(0.02)
Logged years in Canada	−0.00	(0.01)	0.01	(0.02)
Constant	0.77***	(0.11)	0.84***	(0.15)
Observations	862		534	
R-squared	0.03		0.04	

NOTES: OLS regression, with different measures of IDPG as dependent variable. Racialized immigrant respondents only. Standard errors are in parentheses.
$^* p < .1.$ $^{**} p < .05.$ $^{***} p < .01.$

plausible that the effects in the previous model were a result of length of education in a foreign country being confounded with time living in the country of origin. Years in Canada was not statistically significant. In other words, even if immigrants integrate into Canadian society in other ways, their sense of identification with their ethnic group does not decline.

The most interesting finding here is that immigrating to Canada at a later age is correlated with more strongly self-identifying with an ethnic group, as measured by the IDPG. Socialization in the country of origin, presumably in a society where their ethnicity is in the majority, leads to a stronger self-identification with that ethnic group. Put another way, it seems that it is not time residing in Canada that leads to a weaker ethnic identity but rather lack of time lived in another country. The obvious alternative – time spent residing in Canada, where these ethnicities are minorities – does not reduce the strength of ethnic self-identification, perhaps because multiculturalism reduces the "pressure" to assimilate. Certainly, some have argued that multicultural policies emphasize difference rather than reduce it (this position is taken by commentators and politicians, but also see Sniderman and

Hagendoorn 2007). Or perhaps racial and ethnic groups have an innately high barrier to exit; that is, it is simply very difficult to stop being "ethnic," in part because of the way the perspectives of others shape our identities.

Smaller Ethnic and Cultural Groups

In addition to the Statistics Canada ethnic categories, questions were also asked about more specific cultural or national groups, since the distinction between national, ethnic, and cultural groups is often unclear. For simplicity, here, the Statistics Canada categories are referred to as ethnic groups and smaller categories as specific cultural groups. While there are no strong expectations about this measure, it should not be viewed as competitive or in opposition to broader identities. Rather, nested-identity theory suggests that different kinds of identities are likely to be correlated, since identification with narrower groups is likely to result in identification with logically implied superordinate groups. However, specific identities are likely to be stronger since lower-order identities are more likely to shape social life. People therefore self-categorize themselves that way more regularly, increasing the accessibility of that identity.

Following the IDPG questions, respondents were asked an open-ended question: "In addition to [Statistics Canada ethnic category], is there a more specific ethnic or cultural group you belong to?" Respondents could also respond by choosing "No, there isn't a more specific group" (see Table 4.4). The answers were then inserted into another set of the same three IDPG questions. For example, a question might read: "When someone criticizes [Punjabi] people, it feels like a personal insult." By far the most common response was "Chinese," presumably because this is both a national and ethnic group with a (generally) homogeneous definition, although Chinese were also overrepresented in the sample. Conversely, the South Asian category included a wide range of nationalities, minor ethnic groups, different religions, and so on. There were also a significant number of respondents who declared themselves Punjabi, Japanese, or Filipino. However, for some two hundred groups, there were only a small number of responses, the majority with only one response, ranging widely from nationalities such as Lebanese or Vietnamese, to small ethnic groups such as Pashtoon or Yorba, to subnational units such as Hong Kong or Gujarati.

This measure of identity presents some difficulties. A significant number of people simply opted not to provide a response. In addition, some of the

TABLE 4.4

Open-ended responses to specific ethnic or cultural categories

	Number	Percentage
Chinese	454	49
Punjabi	42	5
Japanese	36	4
Filipino	36	4
Korean	15	2
Jamaican	13	1
Tamil	12	1
African	10	1
Caribbean	10	1

NOTES: All categories with ten or more responses are listed. The percentage is based on valid responses (957).

TABLE 4.5

Descriptive statistics for specific cultural IDPG

	Mean	25th	75th	Standard deviation
Chinese	0.65	0.50	0.75	0.20
South Asian	0.70	0.50	0.91	0.23
Other Racialized	0.60	0.50	0.75	0.24

NOTE: Respondents are categorized by ethnicity to facilitate comparison with Table 4.1, but questions reference specific cultural groups.

text-box responses were inappropriate for inserting into the IDPG questions. For example, some people explained their family ancestry rather than giving a one- or two-word answer. These responses were removed from the data. Roughly one-third of the sample had missing values, leaving 957 responses. Given the substantially reduced sample size, these data are not used in the main analysis that follows in the next chapters,[5] but a comparison between the two measures of identity is illuminating.

To examine specific cultural/national identification, the three IDPG questions were merged into a scale (0–1). Krippendorf's alpha was higher for the specific cultural group IDPG (0.76) than for the ethnic group IDPG (0.67).

While both are acceptable, they suggest that respondents gave more consistent answers to questions about identification with their specific cultural or national group. The broad ethnic and specific cultural IDPG scores were strongly, though not perfectly, correlated (0.65, $p < 0.001$), supporting the idea that they were measuring related but distinct identities. The mean score of specific cultural IDPG was higher: 0.65 compared to 0.61. This could reflect that people with weak identities did not bother to fill out the textbox and were excluded from the analysis. However, the finding is also consistent with the expectations of nested-identity theory, where more specific identities tend to be stronger.

Histograms of the three groups are shown in Figure 4.4. They are grouped by ethnic identity for comparison purposes with Figure 4.2, but they show the results of questions about the specific identity group. There are clear differences: in all three categories, there are more strong identifiers at the top end of the scale and considerably fewer indifferent respondents (i.e., at 0.5 on the scale).

Looking at the mean difference in scores, on average, the specific cultural IDPG score is 0.04 higher than the ethnic IDPG (with a standard deviation of 0.15). A closer examination of the cross-tabs (not shown) does not suggest that a group of respondents shifted dramatically from lower on one measure to much higher on the other. Rather, respondents tended to score incrementally higher on the specific cultural IDPG scale than on the ethnic IDPG scale.

Specific cultural identities are likely to be more closely linked to socialization in another country. Conversely, it may require time to identify with an identity group defined by Statistics Canada. That is, it could take time to adopt the racial schema dominant in Canadian society. To test this, Model 4.3 examines the correlation of immigration- and age-related factors, repeating the analysis of Model 4.2 but with specific cultural IDPG as the dependent variable. The results, presented in Table 4.3 above, indicate that years in Canada is not statistically significant: specific cultural identities, like ethnic identities, do not seem to fade with time in Canada. Similarly, both measures are correlated with age at arrival. Interestingly, there is little difference in the correlation between the logged time in Canada and the two measures of IDPG, perhaps because the learning process is nonlinear and the number of truly recent immigrants in this sample was quite small. If immigrants begin to identify with broader ethnic groups in just a few years, this would explain the lack of difference.

FIGURE 4.4

Histograms of cultural/national IDPG measure

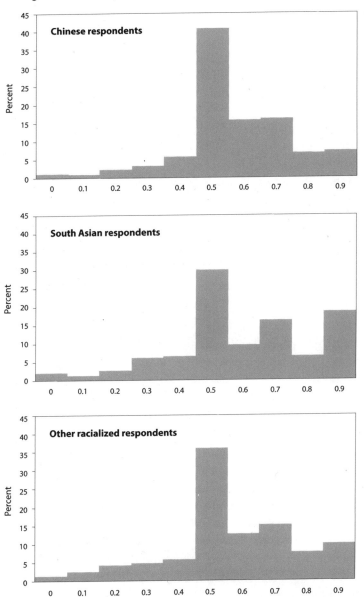

NOTE: Respondents are grouped by ethnicity, but IDPG questions use specific cultural groups such as Punjabi.

Ethnic Self-Identity and Identification with a Psychological Group

As suggested at the beginning of this chapter, group identity is multidimensional and has important cognitive, evaluative, and affective aspects. Most studies of social groups in politics use simple group membership or measures such as the "close to" questions or linked fate for which the psychological content is unclear. Not only are scale measures of identity likely to produce more accurate estimates of effects, they can also help distinguish between explanations for those effects. Using a measure of self-identification rather than cognitive membership, I argue, more accurately taps into the key affective dimension of group identification. Many of the identity-based explanations hinging on in-group bias are actually rooted in the connection between the group and one's self-identity. Conversely, interest-based mechanisms ought to be linked to cognitive group membership rather than to self-identification.

The demographic predictors of the IDPG scale suggest that time living in the country of origin is the most important factor. The lack of correlation with demographic indicators suggests that social situation and interests in Canada are not the primary drivers of ethnocultural identity. For example, there is little difference between the IDPG scores of people with different incomes, education levels, and age. While we might imagine interests based on immigration status (such as settlement assistance, antidiscrimination policies, credential recognition, immigration policy, and so on), there is no reason why they would be related to the age at immigration.

These results have two important implications for ethnic identification over time. First, the effects of self-identification with an ethnic group are probably durable and long-lasting throughout an individual's lifetime, but they will likely be weaker in subsequent generations. The effects of ethnic identities are not confined to recent immigrants but will continue to be strong for decades after immigration. On the other hand, nonimmigrant, racialized respondents do seem to have distinctly weaker ethnic identities. This is not surprising given that time living in the country of origin has such a powerful effect. In the long term, Canada's racialized population will continue to grow, but the percentage of those who are immigrants will decline as the number of racialized Canadian-born citizens increases. Over time, this trend will moderate the effects of ethnocultural identity, which is strong among immigrants but more modest among racialized citizens born in Canada.

In addition, these data suggest that ethnic identity is not primarily caused by the experience of prejudice or discrimination. It is age at immigration, and hence the number of years spent in the country of origin, rather than years spent in Canada, that is correlated with strength of ethnic identity. If identification were related to experiences in Canada, there ought to be an effect from time spent living in Canada – yet there is no such relationship. The fact that perceptions of discrimination are often stronger in second-generation immigrants is consistent with this conclusion (Reitz and Banerjee 2007). Thus, self-identification with one's ethnocultural group seems to be driven primarily by socialization and developing an identity in the country of origin rather than by the social position and experiences of the respondent in Canada.

The more specific cultural IDPG questions incorporated the responses to a prior open-ended question to measure ethnic and cultural groups more narrowly defined, for example, Punjabi rather than South Asian. The two measures were also strongly, though not perfectly, correlated. Identification with these more specific groups was, on average, somewhat higher than for ethnic categories, as nested-identity theory would predict. This suggests that an even broader category, a general racialized or minority identity, would also be correlated with these measures but that average identification would be weaker.

The IDPG scale, I argue, is not a cognitive measure. That is, people would not place themselves high on the IDPG scale for purely cognitive reasons, such as objective group membership, or for reasons relating to their interests. While we cannot test for this directly using these data, there are a number of reasons to think that the IDPG scale is not strongly related to cognitive factors. As already noted, the IDPG score is not correlated with many variables that are usually linked to interests, such as income. In addition, on the face of it, the IDPG questions appear to tap emotional connections to a group rather than cognitive factors. And the measure avoids questions about real social situations, such as the number of friends of that ethnicity or language spoken at home, which some measures of identity use (e.g., McConnaughy et al. 2010). By and large, the cognitive measure (group membership) and affective measure (IDPG) appear to be distinct; we should therefore be able to use them to pull apart the different affinity mechanisms.

One possible complication is whether the IDPG scale is correlated with perceptions of shared group interests. While there is no direct evidence here, some leverage can be gained from thinking about the behaviour of indifferent identifiers – that is, those who place themselves in the middle of the IDPG scale. We would expect that there would be no identity-based affinity voting if the respondents are indifferent to the identity group. Indifference to a group does not suggest in-group bias. Conversely, interest-based explanations would suggest that there should be affinity voting if respondents are at the middle of the IDPG scale. Since they still consider themselves to be members of that group, then there should still be at least some interest-based effect. Even though they do not strongly identify with a group, acknowledging their membership in the group also implies an acknowledgment that their interests are connected to the group, at least to some degree. Membership, even without identification, implies that others see them as a members of the group, and hence they will suffer from discrimination or benefit from policies. Thus, at the middle of the IDPG scale, identity- and interest-based explanations have different implications for affinity effects, which will be discussed at length in the next chapter.

In order to understand the effects of ethnicity on behaviour it is crucial to measure self-identification with the ethnic group rather than simply considering membership in the ethnic group category. Doing so will produce more accurate estimates of effects, but distinguishing between cognitive group membership and self-identification could help distinguish between interest- and identity-based explanations for affinity effects. The IDPG scale appears to work well as a measure of self-identification with an ethnocultural group, and the strongest determinant is age at immigration, suggesting that it is socialization in the country of origin rather than experiences in Canada or material interests that drives ethnic self-identification.

5
Ethnic Identity and
Voter Behaviour

There are indeed ethnic- and racialized-affinity effects in Canada, but they apply to multiple ethnic groups, and the size (but not the direction) of the effects depends on whether the candidate is a member of the same or a different ethnicity group as the voter. The pattern of coethnic affinity voting among racialized Canadians appears to be as follows: strong effects for coethnic affinity voting and more modest, but still positive, effects for racialized affinity voting. The degree of self-identification with an ethnic group, measured by the IDPG scale, is crucial and underpins identity-based explanations. This chapter incorporates the scale into the analysis of coethnic affinity voting.

Identity-based coethnic affinity voting might be caused by a number of mechanisms, including candidate evaluation, persuasion, and expressive voting effects. All of these mechanisms rest on how social identity links the group to the individual's self-esteem. If group affiliation between the candidate and the voter is weak, the victory or loss of the candidate will be unlikely to affect the voter's self-esteem. We would expect little or no direct effect on voting behaviour based on a desire for the candidate to win. Similarly, if a voter does not self-identify as a member of the group, there is no reason to expect bias in candidate attribute evaluations or source effects on the persuasiveness of campaign messages.

To explore identity-based explanations for affinity voting, this chapter tests whether coethnic affinity voting is conditional on self-identifying with an ethnocultural group. If identity-based mechanisms do indeed play an important role, a stronger ethnic identity should be positively correlated with affinity voting.

Ethnic Self-Identification and Affinity Voting

The theoretical framework set out in Chapter 2 and the discussion of self-identity in Chapter 4 suggest several possible effects of ethnic self-identification on vote choice. For coethnic affinity, these effects are relatively straightforward. Self-identification with an ethnic group is likely to be correlated with same-ethnicity affinity effects because it is self-identification with the group that underlies identity-based mechanisms.

For racialized affinity, there are conflicting theoretical predictions. Overall, political research from the United States and sociological and attitudinal research from Europe and Canada suggest that the key identity categories for affinity effects are specific ethnocultural groups, not racialized status more generally. Not only has this research revealed political conflict between minorities, but each minority group seems to prefer affiliation with the white majority over affiliation with other minorities. In Chapter 2, I suggest that this result can be explained by motivated social positioning, since relative group position is a group attribution, and people are motivated to seek positive group attributions. Racialized citizens will associate their group with the high-status white majority, not with other lower-status racialized groups. However, motivated social positioning depends on differences in status, which are probably lower in Canada than in the United States and lower for the ethnic groups in question than for black and Latino Americans.

The alternative explanation is that identification with an ethnic group can promote affinity rather than conflict between ethnic groups, leading to racialized affinity. Self-categorization theory, particularly the common-intergroup-identity model (Gaertner et al. 1993), suggests that context can create broader racialized or minority group identities. It may be that the choice in the present experiment, between a white and a racialized candidate of a different ethnicity, frames the decision in such a way as to activate this kind of broader racialized identity.

There is some empirical evidence that identifying with one's own ethnic group can produce affinity for other racialized groups. Specifically, Latinos who say they have "a lot in common" with other Latinos have been found to be more likely to feel positive toward African Americans (Kaufmann 2003). It is possible that people with particularly strong ethnic group loyalties will have more negative opinions of other minority groups, or perhaps group identities are to some extent mutually exclusive – a stronger specific ethnocultural identity might mean a weaker broader racialized group identity.

However, there is no evidence to indicate this. Although Kaufmann (2003) looks only at general attitudes rather than vote choice, on the basis of these findings, together with the theoretical arguments put forward in Chapter 2, it is hypothesized that stronger identification with one's ethnocultural group should increase both coethnic affinity and racialized affinity:

H5.1: Racialized voters who have a stronger ethnic group identity will be more likely to choose a candidate of the *same* ethnic group than those with a weaker ethnic group identity.

H5.2: Racialized voters who have a stronger ethnic group identity will be more likely to choose a candidate of a *different* racialized group than those with a weaker ethnic group identity.

Testing Identity and Affinity Voting

The models in this chapter are similar to those in Chapter 3 but with the addition of an interaction with strength of identity. The first model merges combinations of ethnic groups to test ethnic and racial affinity in general, and then each combination of specific ethnic groups is examined. The dependent variable in Model 5.1 is voting for Candidate 2, and the key independent variables are dummy variables: showing respondent a candidate of the same ethnicity or of a different racialized ethnicity (seeing a white candidate is the reference category), the IDPG measure, and a set of interaction terms. Demographic covariates (age, income, education, gender, religion, and immigrant status) are also included. Party and independent versions are collapsed, and all models use only racialized respondents.

The predicted probabilities in Figure 5.1 show that there are both coethnic-affinity and racialized-affinity effects, and that they are strongly conditional on self-identity. Respondents high on the IDPG scale are far more likely to support a candidate of their own ethnic group or other racialized ethnic group than an otherwise identical white candidate. Both effects are statistically significant at 0.65 and above on the IDPG scale. This finding is strong support in favour of both Hypothesis 5.1 and Hypothesis 5.2.

At the midpoint of the IDPG scale (.5), there is no evidence of affinity effects. That is, when respondents are indifferent toward their ethnic group, they are also indifferent to the ethnicity of candidates. As discussed in Chapter 4, indifference to the group, or the midpoint on the IDPG scale, implies

FIGURE 5.1

Coethnic and racialized affinity, by strength of identification

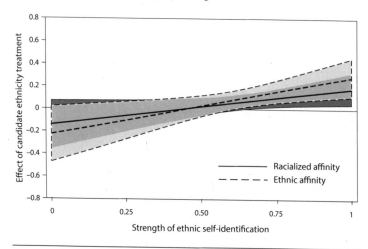

NOTES: Difference in predicted probability of choosing Candidate 2, between white and racialized candidate versions; racialized respondents only; $n = 1{,}125$.

no affinity on the identity-based account. Conversely, there should still be interest-based affinity effects, because these respondents still recognize that they are members of the group (i.e., the Statistics Canada ethnic categories, not the IDPG scale). The evidence here – the lack of effects at the midpoint of the scale – appears to be consistent with identity-based explanations but not with interest-based explanations for affinity effects, which are explored further in Chapter 6.

The size of the racialized and ethnic-affinity effects are different: the size of the racial-affinity effects are roughly two-thirds the size of coethnic affinity. At the 75 percentile of the IDPG scale (.75), respondents were 16 percentage points more likely to support a candidate of the same ethnic group than a white candidate ($p = .002$) and 10 percentage points more likely to support a candidate of a different racialized ethnic group than a white candidate ($p = .01$). At the top of the IDPG scale (1), the racialized-affinity effect is 18 percentage points ($p = .01$), and the ethnic-affinity effect is 28 percentage points ($p = .001$). Notably, these are not extreme values: 0.75 on the strength-of-ethnic-identification scale is the 75th percentile, meaning that 25 percent of the sample scored 0.75 or higher. A large portion of the sample seemed to show high levels of coethnic affinity voting.

There is some evidence that disidentifiers (those at the bottom of the IDPG scale) actually preferred the white candidate over a candidate of their own ethnic group, although the evidence for this effect in the racial affinity analysis is weak ($p = .07$ for coethnic affinity; $p = .19$ for racial affinity). These low scores on the strength-of-ethnic-identification scale are quite rare: only 5 percent of the sample scored 0.25 or below. Thus, it seems that although there were some respondents who identified with their ethnic group very little or not at all and who also discriminated against candidates of their own ethnic group, there were not many of them. Disidentification with one's own ethnic group, and the corresponding rejection of candidates belonging to one's ethnic group, seems to be uncommon. Far more common, at least in this sample, are respondents who seem indifferent about their ethnic self-identification and who show neither affinity nor discrimination.

To examine the effects among specific ethnic groups, Model 5.2 repeats the analysis in Model 5.1 but uses variables for the respondents' and candidates' specific ethnicities: white, Chinese, and South Asian versions of Candidate 2, and "Chinese," "South Asian," and "other racialized" for respondents. To evaluate the effect of strength of ethnocultural identity, the strength-of-identity scale is included in the model and interacted with participant ethnicity and candidate ethnicity to form a three-way interaction (along with its constituent terms).

Figure 5.2 compares the support for the white and racialized versions of Candidate 2 and clearly shows ethnic-affinity effects for both Chinese and South Asian respondents. At 0.75 on the strength-of-ethnic-identification scale, South Asian respondents are 15 percentage points more likely to choose the South Asian candidate than the white candidate ($p = .1$), and at the top of the strength-of-ethnic-identification scale, South Asian respondents are 25 percentage points more likely to choose the South Asian candidate than the white candidate ($p = .08$). In addition, whereas Chinese-origin respondents showed only a small point estimate when strength of identification was not taken into account (Figure 3.2), Chinese respondents with high levels of ethnic group identification are much more likely to vote for the Chinese candidate than the white candidate. At 0.75 on the IDPG scale, they are 13 percentage points more likely to vote for the Chinese candidate ($p = .08$), and at the top of the IDPG scale, they are 30 percentage points more likely to vote for the Chinese candidate than the white candidate ($p = .02$). While ethnic-affinity effects among Chinese respondents are statistically significant, they do not reach conventional levels of significance among South

Figure 5.2

Affinity for same ethnic group, by strength of identification

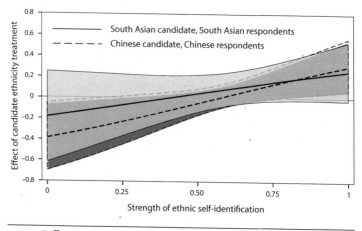

NOTES: Difference in predicted probability of choosing Candidate 2, between white and racialized candidate versions, for respondents of the same ethnicity; *n* = 1,125.

Asian respondents. Nonetheless, the number of South Asian respondents was considerably smaller, and the point estimates are quite close, suggesting that the effects are quite similar for Chinese and South Asian voters.

At the midpoint of strength of ethnic group identification, Chinese- and South Asian–origin respondents are indifferent to whether the candidate is of their own ethnicity. Both Chinese and South Asian low-identifying respondents, at the 25th percentile of the strength-of-ethnic-identification scale (0.5), showed no significant affinity voting, and the point estimates are near zero. At the bottom of the scale, some respondents actually showed discrimination against candidates of their own ethnic group: Chinese respondents scoring 0.25 on the strength-of-ethnic-identification scale are 31 percentage points *less* likely to select the Chinese candidate, which is significant at the 95 percent confidence level. While the point estimates of low-identifying South Asians (i.e., at 0 on the IDPG scale) are also negative, they are not statistically significant.

More generally, these results are a clear confirmation of Hypothesis 5.1. This finding demonstrates that affinity effects are not limited to South Asian respondents. Recall that in the analysis without strength of identification (Chapter 3), Chinese affinity-voting effects were not statistically significant.

FIGURE 5.3

Affinity for different ethnic groups, by strength of identification

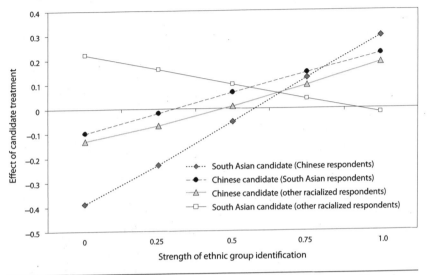

NOTES: Difference in predicted probability of choosing Candidate 2, between white and racialized candidate versions, for respondents of different ethnicity; racialized respondents only; for clarity confidence intervals are not included; $n = 1,125$.

Here, however, there is strong evidence for affinity voting among candidates and voters of the same ethnicity, for both Chinese and South Asian identifiers. This means that these identity effects are broadly generalizable to many different ethnic groups.

To test for racialized affinity voting with specific ethnic groups, we return to Model 5.2, which includes specific ethnic-group variables rather than a white-racialized dichotomy. Predicted probabilities are generated for the difference between the white and ethnic-minority versions of Candidate 2 for each of the four combinations of racialized participant and candidate pairs and at different levels of the strength-of-ethnic-identity measure. Figure 5.3 presents the difference between the white and minority candidate – effectively, the size of the treatment effect for each different-ethnicity combination.

The results are mostly consistent with Hypothesis 5.2: three of four voter-candidate pairs have positive slopes, meaning that respondents who strongly identify with their own ethnic group are more likely to support a candidate of a different ethnic-minority group. These effects are less precisely estimated than for ethnic-affinity effects. Chinese respondents at the top of the strength-of-identity scale are 26 percentage points more likely to support a South Asian candidate than a white candidate ($p = .03$) and 16 percentage points more likely at 0.75 on the strength-of-identity scale ($p = .03$). Similarly, South Asian respondents at the top of the strength-of-identification scale are 24 percentage points more likely to support a Chinese candidate ($p = .01$) and 13 percentage points more likely at 0.75 on the IDPG scale ($p = .08$). However, none of the predicted probabilities for the other racialized respondents are significant. While the "South Asian candidate (other racialized respondents)" line appears to be negative, it is far from statistically significant. The key point here is that the combined results are not being driven by any particular combination, as was the case for affinity-voting results for specific ethnic categories in Chapter 3.

Ethnic and Racialized Affinity

Affinity-voting effects are clearly concentrated among those who have a stronger identification with their ethnocultural group. As Figures 5.1, 5.2, and 5.3 illustrate, a stronger racialized ethnocultural identity increases the likelihood of supporting a racialized candidate. The pattern of results is similar to those in Chapter 3, showing larger ethnic-affinity-voting effects and more modest racialized-affinity-voting effects. Both, however, are strongly conditional on the IDPG measure of ethnocultural group self-identification.

The strongest effects found were for coethnic affinity; that is, strong ethnic identifiers are far more likely to support a candidate of their own ethnicity than an otherwise identical white candidate. Conversely, those who are indifferent to their ethnocultural identity show no effect, and those who reject their ethnic group may actually discriminate against those candidates.

The strength-of-ethnic-identification measure also helps clarify the general applicability of affinity effects. In Chapter 3, the predicted probabilities for the individual ethnic-group combinations showed differences in effect, but the lack of statistical significance hampered the analysis. However, once we modelled the conditioning effect of strength-of-ethnic-group identification, the predicted probabilities clearly showed ethnic-affinity effects for both Chinese and South Asian respondents, suggesting that similar affinity effects apply widely to different ethnic groups.

Nonetheless, the respondents clearly distinguished between their own ethnic group and other ethnic minorities – the size of the effects for racialized affinity were roughly two-thirds the size of those for coethnic affinity. That is, stronger ethnic group identity increases the effect of racialized affinity, but support for a candidate of the same ethnocultural group is still higher.

Racialized-affinity effects are also conditioned by ethnic identity. When the categories are combined, as in Figure 5.2, there is clear evidence for racialized affinity, conditioned by strength of identity measures. When specific ethnic groups are examined for racialized affinity, as Figure 5.3 shows, other racialized respondents were not statistically significant, and for one, the slope is negative. However, there were racialized-affinity effects for both South Asian and Chinese respondents, which suggests the effect is not confined to a single ethnic group.

These results also confirm the usefulness of the IDPG scale for evaluating the influence of ethnicity in politics. While the IDPG scale has previously been used in sociological studies of immigrants (Kester and Marshall 2003), its only use in political science has been to study partisan identities (e.g., Greene 2002; Huddy, Mason, and Aarøe 2015). The results in this chapter demonstrate that the IDPG scale is a useful tool for evaluating the effects of ethnicity on vote choice and is a considerable improvement on focusing on membership in an ethnocultural group.

Open-Ended Responses: "Why Did You Vote for That Candidate?"

To explore the motivations for affinity further, respondents were also asked an open-ended question: "Why did you vote for that candidate?" A text box was provided for respondents to type an answer. Most ranged from a word or two to a few sentences, capped at two hundred words.[1] These responses do not provide direct leverage on causality since they might well be rationalizations. Similarly, social-desirability bias no doubt influenced the responses, since some kinds of considerations are more acceptable when deciding how to vote. Nonetheless, the responses do give a sense of top-of-mind considerations, the kind of responses that people think are acceptable, and a richer sense of how respondents were thinking.

I coded the responses into five categories, which were based primarily on the different explanations for affinity effects. In addition, an inductive reading of the data lead to the separation of two categories ("qualifications" and "personal qualities") and the merging of two planned categories ("party" and "ideology"). The data were recoded following these decisions and before analysis of candidate ethnicity was undertaken. The results are presented in Table 5.1. "Identity" includes mention of *ethnicity, immigrant, minority,* or other racialized terms, including comments such as "He is a minority" and "Because he is Chinese." "Party/ideology" includes references to ideological positions and either the respondent's or the candidate's party affiliation, such as "tax and government spending" or "I am a Liberal." References to ideology and party were often difficult to tell apart, a point which is explored in the following chapter. Because of the challenges of telling these two terms apart, they are coded as a single category. "Qualifications" includes references to the candidate's career and experiences, such as "successful businessman" or "like the charities he supports." "Personal qualities" includes general references to the candidate's quality, such as "He sounds like more of a leader" or "honest." Personal qualities were coded separately from qualifications since the latter are based on actual features of the treatment, while the former were generated entirely by the respondent and are perhaps more likely to be a product of in-group bias. Finally, the "Other" category includes responses indicating uncertainty or are otherwise uninformative, such as "personal preference," "no specific reason," or unintelligible responses. Generally, only a single reason was given, but multiple categories were coded where appropriate.

Why do respondents say they voted for candidates? According to Table 5.1, candidate qualifications were by far the most common answer, but this finding might be an artifact of the experimental design, which gives more prominence to this information than a real election does. Personal qualities were also a common response. While this explanation might be an effect of in-group bias about candidate evaluations, it is also an obvious way to rationalize any decision. More interesting are the sixty-two racialized candidate supporters who explicitly cited identity factors as the reason for supporting the vote choice. Roughly half of them explicitly cited the candidate's ethnicity and culture with statements such as "I like to support South Asian candidates," "being of south asian roots," "he's indian," "Because he helps the local community and also because he is an Indian (I mean East Indian)," "Chinese," "because he is chinese," "of asian ethnicity," "related cultural background," and "Mr. Zhang is probably Chinese and may relate to my heritage." Clearly, many respondents consciously and explicitly supported candidates because of their ethnicity. They also seemed to think this was a socially acceptable reason to give for their choice. This is significant since it is generally unacceptable for people to say they voted for a candidate because he or she was white; in fact, only one respondent did so, saying "the primary reason is because Mr. Hawkes has a 'white' name." (this was one of

Table 5.1

Open-ended reasons for support

	White Candidate 2		Racialized Candidate 2	
Identity***	0	(2)	6	(62)
Party/ideology	13	(66)	12	(122)
Interests	1	(4)	1	(7)
Qualifications*	57	(289)	52	(523)
Personal qualities	15	(75)	15	(147)
Other	18	(89)	17	(174)

NOTES: Includes racialized respondents only. Rounded column percentage reported, with raw numbers in brackets. Chi² test of difference between white candidate and racialized candidate for each category.
* $p < .05$. ** $p < .01$. *** $p < .001$.

one thousand white respondents, who were not included in the analysis). Conversely, respondents were much more willing to cite minority ethnicity as a reason to vote for a candidate.

A small number (2) of racialized respondents who *opposed* the racialized candidate also cited identity considerations. For example, one respondent said, "I do not vote for someone with same background if I do not like what he does." This statement supports the point discussed earlier in the chapter: just as voters at the bottom of the IDPG scale discriminate against candidates of their own ethnicity, some racialized voters explicitly distance themselves from their ethnic identity or do not want to be seen as supporting a candidate just because of his or her ethnicity. While few in number, these responses support the experimental results in suggesting that there is a group of disidentifiers who have a distinct behavioural response.

A few respondents (5) who gave identity-related responses specifically mentioned general representation issues: "We have many Asians living in my riding, if he were the elected one he would better represent us," "to support more minority in politics," "to give a chance for a minority person to get into a political position," "we need more minority politicians," and "to promote diversity." The motivations for these comments about representation are not clear – when they say *represent*, do they mean advocating for policy or purely for symbolic representation? These kinds of responses were few in number, but the issue deserves future exploration. Notably, these responses are similar to focus-group research in Toronto, which also found a desire for symbolic representation among ethnic-minority citizens (Bird 2015).

A good number of respondents (24) seemed to express more general racialized, minority, or immigrant identities. One respondent said, "because he's the minority," while others gave statements such as "Minority like myself giving back to the community," "Primarily because he belongs to a visible minority," "he is from minority," "minority like me," "he's not white," and "he is an immigrant like me." These statements all fit with racialized affinity as an identity effect: they stem from an understanding of racialized ethnic groups as belonging to a broader, superordinate group ("minorities," "immigrants") and an understanding of candidates of other racialized ethnic groups as in-group members.

Identity and Affinity Voting

The results presented in this chapter provide strong evidence for the important role of ethnic self-identity in affinity voting. As noted in Chapter 2, affinity research to date has, surprisingly, neglected identity-based explanations. These findings confirm the crucial role that self-identification, rather than simple group membership, plays in influencing behaviour. The data in Chapter 3 produced evidence of affinity voting for candidates of the same ethnicity, and to a lesser extent, for those of a different racialized ethnicity. Chapter 4 argued that we need to focus on self-identification, rather than membership, since it is self-identification that is likely to drive key psychological processes, such as in-group favouritism. The evidence here confirms that self-identification does indeed condition the effect of seeing a racialized candidate and in fact does so quite strongly. Moreover, the open-ended responses are consistent with the experimental data: many respondents explicitly stated that they were supporting the candidate because of a shared ethnic group (co-ethnic affinity) or a shared minority or immigrant group (racialized affinity).

These outcomes are in sharp contrast to two studies that found no conditioning effect of ethnic identity (McConnaughy et al. 2010; Fisher et al. 2015). This divergence might be explained by the measures used: for the former, an ad hoc scale measure composed of a series of behavioural variables; for the latter, a measure of relative ethnic versus national identity. If so, this underlines the importance of using carefully constructed measures of identification, such as the IDPG scale.

The conditioning effects of identity are also consistent with the results of linked-fate research, but this analysis tests a different, and more precisely identified, mechanism. As is argued in Chapter 2, linked fate combines considerations about self-identity, social discrimination, and the impact of group membership. This research suggests that higher levels of linked fate are correlated with affinity voting among black and Latino Americans (e.g., Dawson 1994; Tate 1994; McConnaughy et al. 2010). However, while linked fate may be related to a series of considerations, including categorization by others or expectations of discrimination, self-identification need not be. A person might well not self-identify as Latino yet still believe that his or her success or failure is related to those of other Latinos because of general discrimination against the group. Linked fate is a belief about the world, not about the self. As a result, the findings here demonstrate something different from the research on linked fate. If we are interested in the effects of identity, then we need a measure of self-identification. The IDPG scale is just such a measure, and it strongly conditions the response that people have to candidates of their own ethnic group.

Racialized affinity voting and ethnic identities are positively correlated, and this finding is consistent with the generation of a broad racialized identity but not with motivated social positioning. Recall that Chapter 2 discussed two possible ways for identity to affect racialized affinity – motivated social positioning and the generation of a common intergroup, racialized identity. While we do not have direct evidence of a common racialized identity, readiness to identify with a specific racialized ethnic group plausibly implies readiness to identify with a broader racialized group. Thus, respondents were more likely to support racialized candidates because they see them as belonging to the same in-group of racialized people. At the same time, specific coethnic affinity-voting effects are significantly stronger, perhaps because self-identification with a specific ethnocultural identity is personally important, or perhaps because people identify that way more often – hence, the identity is more accessible.

Importantly, this analysis shows no evidence of motivated social positioning – that is, of discrimination against other racialized ethnic groups as a way of distancing one's own group and bring it closer to higher-status whites. This finding could reflect relatively small status differences. That is, perhaps in Canada neither Chinese nor South Asian candidates are perceived as especially low status, and therefore there is little motivation for distancing. If correct, this suggests that motivated social distancing might still operate in other circumstances. Though speculative, it might apply to black or Indigenous candidates.[2]

That said, the important role played here by strength of ethnocultural identity is consistent with a small number of studies that found that the primary variable associated with interminority cooperation is group identity. Specifically, both Kaufmann (2003) and Sanchez (2008) found that, for Latinos, identifying strongly as Latino was correlated with positive views of blacks. Similarly, McClain and colleagues (2006) also suggested that a sense of linked fate between Latinos was correlated with fewer negative stereotypes of blacks. These studies, however, only ask about general dispositions and attitudes toward racial groups. The present research goes a step further and confirms that these effects have electoral implications – minorities who identify strongly with their own ethnic group also seem more likely to support a candidate of a different minority group.

Notably, some have suggested that identity effects such as these are really composed of sensitivity to negative evaluations of their group, rather than strictly in-group bias: Goodyear-Grant and Tolley (2017) find that coethnic affinity voting occurs for respondents who scored highly on the IDPG question about "criticism ... feels like a personal insult," but not for the questions about "we rather than they" or "feels like a personal compliment." This result is not reflected here, in that although effects from the "personal insult" question seem to be the largest, the results for all three questions are similar (not shown). A better test might be to include the three questions together in the same model to examine the effects of one controlling for the others, but unfortunately (though not surprisingly) this model structure produces substantial multicollinearity. Nonetheless, whether this is a form of negativity bias, and the degree to which these are really separate constructs, is worth further examination in future research.

One question might be whether the results really reflect affinity effects or, rather, an aversion to the white candidate. That is, coethnic affinity voting might really be a measure of antiwhite sentiment rather than proethnic group sentiment. Unfortunately, it is not possible to test this hypothesis with these data, and, in fact, questions about antiwhite sentiment are quite rare. As far as I am aware, there are no such questions in Canadian surveys. Perhaps this is itself a symptom of the normalization of whiteness. In the United States, there are questions related to antiwhite sentiment on some surveys, but no studies have linked it to affinity voting. However, there are two reasons to think affinity voting is not primarily the product of out-group hostility, rather than in-group favouritism. Generally speaking, research suggests that in-group bias and out-group hostility are actually separate phenomena (Brewer 1999). This means that a high IDPG score implies preference for one's own ethnic group but not necessarily hostility toward other groups. In addition, research in Canada suggests that perceived discrimination – and, likely, antiwhite sentiment (see Monteith and Spicer 2000; see also Wilson and Davis 2017) – is higher among second-generation than first-generation immigrants (Reitz and Banerjee 2007). Yet, it was immigrants rather than Canadian-born, racialized respondents who had higher levels of IDPG (see Model 5.2). Thus, Canadian-born, racialized respondents have lower rather than higher levels of coethnic affinity voting, as we would expect if these findings were driven by discrimination and antiwhite sentiment, a point examined in the next chapter.

Finally, the results provide important evidence for identity-based explanations of affinity voting. It is clear that ethnic self-identification strongly conditions ethnic and racialized affinity voting. The implication, I argue, is that affinity-voting effects are a result of social identity and in-group bias. The conditioning effect of self-identification is far stronger than it is for objective membership in the group alone. In fact, respondents low on the IDPG scale actually may discriminate against their own group. Moreover, the IDPG measure specifically focuses on self-identity. The questions explore whether attributions of the ethnic group are taken on by the individual. This kind of depersonalization, where self-identity is fused to the group identity, happens precisely when the social-identity perspective suggests in-group favouritism will occur (Tajfel and Turner 1986).

The evidence shows that membership in ethnocultural categories has no significant effect at the midpoint of the IDPG scale, when respondents are indifferent to the group in terms of their self-identity but still claim membership in the group. This finding fits with the argument put forward in Chapter 4 that cognitive group membership, affect toward the group, and self-identification toward the group are distinct phenomena. Interest-based explanations would suggest that even at the indifference point, membership in a group should produce some affinity effects – but there is no evidence of that here. Simple membership in a category, in and of itself, does not produce affinity voting, according to an identity account. Instead, self-identification, with its implications for in-group bias, is more important than cognitive group membership. This point does not rule out interest-based explanations, but it does suggest that identity has important effects separate from the effects of interests.

6
The Role of Interests, Ideology, and Policy

The affinity voting demonstrated in previous chapters demands an explanation – why are racialized voters more likely to support racialized candidates? Clear evidence was presented for identity-based effects in the previous chapter, showing that affinity voting is strongly conditional on strength of identification with one's ethnocultural group. This chapter examines three types of interest-based explanations: ideological stereotyping, policy attitudes, and general group interest.

Ideological stereotyping is suggested as an explanation by McDermott (1998) for both race and gender affinity: citizens attribute ideological characteristics to certain social groups, these attributes are transferred to candidates via stereotyping, and then support for the candidate depends on the voter's opinion of the attributes. Two versions of ideological stereotyping will be tested here: 1) racialized candidates being perceived as more left-leaning and 2) racialized voters seeing racialized candidates as ideologically closer to them than white candidates, be they left- or right-leaning.

But affinity voting might be a product of specific policy stereotypes rather than broad left-right ideological stereotypes. Racialized voters might want more liberal policies on immigration, racial inequality, government job creation, and crime, and they may think that racialized candidates are likely to provide them. To test this, a series of models are introduced that include interactions with the respondents' policy attitudes.

Finally, voters may support a candidate of the same ethnicity because they believe the candidate will be more likely to act or take positions that benefit them. They might not have a particular policy or ideological position in mind, simply a general sense that the candidate would work for them. To test the general-interest explanation, a subset of respondents were asked which candidate would serve their financial interests, rather than the standard question about who they would vote for.

Ideological Stereotyping

To test the ideological-stereotyping explanation, I employed an ideological position question about the candidate, since it is necessary (though not sufficient) that the ethnicity of the candidate be correlated with his or her perceived ideological position. Respondents were shown a biography of a candidate and asked: "Where would you place this candidate on a left-right spectrum?" A ten-point scale was shown, with the endpoints labelled "left-wing" and "right-wing." Then a biography of the second candidate was shown and the question repeated. The same candidate biographies were used for this question as for the vote question – i.e., with names manipulated to imply ethnicity. That is, each respondent was shown a set of candidates and asked to make a vote choice (as analyzed in Chapters 3 and 5). Later, respondents were shown the same candidates again, first one and then the other, and asked the ideological perception question. The ideology question was placed after the vote question to minimize the bias on vote-choice, although, of course, the reverse is still possible. The ideology question was asked for all versions of the biography, including the party and independent versions. Of course, we would expect party labels to have a large effect on perceived ideology, so the main analysis is performed on the independent version, but the party version allows for validation of the measure. While the ideology question was asked for both Candidate 1 and Candidate 2, the analysis here focuses only on Candidate 2, the one whose ethnicity was manipulated.

Validating the Measure of Perceived Ideology

It was necessary to validate the measure before testing the impact of candidates' racialized status on perceived ideological position. After all, it could be that respondents did not understand the question, or that the left-right scale held little meaning for them. Given the conflicted history of the study of ideology and vote choice, this is entirely possible. To test this, I drew on an experimental manipulation that alters the party affiliation of the candidate.[1] While most of the analyses so far have drawn on candidate biographies with an independent candidate, a subsample of respondents was shown candidate biographies that included political party labels. Only the Liberal Party and the Conservative Party were used because of concerns about sample size and conserving power. Although the NDP held more seats than the Liberal Party in 2011, the Liberal Party is often associated with multiculturalism, and the NDP has never formed a government at the federal level. Therefore, the experiment used the Liberal Party rather than the NDP. The subsequent return of the Liberal Party to power and the substantial decline in seats held by the NDP provide some validation of this approach. The party labels were randomly assigned to Candidate 1 or Candidate 2, producing a three-by-three factorial design with three possible candidate ethnicities (white, Chinese, or South Asian) and three possible party labels for Candidate 2 (Liberal, Conservative, or independent). Note that since some of the manipulations in this case had fewer respondents than in the main ethnicity manipulations, I began by merging all racialized respondent and candidate categories to gain maximum leverage. I also examined specific ethnic groups to determine if effects were driven by particular combinations, although the estimates are less precise.

If respondents did comprehend the ideology question and understood the measure in conventional terms, then they should have associated candidates of different parties with different ideological positions. If party labels have an effect on perceived candidate ideology, then the measure itself functions properly. Model 6.1 has perceived candidate ideology as the dependent variable, scaled 0 to 1, with higher values further to the right. The independent variables are party labels (Conservative, Liberal, independent), respondents' racialized or white status, and candidates' racialized or white status. These variables are interacted, and constituent terms are included. Note that unlike most of the models, white respondents are included here in order to estimate the impact of party labels on perceived candidate ideology, for both white and racialized respondents and for the Conservative and Liberal version. If the candidate ideology measure functions properly, there should, at least, be a difference between Liberal and Conservative candidates.

The perceived ideology of (white) Liberal candidates is clearly lower (more left-wing) than that of (white) Conservative candidates, as Figure 6.1 shows. Independent candidates are in the middle, as we might expect. The difference between Liberal and Conservative candidates for white respondents is 0.19 ($p < .001$). For racialized respondents, the difference is smaller (0.06) but still in the expected direction ($p = .06$). Interestingly, the racialized respondents perceived both Liberal candidates and Conservative candidates as being more centrist than did white respondents, possibly because racialized respondents are less well informed about politics, the positions of political parties, and concepts such as left and right – recall that most racialized respondents are immigrants. If anything, this lower knowledge among racialized respondents would make ideological-stereotyping explanations of

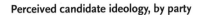

FIGURE 6.1

Perceived candidate ideology, by party

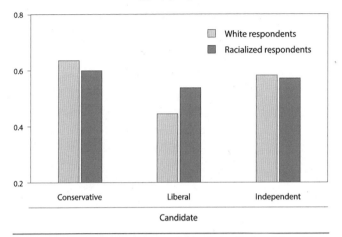

NOTES: Perceived candidate ideology, higher being further right; white candidate only; n = 2,223.

affinity even less plausible. In any case, these results indicate that respondents did understand the ideological-position questions and were capable of discerning between candidates. Of course, the effects of race may be smaller than the effects of party – party labels are a strong treatment with clear ideological content – but clearly the measure functions as intended.

TESTING IDEOLOGICAL STEREOTYPING OF RACIALIZED CANDIDATES

As noted earlier, it is difficult to establish ideological stereotyping as the cause of affinity voting. Support for a candidate might influence perceived candidate ideology rather than the other way around. Correlation is a necessary, though not sufficient, condition for demonstrating ideological-stereotyping explanations of affinity effects. The test here is simple: if racialized candidates are perceived as systematically more left-wing, then the ideological stereotype explanation is plausible. On the other hand, if there is no systematic difference in ideological perceptions of the white and racialized versions of the candidate, then left-right ideological stereotypes cannot possibly explain the affinity effects found in the data. The hypothesis is as follows:

H6.1 Racialized candidates will, on average, be perceived as more left-leaning than white candidates.

FIGURE 6.2

Perceived ideological position, by candidate ethnicity

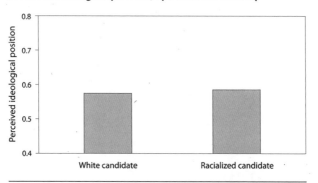

NOTES: Higher score is further right; quantity of interest is difference between the bars (p = .49); racialized respondents only; n = 1,125.

To test the hypothesis, predicted probabilities were generated using Model 6.1, which estimates the effect of candidate racialized status on perceived candidate ideology. Figure 6.2 displays the difference in predicted values for candidate ideology for white and racialized candidates. That is, it shows the effect of candidate racialized status on ideological perceptions of the candidate. The predicted values here are also generated for the independent version and racialized respondents. As Figure 6.2 shows, the difference in perception of ideology between the white and racialized candidates is very small, only 0.01, and not statistically significant (p = .49). Clearly, the ethnicity of the candidate does not seem to affect the perceived right- versus left-wing position of the candidate, suggesting that ethnicity as an ideological heuristic cannot possibly be the explanation for coethnic affinity voting.

Ideological stereotypes may emerge only as interactions with specific ethnicities. Perhaps, for example, the South Asian candidate was stereotyped as left-wing, and the Chinese candidate was not. Alternatively, stereotyping might occur only among respondents of a different ethnicity – South Asian respondents would not stereotype South Asian candidates, but other racialized respondents might. Model 6.2 examines this possibility using ordinary least squares (OLS) regression to look at the impact of specific ethnicity on candidate ideology. The dependent variable is, as before, perceived candidate ideology. The independent variables are candidate ethnicity (white, Chinese, South Asian) and respondent ethnicity (Chinese, South Asian, other racialized respondents).

FIGURE 6.3

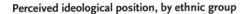

Perceived ideological position, by ethnic group

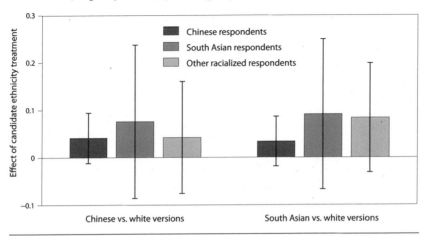

NOTES: Difference in perceived ideological position between white and racialized candidate versions; *n* = 1,125.

Figure 6.3 shows the difference in predicted values for candidate ideology – that is, the difference between the white and the Chinese or South Asian candidates. None of the differences are statistically significant, and the point values are very small. For example, the largest effect is found among South Asian respondents who see Chinese candidates as 0.05 further right than the white candidate, but this is not statistically significant ($p = .23$).

So far, the data seem to rule out the ideological-stereotype explanation. There is simply no evidence that racialized candidates, either Chinese or South Asian, are perceived as more left-wing than white candidates. Nor, indeed, is there any evidence that they are perceived as more right-wing than white candidates – candidate ethnicity seems to have no systematic relation to ideology at all.

A second version of the ideological-stereotyping explanation posits that ethnicity is simply a heuristic about ideological proximity, rather than a specific ideological direction. Racialized respondents might see the racialized candidate as more ideologically similar to themselves than a white candidate, whether that be more left-wing or more right-wing. This version is empty of substantive content. Unlike the previous account, it does not imply knowledge of the policies of political parties or beliefs about ethnic groups.

It is certainly a less demanding account, but it is also less encouraging from a democratic point of view. The hypothesis is as follows:

H6.2: Racialized respondents will perceive racialized candidates as more ideologically similar to themselves than white candidates.

Model 6.3 tests Hypothesis H6.2. The dependent variable is a measure of respondent-candidate ideological distance. Before placing candidates on a left-right scale, respondents were asked to place themselves on the same scale. This measure was then subtracted from the candidate ideological scale, and the result was converted to an absolute value, with 0 being the same ideological score for candidate and respondent, and 1 being the opposite end of the ideological spectrum. This, then, is a measure of how different (or similar) the respondent perceives the candidate compared to him or herself. The independent variables are candidate racialized status and demographic covariates, and the analysis is restricted to racialized respondents and the independent condition.

On a scale of ideological difference, Figure 6.4 shows that white candidates are rated an average of 0.57, racialized candidates 0.58. In other words, the effect of candidate ethnicity on ideological difference is 0.01, a tiny difference that is certainly not statistically significant ($p = .49$). Hypothesis 6.2 is rejected; as with Model 6.2, Model 6.3 provides no evidence that racialized candidates are perceived as being ideologically different from white candidates.

Model 6.4 repeats the analysis of the ideological-distance heuristic using specific ethnic groups. The dependent variable is, again, the ideological-distance measure, and the independent variables are candidate ethnicity (white, Chinese, South Asian) and respondent ethnicity (Chinese, South Asian, other racialized respondents), interactions between candidate and respondent ethnicity, and demographic controls.

As with Figure 6.4, Figure 6.5 reveals only small effects, and no significant differences between the white and racialized candidates for any of the respondent ethnic categories. We should note that one category is statistically significant: South Asian respondents viewed the Chinese candidate as 0.07 points ($p = .04$) less ideologically different from themselves than the white candidate. However, we have no theoretical reason to imagine that this pair should be more likely to be seen as more ideologically different than any other pair. Given the large number of coefficients generated in this

FIGURE 6.4

Perceived ideological distance, by candidate ethnicity

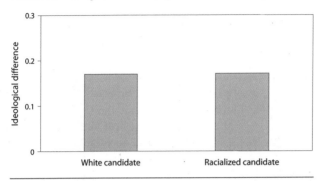

NOTES: Higher score is greater ideological difference; quantity
of interest is difference between the bars (*p* = .92); racialized
respondents only; *n* = 1,125.

FIGURE 6.5

Perceived ideological distance, by ethnic group

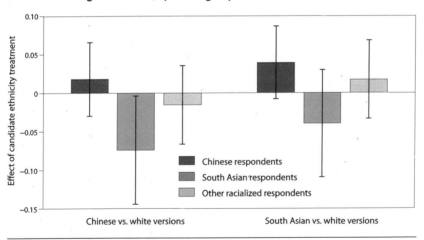

NOTES: Difference between perceived ideological positions of candidate and respondent,
between white and racialized candidate versions; *n* = 1,125.

analysis, and the otherwise null finding of ideological perceptions, this may
simply be a chance finding.

Despite null findings, one further possibility is that ideological stereotyping only occurs among the more politically knowledgeable. As famously

noted by Converse (1964), the politically sophisticated generally have more coherent ideological beliefs than the politically unsophisticated. Similarly, more recent research on heuristics emphasizes that many heuristics actually require a significant amount of political knowledge (Lau and Redlawsk 2006). The heuristic here, that racialized candidates are more likely to take left-wing positions on policy issues, might indeed require at least moderate levels of political knowledge, since it requires both ideological opinions and some knowledge of the political system. For perceptions of ideological distance, on the other hand, political knowledge is unlikely to matter since this is simply a kind of restatement about ethnic similarity. If there is any systematic difference in perception of the ideological position of racialized candidates, it would probably be by the most politically knowledgeable respondents.

To test this, Model 6.5 includes an interaction with political knowledge (not shown; for details, see Appendix C). The measure of political knowledge is composed of three multiple-choice questions: "Who is the current prime minister of Canada?," "Which party is the official opposition in Ottawa?," and "Whose responsibility is it to determine if a law is constitutional or not?" The additive scale is 0–1. Model 6.5 is similar to Model 6.1 but includes an additional interaction with political knowledge. There is no statistically significant effect from political knowledge even at the top of the political-knowledge scale ($p = .14$): respondents high in political knowledge are no more likely to view a racialized candidate as left-wing than those with low political knowledge.

Policy Attitudes and Affinity Voting

Another explanation for affinity voting is policy attitudes – stereotyping about specific policies rather than general left-right ideology. For example, if racialized voters are especially concerned about immigration policy, and if they believe that a racialized candidate will be more pro-immigration than a white candidate, then they might support the racialized candidate as a way to influence immigration policy. A concern is that the identity effects identified in the previous chapter might be spurious if ethnic self-identity is correlated with policy attitudes. Since candidate policy positions and respondent attitudes are not manipulated, it is not possible to demonstrate a causal relationship, but we can test a minimum requirement of this explanation. That is, are policy attitudes correlated with affinity voting after controlling for ethnic self-identity? And do IDPG scores still predict affinity voting even when controlling for policy attitudes?

Four policy attitudes are tested here: immigration, racial inequality, government job creation, and crime. The immigration statement was worded as follows: "Canada should have more immigration than we have now." The racial inequality statement was taken from the Canadian Election Study: "It is more difficult for nonwhites to be successful in Canadian society than it is for whites."[2] The job-creation question was reverse worded: "Government should leave it entirely up to the private sector to create jobs" (also taken from the Canadian Election Study). Since racialized respondents are more likely to be unemployed (Statistics Canada 2017), they might support racialized candidates because they are less trusting of the private sector and more likely to want the government to create jobs. Finally, crime policy is often viewed as racialized. Affinity voting might be caused by racialized respondents supporting racialized candidates because they oppose "tough on crime" policies. The statement presented was "Punishment for criminals is sometimes too severe; we should focus on rehabilitation instead." All responses were on a five-point agree/disagree Likert scale, and were coded 0–1 so that the left-wing response is high. The formal hypotheses are as follows:

H6.3: Racialized voters who are pro-immigration will be more likely to support a racialized candidate than a white candidate, controlling for ethnic identity.

H6.4: Racialized voters who believe racialized people have more difficulty succeeding than white people will be more likely to support a racialized candidate than a white candidate, controlling for ethnic identity.

H6.5: Racialized voters who think the government should create jobs will be more likely to support a racialized candidate than a white candidate, controlling for ethnic identity.

H6.6: Racialized voters who oppose "tough on crime" policy will be more likely to support a racialized candidate than a white candidate, controlling for ethnic identity.

To examine the separate effects of policy attitudes and identity, Models 6.6, 6.7, 6.8, and 6.9 include interactions between candidate treatment and policy attitudes and also between the candidate treatment and ethnic self-identification. Given the additional interactions, ethnic- and racialized-affinity conditions are merged to maximize statistical power. Since these policy attitudes are quite likely correlated, separate models are estimated for each policy. As Table 6.1 shows, ethnic self-identification strongly conditions affinity voting, even controlling for policy attitudes. Identity effects are not simply confounded with policy attitudes. Conversely, attitudes about immigration, racial inequality, creating jobs, and crime show no significant effect on the likelihood of affinity voting (controlling for ethnic self-identity): none of the interactions are statistically significant (the same goes for marginal effects, not shown). Notably, the interaction of racial inequality with identity tests the group-consciousness model discussed in Chapter 2, but finds no support for it, suggesting that racialized voters do not support racialized candidates because of beliefs about the kind of policy positions the candidates hold.

It should be noted that the results for immigration are not far from being statistically significant ($p = .14$). With a larger sample or a broader distribution of attitudes, it is possible that there might be evidence for the attitudes about immigration affecting affinity voting. On the other hand, attitudes about immigration are quite likely to be symbolic because they express positive or negative attitudes about immigrants. That is, responses to the immigration question may not reflect a desire for change in the federal government's admissions policy so much as positive sentiments toward immigrants. Moreover, because there is no manipulation of the policy positions of these candidates (or the opinions of respondents), we cannot be certain that these attitudes are causally related to their vote choice. On the contrary, both vote choice and policy attitudes might be caused by identity. These results for immigration are suggestive and would benefit from further research, but the evidence here is weak. Conversely, the evidence for identity is still quite strong, even controlling for a series of policy attitudes.

Open-Ended Responses: Ideology, Policy, Parties

What kind of open-ended statements did respondents provide about ideology, policy, and parties? The categorization of these responses was initially discussed in Chapter 5, but they are examined in more detail here. Ideology is a difficult concept to examine because the terminology of ideology is quite similar to that of party (and, sadly, survey respondents do not reliably capitalize proper nouns). For example, one respondent said she voted for a candidate because "my values are more liberal values," but it is not clear if

TABLE 6.1

Policy attitudes and affinity voting

Variable	Model 6.6 Immigration		Model 6.7 Racial inequality		Model 6.8 Government job creation		Model 6.9 Crime	
Racialized candidate	-1.01**	(0.47)	-0.96*	(0.49)	-0.61	(0.44)	-0.74*	(0.43)
IDPG	-0.72	(0.52)	-0.74	(0.52)	-0.80	(0.53)	-0.73	(0.52)
Racialized candidate* IDPG	1.44**	(0.64)	1.47**	(0.65)	1.58**	(0.65)	1.53**	(0.64)
More immigrants	-0.23	(0.41)						
Racialized candidate* More immigrants	0.73	(0.50)						
Racial inequality			-0.21	(0.38)				
Racialized candidate* Racial inequality			0.48	(0.48)				
Government job creation					0.48	(0.37)		
Racialized candidate* Job creation					-0.28	(0.46)		
"Not Tough on Crime"							-0.06	(0.35)
Racialized candidate* Crime							0.13	(0.43)
Income	-0.26	(0.20)	-0.26	(0.20)	-0.26	(0.20)	-0.26	(0.20)
Education	0.28	(0.29)	0.30	(0.29)	0.34	(0.29)	0.31	(0.29)
Age	-0.00	(0.01)	0.00	(0.01)	-0.00	(0.01)	0.00	(0.01)
Gender (male)	0.23*	(0.12)	0.24**	(0.12)	0.23*	(0.12)	0.24*	(0.12)
Religion (non-Christian)	-0.47***	(0.15)	-0.46***	(0.15)	-0.45***	(0.15)	-0.46***	(0.15)
Religion (non-religious)	-0.30*	(0.17)	-0.31*	(0.17)	-0.29*	(0.17)	-0.30*	(0.17)
Immigrant	-0.01	(0.13)	0.00	(0.13)	-0.03	(0.13)	-0.01	(0.13)
Intercept	0.40	(0.49)	0.38	(0.51)	0.10	(0.47)	0.27	(0.47)
Pseudo r²	.018		.017		.018		.016	
N	1,125		1,125		1,125		1,125	

NOTES: Logistic regression. Left-wing policy attitude is high. Candidate vote is dependent variable. Standard errors are in parentheses.
* $p < .1$.   ** $p < .05$.   *** $p < .01$.

TABLE 6.2

Open-ended reasons for support by party condition

	Independent		Party affiliation	
Identity	7	(48)	5	(17)
Ideology/party	0	(2)	37	(117)
Interests	0	(3)	0	(1)
Qualifications	60	(425)	30	(97)
Personal characteristics	14	(99)	12	(39)
Other	19	(137)	15	(48)

NOTES: Racialized respondents and racialized candidates only. Rounded column percentage reported, with raw numbers in brackets.

this is a reference to ideology or the Liberal Party. In general, clear ideological references were few and far between: there was no, for example, single unambiguous reference to ideology, such as "left" or "right." Even using a broader definition of ideology, including policy-related references, these kind of considerations were mentioned only by a small number of respondents (6). One respondent supported the candidate because he was "close to my political views," another because "my vote is based on tax and government spending," but these kinds of responses were rare.

Despite possible ambiguity, most references to being conservative or liberal seemed to relate to political party affiliation, of either the candidate or respondent: "I'm a Liberal," "My views are more in line with liberal party," "I traditionally vote Conservative," "prefer that party," and "Because of the political party the candidate belongs." Other times, they provided negative responses: "better than liberal guy" or "he's not a Conservative." That these are references to party rather than ideology is reinforced by the differences between the party and independent conditions: as Table 6.2 shows, in the absence of party labels, very few respondents (2) mentioned these kinds of considerations. The "ideology/party" responses are frequent in the party condition – more than any other category – but practically absent in the independent condition. Most importantly, there is little evidence that ideology caused respondents to vote for a racialized candidate. For example, not a single respondent said he or she supported the independent racialized candidate because (he or she assumed) the respondent was a Liberal or Conservative.

Some comments about group interests might be interpreted as ideological policy positions, for example: "He will take better care of minorities," "Visible minority – so he likely understands the difficulties of being a visible minority," "I think he would understand my concerns as an immigrant Canadian," and "Mr. Zhang has a better idea of how people struggle due to their nationality and will understand and appreciate minorities more." However, these comments are still few in number (3), and it is unclear what, exactly, they refer to.

These open-ended responses are consistent with the null results of the quantitative models of ideological perceptions. Respondents did not view the racialized candidates as ideologically different, and given that they provided few ideological reasons when the racialized candidate was independent, they did not assume that they lean toward one party or another. There is little reason, then, to think that affinity effects are caused by ideological stereotyping or that racialized voters support racialized candidates because of their perceived policy positions.

Overall, there was little support for any version of ideological stereotyping. Ethnicity is essentially irrelevant to ideological perceptions of candidates, at least in Canada. Respondents understood the survey questions and correctly placed parties, but they did not view the ideological position of racialized candidates as more left-leaning than white candidates. Nor did racialized respondents view racialized candidates as ideologically closer to themselves. When asked an open-ended question, very few respondents mentioned ideological or policy-related reasons for supporting the candidate. Reasons related to party were given only when the candidate had a party affiliation, suggesting that the respondents did not assume that racialized candidates were associated with a particular party. Nor is there clear evidence that specific policy attitudes condition the effect of the racialized candidate treatment. There is some evidence that pro-immigration racialized respondents showed affinity voting while those lower on the scale did not. However, the statistical evidence is ambiguous; there may be issues with causality, and there is good reason to think that attitudes about immigration are, at least in part, symbolic rather than purely about government policy.

Self-Interest and Coethnic Affinity Voting

At its most basic, the general-group-interest explanation posits that citizens vote for candidates of their own ethnicity because they expect that the candidate will pursue policies that will benefit them. It is a heuristic in the classic sense: candidate ethnicity is a mental shortcut for the candidates' future actions and policy positions, and voting for a racialized candidate is in the interest of a racialized voter. This account is quite different from identity-based explanations that rely on in-group favouritism or on the persuasiveness of campaign messages.

In defining self-interest, the definition adopted here is that of the symbolic politics school: "1) short-to-medium term impact of an issue (or candidacy) on the 2) material well-being of the 3) individual's own personal life (or that of his or her immediate family)" (Sears and Funk 1990, 248). Chong, Citrin, and Conley (2001, 542) take a similar position, defining self-interest as "tangible, relatively immediate, personal or family benefits of a policy." This is self-interest defined narrowly – that is, the voter supports the candidate because he or she believes the candidate will benefit them in some concrete way. In addition, this definition of self-interest is based on subjective knowledge and intention, not objective measures of group interest or competition, as in some interminority-conflict research (e.g., Gay 2006). While there is likely a strong connection between objective and subjective self-interest, *self-interest* in the present analysis does not include objective conceptions of self-interest that do not involve subjective awareness on the part of the citizen. The issue is not whether objective interests have some role to play – they surely do. Rather, the question is whether the motivation at the individual level is a self-interested one: do racialized respondents support racialized candidates because they believe that a racialized candidate will be good for their interests?

While self-interest is often taken for granted in politics, research on self-interest in voting behaviour suggests its influence is actually very constrained. Research on self-interest suggests that it can have an effect when the stakes are clear, direct, and significant (Chong, Citrin, and Conley 2001). For example, homeowners are more likely than nonhomeowners to support a property tax cut (Sears and Citrin 1982). However, in general, matters of public policy do not have a clear and immediate benefit to individuals, and so, for most political situations, political values and attitudes toward groups are much more influential than self-interest (Sears and Funk 1990).

At the same time, the methodological difficulties here are similar to those for ideological stereotyping – asking about candidate support is likely to bias other measures. Because of bias toward consistency, we cannot ask respondents to choose a candidate and, at the same time, ask if choosing that candidate is in their own self-interest. Similarly, distinguishing between self-interest and symbolic-identity motivations for coethnic affinity voting is actually quite difficult. If social-identity considerations bias the voter toward supporting a candidate, the same in-group bias might well affect the voter's perceptions of self-interest in relation to that candidate. Ruling out social-identity explanations in favour of self-interest is, therefore, not possible here. However, it is possible to do the reverse: we could show that self-interest is not a relevant consideration. If self-interest considerations are primed, then the effect of coethnic affinity voting should be larger, if self-interest is a relevant motivation.

Testing Self-Interest Motivations

To test the general-group-interest explanation, a subset of the sample were asked a different question about the candidate to prime self-interest considerations. Rather than being asked "Which candidate would you vote for?," these respondents were asked: "Which candidate would be financially better for you and your family?" The reference to family follows the definition used in the symbolic politics literature (e.g., Chong, Citrin, and Conley 2001) to capture a wider range of policy benefits. *Financial considerations* covers a wide range of racialized issues, including employment, credential recognition, housing discrimination, and so on. More generally though, the reference to economic benefits likely primed self-interest considerations, even those that are not strictly financial (Chong, Citrin, and Conley 2001).

Since the question asked explicitly about self-interest considerations, if candidate ethnicity is relevant to self-interest then we could expect that priming these considerations would increase the effect of candidate ethnicity. Conversely, if there is no link between candidate ethnicity and self-interest, then the prime would have no effect. Of course, this is assuming that the effect of self-interest considerations is not already maximized, thus leaving no room for the prime to increase the effect of self-interest. However, this is unlikely given the relatively low level of self-interest in most political decisions (Sears and Funk 1990) and that self-interest effects are strongest when the benefits are large and clear (Chong, Citrin, and Conley 2001), neither of which is the case here. Thus, the hypothesis reads:

H6.7: The likelihood of affinity voting will be greater when self-interest is primed.

In Model 6.10, the dependent variable is vote for Candidate 2, as in previous models. An independent variable with the question wording (self-interest, vote choice) is included, as well as independent variables for candi-

FIGURE 6.6

Vote choice and self-interest prime

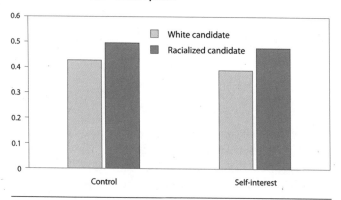

NOTES: Predicted probabilities for Candidate 2; racialized respondents only; quantity of interest is difference between two treatment effects $(p = .8)$; $n = 1,125$.

date racialized status and racialized respondent status, two- and three-way interaction terms for these variables. Given the smaller number of respondents in the self-interest treatment, analysis of specific ethnic groups is likely to be unreliable; no similar model with specific ethnicities is estimated.

The likelihood of voting for the racialized candidate under the two conditions, self-interest and vote choice, is shown in Figure 6.6 for racialized respondents. The treatment effect of candidate ethnicity is nearly identical for the vote and self-interest questions: there is a 47 percent chance of choosing the racialized version of Candidate 2 when the question is about voting, and a 49 percent chance with the self-interest wording. The effect of the candidate treatment – the difference between a white and racialized candidate – is 0.07 under the standard "Which candidate would you vote for?" question and 0.09 under the "Which candidate is in the financial interest of you or your family?" question. The difference between these two numbers is only 0.02 – that is, the conditioning effect of the self-interest manipulation on the racialized candidate treatment is very small. It is also not statistically significant $(p = .8)$. Respondents showed no greater level of affinity effects when asked which candidate was best for their own self-interest than they did when asked which candidate they would vote for. This finding is contrary to Hypothesis 6.7, which suggests weaker effects under the self-interest manipulation than under the vote-choice manipulation. Other specifications, such as ethnic- and racial-affinity groups and examining combinations of specific ethnic groups result in the same finding – there is no evidence that priming self-interest increases the size of affinity effects.

Finally, the interaction of the self-interest question with the IDPG scale was tested. While it is argued in Chapter 4 that self-interest should be determined primarily by cognitive group membership, it is possible that perceptions of self-interest are conditional on group self-identification. That is, high identifiers would see a candidate as being in their interest, but low identifiers would not, making self-interest a mediator between identity and vote choice – a related but slightly different version of the identity motivation. This would mean that self-identity was the ultimate cause of identity effects but that the mechanism was interests rather than the mechanisms described as identity effects (in-group bias, persuasion effects, and so on). If identity is linked to perceived self-interest, the IDPG scale should be correlated with the likelihood of a respondent seeing a racialized candidate as being in his or her own interest. As a result, the slope of the self-interest line should be steeper than the vote-choice line – the effect of IDPG on affinity effects should be greater in the self-interest condition.

H6.8: The conditioning effect of strength of ethnic identity on affinity will be greater when self-interest is primed.

To test Hypothesis 6.8, the IDPG scale was added to the model (Model 6.11), producing a three-way interaction (and constituent terms) with racialized candidate status, the IDPG scale, and a set of dummy variables for the biography versions. Since this hypothesis and the identity hypothesis from Chapter 5 have opposite implications, the confidence intervals below represent two-tailed tests. Because the confidence intervals here are wide, these results should be taken with caution – but they still shed some light on the relationship.

Figure 6.7 shows that there were clear differences between the self-interest question and the vote-choice question – the slope of the vote question is positive, but the slope of the self-interest prime is negative. Certainly, this is inconsistent with Hypothesis 6.8. Rather than identity affecting perceptions of self-interest, here there is no such effect. Identity and self-interest do not seem to be tightly linked.

The left-hand side of the figure shows that racialized respondents with low IDPG scores (i.e., weak ethnic identities) are more likely to say racialized

FIGURE 6.7

Affinity voting in control and self-interest conditions, by IDPG

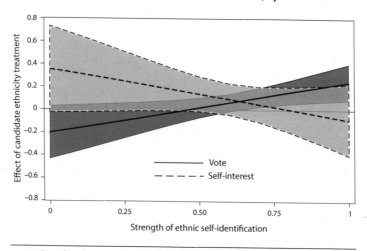

NOTE: Racialized respondents only; difference in predicted probability of choosing Candidate 2, between white and racialized candidate versions; racialized respondents only; $n = 1,335$.

candidates are in their self-interest, but they are *not* more likely to vote for them. Why might this be so? Perhaps people who are members of an ethnic group but do not strongly identify with it cognitively recognize that a racialized candidate is in their interest, yet for other reasons (perhaps social positioning or symbolic considerations) do not vote for that candidate. These reasons might include a desire to not be seen as someone who "blindly" supports members of his or her own ethnic group. Conversely, high ethnic self-identifiers *are* more likely to vote for the racialized candidate, pointing toward quite different effects for group membership and group identification.

One puzzle is that in Figure 6.7, high ethnic identifiers do not seem to see racialized candidates as in their interest; in other words, why is the slope negative? It seems strange that strongly identifying with an ethnic group would make a voter *less* likely to see racialized candidates as being in their self-interest. But this apparent relationship could be misleading because the confidence intervals are wide. The difference in the effect of racialized candidate status between high and low ethnic identifiers (0 and 1 on the IDPG scale) is not significant ($p = .18$). In other words, the slope shown in Figure 6.7 might, in fact, be flat in the population as a whole. In addition, there is no theoretical reason to think that high ethnic identifiers would not see racialized candidates as in their own interest, and we should be skeptical about the negative correlation. The situation is essentially the same as in the immigration policy-stereotype model: while the lack of a statistically significant effect might be surprising, it should not be taken as clear evidence of no effect. The other pieces of evidence – in particular, the fact that low ethnic self-identifiers say that racialized candidates are in their interests but do not vote for them – are consistent with the interpretation that it is identity-based factors that primarily drive vote choice. The key piece of information is the left-hand side of Figure 6.7, where the difference between the vote and self-interest is statistically significant ($p = .02$ at 0.25 on the IDPG scale): low ethnic-identifiers seem to recognize that, objectively, a racialized candidate is in their interest, yet they do not vote for that candidate. In other words, perceptions of interests do not drive vote choice.

Open-Ended Mentions of Interests

In the previous chapter, responses to open-ended questions about why respondents supported candidates showed a number explicitly citing identity considerations. What about interests? As previously reported in Table 6.1, there were very few respondents who noted considerations such as self-interest or group interests, broadly defined: there were eleven comments, but seven of them were unrelated to candidate ethnicity. One respondent did state that he or she had supported the racialized candidate because "he will take better care of minorities." More ambiguously, another commented that he or she was supporting the racialized candidate because he was a "visible minority – so he likely understands the difficulties of being a visible minority." In addition, responses included: "I think he would understand my concerns as an immigrant Canadian," and "Mr. Zhang has a better idea of how people struggle due to their nationality and will understand and appreciate minorities more." These responses were noted earlier in the chapter as possible policy positions or symbolic representation, but they might also be interpreted as general interest. One (Chinese) respondent said he or she supported the candidate because "I think that candidate know our languages better for communication," which could also be interpreted as a kind of interest, given that the ability to provide constituency services in nonofficial languages is a theme that Bird (2015) notes came out of focus groups. These responses are ambiguous in the sense that they might reflect either a desire for a candidate that understands their problems in order to address those problems through policy change, or might be simply a desire to be heard, understood, and respected for its own sake. After all, the need to be understood not only has deep psychological roots (e.g., Baumeister and Leary 1995, Lun et al. 2013; Reis et al. 2017), but is regularly practiced by politicians; recall Bill Clinton's "I feel your pain" strategy of appealing through empathy.[3]

Overall, these interest-related reasons were few in number (four, using quite a broad definition) and ambiguous in content. There were no comments that suggested that a racialized candidate would fight for specific policies and certainly no suggestion that policy change would be achieved. It is also unclear the degree to which voters wanting a politician who understands them is an end in itself, or if it is so that the politician will achieve policy goals the voter cares about. On the other hand, it could be that expressing self-interest is seen as not socially desirable, so this small number of responses might be an underestimate. Still, these open-ended questions provided little support for the interest-based account of affinity, even if we interpret the category quite broadly.

Little Evidence for Ideology or Self-Interest

Three possible explanations for coethnic affinity voting were tested, and all were found wanting. Ideological stereotyping as an explanation for affinity voting has been suggested by research on gender affinity as well as in McDermott's study of racial affinity among African Americans (1998). Two versions of this explanation were tested: 1) that racialized candidates are stereotyped as left-leaning and racialized citizens are left-leaning and 2) that racialized citizens perceive racialized candidates as ideologically closer to them. Both were rejected. There is no evidence that racialized candidates are stereotyped as left-leaning, either by white or racialized respondents. Nor is there any evidence that racialized respondents see racialized candidates as ideologically closer to themselves than white candidates. Together, these findings provide quite strong evidence that ethnicity does not have clear ideological associations in Canada. Since a link between ideology and ethnicity is a necessary condition of both versions of the ideological heuristic explanations, this finding suggests that coethnic affinity voting cannot be explained by ideological-stereotyping heuristics. Whatever its cause, the affinity voting found in Chapter 3 is not a result of the perceived ideological positions of racialized candidates.

Similarly, there is little evidence that opinion in more specific policy areas is responsible for affinity voting. Four policy attitudes were tested: immigration, racial inequality, government job creation, and crime. These models tested the conditioning effect of policy attitudes of respondents on affinity voting, since this is a requirement of the theory, even if it does not establish causality. There was no strong evidence that policy attitudes are correlated with stronger (or weaker) affinity effects. There is some evidence that opinions on immigration may affect affinity voting, which deserves further research. However, the statistical evidence here is weak, and there is good reason to think that it is a symbolic attitude, especially as there was no evidence about a causal relationship. Importantly, ethnic self-identity was still a strong predictor of affinity voting, even controlling for policy attitudes, which demonstrates that the findings in Chapter 5 were not simply caused by a correlation between identity and policy attitudes.

A final possible explanation for affinity voting is general interest. According to this theory, candidate ethnicity is a shortcut for the candidate's future actions or policy positions, and racialized voters use this information to vote according to their own interests, however defined. To test this possibility, respondents were asked which candidate would be in their financial interest or the interests of their family. Asking about financial interest should have primed self-interest considerations. However, Hypothesis 6.7 was rejected – priming self-interest had no effect on coethnic affinity, which suggests that self-interest is not strongly connected to coethnic affinity voting. To this we might add that many of the policy-stereotype models can also be interpreted as being about self-interest. Racialized Canadians might care about immigration or racial inequality because they, or their family and friends, are impacted by these policies. Yet there is little evidence that these attitudes are related to affinity voting.

Establishing a null finding is not easy. There are many possible policy attitudes and many ways to ask questions about them. Thinking that it is more difficult for nonwhite people to succeed, for example, is not quite the same as thinking the government needs to do something about discrimination. Separating out the symbolic content of responses from actual policy desires may not be possible, especially when the respondent and the policy are, of necessity, closely connected. To definitively establish a causal relationship would also require a whole separate set of manipulations and, therefore, a far larger data set. The self-interest prime might simply have failed, or affinity voting could be strongly driven by self-interest considerations that have no relation to the financial impact on voters. This, though, seems unlikely, given the wide range of policies that have a financial impact, and the null effects of policy-attitude models, but it does underline that these results are not definitive. Still, a series of different tests using multiple measures turned up essentially no evidence of interest-based explanations for affinity voting.

Putting this in broader context, it is worth keeping in mind that there is no clear evidence of interest-based effects from other sources either. McDermott (1998) uses an analysis quite similar to the policy-stereotype models. However, the measure of ideology is "do more for Blacks," which is not obviously an ideology, or even a policy attitude, and is probably deeply influenced by identity. Linked-fate research certainly shows that those measures are correlated with affinity voting (e.g., Dawson 1994; McConnaughy et al. 2010), but it does not separate identity from interests.

In conclusion, these research findings rule out one possible motivation for coethnic affinity voting – ideological stereotyping. The results directly contradict one of the few studies to date that has examined the causes of racial affinity (McDermott 1998). Nor is there any evidence for more specific policy stereotypes, though there were some suggestive findings about immigration attitudes. In particular, having controlled for identity, there is no effect of racial inequality despite its prominent role in group-consciousness theory. Conversely, ethnic self-identity still had strong effects, even controlling for policy attitudes. Finally, priming self-interest did not affect affinity effects. While the findings here do not conclusively rule out interest-based explanations for affinity voting, there is little to no evidence to support them.

7
Affinity Voting
..... in Federal Elections

Are ethnic- and racialized-affinity effects likely to occur in federal elections in Canada, and how widespread will they be? There is clear evidence for the existence of both coethnic affinity and racial affinity voting in Canada, and the key driver of these effects is identity, not interests. This chapter evaluates these effects in the context of Canadian electoral politics in three ways: by examining the effect of political party labels, by considering the distribution of racialized candidates, and by analyzing the geography of racialized voters. To undertake these analyses, two new data sources are introduced: data on some four thousand candidates, for all major parties, from federal elections in 2004, 2006, 2008, and 2011 and census data on visible-minority Canadians, by federal electoral district.

The first part of the chapter evaluates whether political party labels condition the effect of candidate ethnicity. This question arises from research that suggests racial or ethnic heuristics are not influential when voters have access to party cues (Kam 2007). In other words, when candidates have party labels, the ethnicity of the candidate might not matter. If this is the case, then elections at the provincial or national level are unlikely to be influenced by ethnic or racialized affinity voting. To test this, the presence and type of party label were manipulated.

The second part examines how widespread affinity voting is likely to be by evaluating the distribution of racialized candidates and voters. If a racialized candidate competing against white candidates is an uncommon occurrence at the electoral district level – perhaps because racialized candidates are concentrated in a handful of ridings – then the experimental set-up might not represent the electoral choice set of many racialized voters. Recall that the choice set might have important effects on the way that voters identify, so differences between the experimental set-up and real electoral choice sets might affect the generalizability of the results.

Finally, the geographic extent of racialized voters is pivotal: do racialized voters actually have a chance to vote for racialized candidates? Local ethnic homogeneity – the proportion of different racialized ethnic groups – also determines the degree of ethnic versus racialized affinity voting. Perhaps electoral districts that tend to have a single large, racialized ethnic group are likely to nominate candidates of that ethnic group. In that case, the amount of racialized affinity voting might be low and coethnic affinity voting high.

Partly labels, candidate distribution, and geographic concentrations are important to understanding how influential affinity voting is in Canadian elections. The findings here suggest that affinity voting still occurs, even when candidates are affiliated with a political party, which means that these effects will apply to a wide range of federal and provincial elections. Moreover, there are racialized candidates in a large percentage of electoral districts, and the most common composition of these electoral slates is one racialized candidate and several white candidates – just like the candidate experiments in previous chapters. Finally, most racialized candidates face electorates in which the size of their own ethnic group is significant but that group represents only a plurality of racialized voters. These results suggest that ethnic and racial affinity voting are both relevant to elections at all levels of government and to a large percentage of the racialized Canadian population but that racialized affinity voting is particularly important.

Political Party Labels

Political parties dominate electoral politics at the national and regional level in essentially all established democracies, and citizens rely heavily on partisan cues in making political judgments (Lau and Redlawsk 2006; Rahn et al. 1993; Campbell et al. 1960). This is an especially important consideration for the present research because of a study by Cindy Kam (2007), which finds that partisan cues eliminate the effect of racial cues. In partisan elections, candidate ethnicity may not matter, or it may matter less. Although there is not a great deal of direct evidence, these findings are consistent with several other studies, as Sigelman and Sigelman (1982) suggest (see also Citrin, Green, and Sears 1990; Rahn 1993). On the other hand, although they included party labels in candidate biographies, King and Matland (2003) found gender effects for candidates, and McDermott (1998) found both gender and race effects. Finally, Barreto (2010) found that Latino voters are willing to vote for a Latino candidate of a different party. This evidence suggests that while party labels are important, they do not have the straight-forward suppressing effect that Kam found in her research.

To examine this issue, the candidate biographies in the voting experiment were manipulated to list party affiliation.[1] A subset of respondents were shown candidates that were labelled Liberal or Conservative rather than independent. Rather than the last sentence of the biography reading, "Mr. Hawkes is an independent candidate," it read, "Mr. Hawkes is running for the Liberal Party" or "Mr. Hawkes is running for the Conservative Party." Otherwise, candidate biographies and manipulations of candidate ethnicity were the same as in the rest of the experiment. We might expect, for instance, that a Liberal candidate already benefits from being seen as the "tolerant" candidate and thus receives no further increase in support from being of a racialized ethnic group. Therefore, under the partisan condition, Candidate 2, the candidate whose ethnicity was manipulated, had a 50 percent chance of being Liberal and a 50 percent chance of being Conservative. The independent versions of the candidates are the same as in the previous chapters. Given previous research, especially Kam's study (2007), the hypothesis is that party labels will reduce the effects of ethnic identification.

H7.1: Affinity effects will be smaller when candidates have party affiliations than when candidates are independent.

To test Hypothesis 7.1, the Conservative and Liberal cells were merged, since the hypothesis states that party labels in general will suppress the effect of candidate racialized status. This increased the size of the cells and, therefore, the precision with which the parameters could be estimated. Model 7.1, as before, has support for Candidate 2 as the dependent variable. The independent variables are candidate racialized status, strength of ethnic self-identification, and the party label/independent variable, which forms a three-way interaction and constituent terms, as well as demographic controls. As in previous models, since the strength-of-ethnic-self-identification question was only asked of racialized respondents, white respondents were not included in this analysis.

The predicted values are shown in Figure 7.1. With party labels at the top of the strength-of-identification scale, racialized respondents are 17 percentage points more likely to support a racialized candidate than a white candidate ($p = .1$), compared to 24 percentage points for the independent version

FIGURE 7.1

Affinity voting in party label and independent conditions

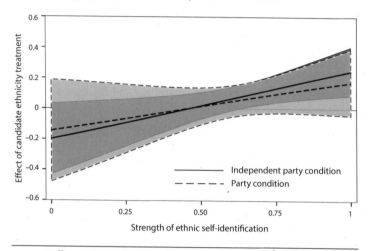

NOTES: Difference in predicted probability of choosing Candidate 2, between white and racialized candidate versions; racialized respondents only; n = 1,335.

(p = .02). While the confidence interval for the party condition is certainly wider, this is likely a result of the smaller cell size in that condition. These results seem to be contrary to Kam's findings and to Hypothesis 7.1.

The crucial test is the difference between the party and independent conditions, which is not statistically significant – the difference has a p-value of 0.32 at 0.75 on the IDPG scale, and a p-value of 0.32 at 1 on the IDPG scale. Clearly, the difference between the party version and the independent version does not even approach statistical significance, so there is no solid evidence that party labels reduce affinity effects.

The two-party label conditions – Liberal and Conservative – are separated in Model 7.2, which is otherwise the same as the previous model. Figure 7.2 shows the difference in the probability of voting for a white Candidate 2 as compared to a racialized Candidate 2. Effectively, this is the size of the candidate-ethnicity treatment effect. Three sets of values are shown – one for the independent version of the candidate, one where Candidate 2 is Liberal, and one where Candidate 2 is Conservative. There is not a great deal of difference in coethnic affinity voting between the independent, Liberal, and Conservative versions – although there may be a possible interaction with the Conservative Party label.

FIGURE 7.2

Affinity voting with Conservative, Liberal, and independent candidates

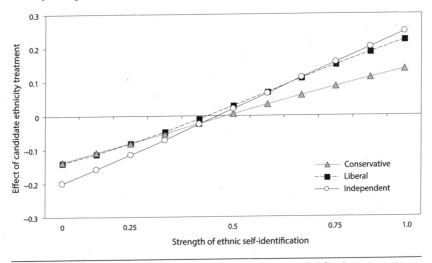

NOTE: Racialized respondents only; confidence intervals not included for clarity; quantity of interest is difference between lines, not statistically significant; $n = 1,125$.

Consider the predicted probabilities at 0.75 on the IDPG scale. For the independent candidates, the effect of candidate racialized status is 0.13 – that is, racialized respondents are 13 percentage points more likely to support a racialized, independent Candidate 2 than a white, independent Candidate 2. The Liberal condition is also 13 percentage points – identical to the independent condition. However, racialized respondents are only 7 percentage points more likely to support a racialized, Conservative Candidate 2 than a white, Conservative Candidate 2. At the top of the IDPG scale the pattern is the same: 0.25 for the independent candidate, 0.22 for the Liberal candidate, and 0.14 for the Conservative candidate. These differences, however, are still not statistically significant – the difference in the treatment effect, between the independent and Conservative party conditions, at 0.75 on the strength-of-identification scale has a p-value of .27; at 1 on the strength-of-identification scale, it has a p-value of .26.

The effects of candidate racialized status under the party conditions are not significantly different from those under the independent condition, leading to the rejection of Hypothesis 7.1. Contrary to expectations based on Kam's study, there is no evidence of weaker ethnic-affinity effects when candidates have party labels, as compared to independent candidate characteristics. If anything, there might be an interaction with the Conservative Party – affinity effects for the Conservative version might be smaller, although the difference is not statistically significant. For the Liberal version, the point estimates of affinity effects are nearly identical to the independent version. While it is difficult to definitively rule out Kam's theory, the effects that she found failed to materialize here.

Explaining Affinity Voting with Party Labels

When candidates have party affiliations, there is evidence that coethnic affinity voting persists rather than is attenuated. To what extent do these results clash with Kam's (2007) findings? Perhaps less so than it seems. Kam has no strong *a priori* reason to expect weaker candidate-ethnicity effects with party labels, other than that parties are important in evaluating candidates in many ways. Nonetheless, Kam interpreted the results in light of a primary mechanism (heuristics) and a secondary mechanism (aversive racism).

The heuristic mechanism is not explored at much length in Kam's (2007, 362) research, but she suggests that "citizens will use party cues over attitudes toward an ethnic group because party cues are widely shared heuristics that seem more appropriate and more legitimate for political decision-making." However, it is not obvious why this would be so. Certainly, citizens use inappropriate or illegitimate information to make political decisions all the time, as the large body of research on prejudice and discrimination illustrates. What might be at play is *relevant* information – citizens believe that party is a more accurate heuristic than race and therefore abandon race as a heuristic when party labels are available. However, this account relies on the assumption that citizens have an idea about which heuristics are more accurate, and that they will abandon worse heuristics in favour of better ones. This is a rationalistic account of heuristics, and it is plausible but hardly certain. In any case, we do not have a strong theoretical reason to think that party heuristics are necessarily privileged over racial heuristics. A third possibility is that these results simply reflect proportional influence: when only a few pieces of information are offered about a candidate, each piece of information is very influential; when more information is available, each piece of information is less influential. Thus, adding party labels might decrease the relative weight of candidate ethnicity but certainly not eliminate it.

Aversive racism is the second mechanism that Kam suggests may be responsible for the attenuation of candidate race effects when party cues are present. The theory of aversive racism holds that people are likely to discriminate under ambiguous conditions. In other words, given a lack of knowledge, people tend to assume the worst about racialized candidates and vote accordingly. Party labels reduce ambiguity about factors such as policy positions and therefore should reduce discriminatory behaviour. The theory also provides a possible explanation for the divergent findings here. As ambiguity declines, there is less bias because people are unwilling to engage in obvious discrimination – either recognizing that this behaviour is wrong or fearing what others might think. Affinity voting, however, is probably not socially unacceptable in the way that discrimination is. In other words, these respondents may be perfectly willing to vote *for* a racialized candidate consciously or publicly, in a way that Kam's respondents would be unwilling to vote *against* the racialized candidate.

The divergence between these findings and Kam's research lends more credence to identity-based over interest-based explanations. If candidate ethnicity is a heuristic for future actions or policy positions, then party labels ought to reduce this influence. Party affiliation, after all, would be an excellent heuristic for policy positions and other similar considerations. On the other hand, if coethnic affinity voting is driven by identity-based mechanisms, such as desiring a member of one's group to succeed, or in-group bias in evaluating candidate characteristics, then party labels should have no particular effect on candidate ethnicity. Of course, party labels would still have an independent effect, but they would not replace the effect of in-group favouritism the way they would replace ethnicity as a policy heuristic.

There is no evidence here that party labels suppress the effect of candidate ethnicity, as previous research has shown. If anything, the somewhat smaller (though still not statistically significantly different) effect for the Conservative (but not the Liberal) Party manipulation suggests that there may be interactions between coethnic affinity and specific parties rather than a universal attenuating effect. In addition, the fact that the effect of ethnicity is not replaced by party heuristics when they are available suggests that these effects are more a function of identity considerations than interest-based candidate heuristics.

Distribution of Federal Candidates

The final major issue is the extent to which visible-minority candidates actually run for office and how widely they are distributed. If minority candidates run in many electoral districts, then affinity voting will be more widespread than if they are concentrated in only a few districts.

In addition, the experiment was set up as a choice between a white and (sometimes) racialized candidate, but a choice between multiple racialized candidates might lead to significantly different results. It is certainly plausible that the likelihood of the nomination of racialized candidates is related to the size of the visible-minority population in a geographical area, meaning that racialized candidates may tend to be concentrated in the same ridings. If most racialized candidates compete in ridings with multiple racialized candidates, then the experimental set-up might not be a good representation of the circumstances of actual elections.

To test this, I developed a data set of candidates in four federal elections (2004, 2006, 2008, and 2011). The list of candidates, ridings, and political affiliations was provided by Elections Canada. It included 60 candidates for the Bloc Québécois and 308 candidates for the Conservatives, Liberals, and NDP, in each election. In a small number of cases, the major parties did not run candidates, such as when the Conservatives did not run a candidate against the independent André Arthur in 2008 and 2011 and when the Liberals did not run a candidate against Elizabeth May in 2008. Other candidates and parties were not included, even when they won: for example, independent candidates André Arthur in Quebec and Bill Casey in Nova Scotia or the Green Party's Elizabeth May in British Columbia. There was a total of 3,993 candidates.

The candidates were coded using the same method as a number of other studies, including Black (2008) and Tossutti and Najem (2002). The coding involved drawing on publicly available data, such as candidate biographies, newspaper articles, websites, and, where necessary, surname analysis. For the most part, the sources were quite accurate – multicultural media such as the *South Asian Times* often publish lists of South Asian candidates. In addition, the CBC and the *Globe and Mail* published riding profiles with candidate photos and biographies dating back to 2004.

The coding of ethnicity drew on Statistics Canada categories; however, it combined two sets of categories. Chinese, Korean, Japanese, Filipino, and Southeast Asian candidates were combined into a single "East Asian/

TABLE 7.1

Visible-minority candidates per riding

Number of candidates	2004	2006	2008	2011
0	240	236	226	231
1	53	53	62	54
2	14	18	16	14
3	1	1	4	9

Southeast Asian" category. Similarly, Arab, other Middle Eastern, and West Asian candidates (e.g., Iranian, Afghan) were combined into a "Middle Eastern/West Asian" category. This was done because the numbers are quite small but also because distinguishing between these groups can be quite difficult. Note that, as discussed in Chapter 2, the dynamics of affinity voting might be quite different for Indigenous and immigrant racialized groups. In addition, because they are defined as nonvisible minorities by Statistics Canada, Indigenous candidates are not coded as visible-minority candidates here.

The number of districts with visible-minority candidates and the number of visible-minority candidates per district are shown in Table 7.1. It sets out the number of visible-minority candidates per riding, by election year. In the most recent election in this data, 2011, fifty-four ridings had a single visible-minority candidate, fourteen had two visible-minority candidates, and nine had three. Clearly, the most common situation is one visible-minority candidate competing against multiple white candidates. This situation replicates the experimental set-up, though affinity effects should also apply to ridings with multiple visible-minority candidates. The relatively high dispersal of minority candidates in many ridings, rather than being concentrated in a few, suggests that coethnic affinity voting has a large potential influence.

These numbers are essentially stable across all four elections, with the exception of ridings with three candidates or more, where there is a sharp increase in more recent elections. Since the raw numbers are still relatively small, it is hard to tell if this is a real trend. Put in terms of percentages, the election with the lowest percentage of ridings with at least one visible-minority candidate was 2004 (with 22 percent), and the highest was 2008 (with 26 percent). Visible-minority candidates clearly run in a large portion of ridings; thus, attitudes toward them are potentially influential for a large percentage of the population.

Distribution of Visible-Minority Voters

Having established that visible-minority candidates run in a large percentage of ridings, how does the distribution of visible-minority candidates relate to the distribution of visible-minority citizens? Are there, in fact, many visible-minority citizens who are exposed to affinity effects? To answer this question, the candidate data were merged with riding-level census data on population ethnicity from 2006. Because the 2011 long-form census was cancelled and questions about ethnicity moved to the nonmandatory National Household Survey, this more recent data is not easily comparable. Nonetheless, the 2006 data are not far removed from most elections included in this data set and should be relatively accurate for the period.

Riding-level census data are linked to the candidate data discussed previously in order to calculate the number of visible-minority citizens living in ridings with visible-minority candidates. For example, the riding of Beauharnois–Salaberry had one visible-minority candidate in 2011 (Anne Minh-Thu Quach) and 43,930 visible-minority citizens. Similarly, the riding of Willowdale had two visible-minority candidates (Mehdi Mollahasani and Chungsen Leung) and 62,235 visible-minority citizens. How many visible-minority Canadians can vote for visible-minority candidates? To show this, I summed the visible-minority populations living in those ridings with visible-minority candidates in the most recent election (2011). This number was then converted to a percentage of visible-minority citizens across the country. The calculation showed that in 2011, 4.1 million visible-minority Canadians (31 percent) lived in ridings with at least one visible-minority candidate. Clearly, large numbers of visible-minority Canadians are faced with electoral choices that might produce affinity voting.

Another issue might result from the potential for national diversity (but regional concentration) of ethnic groups. If ridings are often dominated by single ethnocultural groups, relations between racialized ethnic groups would be irrelevant at the local level. For this to matter, visible-minority candidates would have to be nominated often in ridings where their own ethnic group is demographically dominant. To test if visible-minority candidates are nominated in ridings dominated by their own ethnic group, I compared the percentage of the population belonging to the same ethnic group

FIGURE 7.3

Electoral district voter ethnicity, by candidate ethnicity

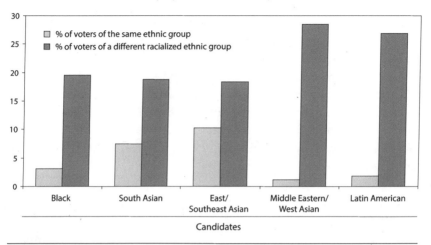

NOTES: 2004–11 elections, 2006 census data; $n = 3,998$.

as the candidate with the percentage of the population of all other visible-minority groups. As Figure 7.3 shows, the average racialized candidate does not run in a riding dominated by his or her own ethnic group. In fact, for most ethnocultural categories, the mean percentage of the candidate's ethnic group is less than half the percentage of other visible-minority groups. The one exception is the East Asian/Southeast Asian ethnicity, where the average candidate ran in a riding where 10.1 percent of the population was East Asian/Southeast Asian and where 18.4 percent of the population was of other ethnic minorities. There are certainly some electoral districts dominated by one racialized ethnic group, but most racialized candidates face electorates where their own ethnocultural group is a plurality.

Of course, it is still probably true that visible-minority candidates are more likely to be nominated in diverse areas and in areas with greater numbers of people of the same ethnic background. Not only do more potential candidates live there, but they could recruit people of the same cultural community to vote in nomination meetings. In other words, there is likely a correlation between the local size of an ethnocultural group in a riding and the likelihood of a candidate belonging to that ethnocultural group. However, this does not mean they dominate the riding in total numbers. As Figure 7.3 shows, visible-minority candidates generally run in a riding where their own ethnic group is outnumbered by people of other visible-minority ethnicities by a large margin.

Nonetheless, for some ethnicities – South Asians and East Asians – their own group is a substantial portion of the racialized population. Conversely, black, Middle Eastern/West Asian and Latin American candidates generally face electorates where, even compared to other racialized groups, their own ethnic group is quite small, no doubt because, in absolute terms, there are far more South Asians and East Asians in Canada than other racialized groups. Because ethnic-affinity effects are substantially larger than racial-affinity effects, this might be an important advantage. South Asian and East Asian candidates are not only more likely to be elected because there are more potential candidates but because the structure of affinity voting means they face a friendlier electorate.

Affinity Effects in Federal Elections

The above analysis examined how likely ethnic and racialized affinity voting are in federal elections in Canada and how widespread these effects might be, with a focus on three issues: the effect of party labels, distribution of racialized candidates, and the geography of racialized voters. The first issue was investigated by drawing on Kam's (2007) research, which suggests that the effects of candidate ethnicity would be suppressed by party labels. If this is the case, then affinity voting would be unlikely to occur in federal and provincial elections. Model 7.1 tests this by comparing coethnic affinity voting when the candidates are independent and when they have party labels. Contrary to Kam's findings, there was no clear difference between the independent and party conditions.

Three important conclusions can be drawn from the findings regarding party labels. The first is that coethnic affinity-voting effects also apply to party-based elections. Had there only been affinity effects under the independent condition, as is suggested in Kam's work, coethnic affinity voting might be prevalent in municipal elections, where the candidates do not have party affiliations, but not in provincial or federal elections. As it turns out, this is not the case; all else being equal, the racialized status of candidates had essentially identical effects for independent candidates and candidates with party labels. Therefore, there is no reason to think that coethnic affinity voting will not occur in elections at all levels of government. Of course, there may be other reasons that affinity effects would be smaller than demonstrated here; for example, knowledge about local candidates, especially of their ethnicities, is no doubt greater in this experiment than in real-world elections. Nonetheless, this analysis suggests that candidate ethnicity is influential at a psychological level, even when candidates have party affiliations.

While there is also no clear evidence of an interaction between party and candidate ethnicity, there is some suggestion that affinity voting was lower for Conservative racialized candidates, although the difference was not statistically significant. Interestingly, this would be consistent with King and Matland's (2003) finding that gender affinity functions differently for Republicans and Democrats, as well as other research on differential effects of candidate identities by party label (Bauer 2018; Besco 2018; Street 2014). However, these differential effects only appear to manifest when the attitudes toward identity/stereotypes vary by party. For example, (some) Democratic women may view electing more women as an important goal while Republican women do not, which leads to different effects of gender affinity for women candidates. While only the Liberal and Conservative parties were tested, it seems unlikely that the NDP and Liberal parties are perceived as very different on issues related to ethnicity, immigration, racial inequality, or multiculturalism, and the respondents in this survey do not differ on the IDPG by party. Therefore, it seems plausible that these results should apply to NDP candidates as well.

Another implication of these findings is that the party-label analysis reinforces the importance of identity, rather than interests, as the explanation for affinity effects. If candidate ethnicity was a heuristic for the actions of the candidate in office, as all of the interest-based explanations suggest, then party labels ought to reduce this effect. Party affiliation, after all, might seem to be a good predictor of what a candidate will do in office – at least better than ethnicity. As noted earlier, if voters do, indeed, chose "better" heuristics over less reliable ones, then party cues ought to replace ethnic cues. The fact that coethnic affinity voting is not lower in the party affiliation condition than in the independent condition suggests that respondents are primarily motivated by factors other than interest-based considerations about the candidate's actions in office.

The persuasiveness of this evidence is greater in conjunction with the results of the ideological-stereotypes test. Recall that there was no evidence that racialized candidates are stereotyped as more left-leaning than white candidates (see Chapter 6). In fact, the perceived ideological position of white and racialized candidates was essentially identical. The results of the party manipulation are similar – if ethnicity was a heuristic for candidate policy positions, then we would expect to see the effect of ethnicity decline when party labels are provided. In fact, candidate party affiliation does not supersede the effects of candidate ethnicity. In other words, explanations for coethnic affinity voting that rely on heuristics about what a candidate would do in office – interest-based explanations – are not the primary driver of coethnic affinity voting.

In regard to the number of districts that have visible-minority candidates and the number of visible minorities who can vote for them, the data set on actual candidates who ran in federal elections showed that visible-minority candidates are widespread – in most elections, one-quarter of ridings had at least one visible-minority candidate. Moreover, some 4.1 million visible-minority voters lived in those ridings, demonstrating the potential reach of ethnic- and racial-affinity effects.

Finally, census data were combined with the candidate data to evaluate the degree of ethnic homogeneity in electoral districts. Despite the diversity of ethnicity at the national level, local homogeneity might make racialized-affinity effects unimportant. However, the data considered show this is not the case: the mean percentage of the population of the candidate's ethnic group is generally less than half the size of other ethnic groups. That is, the candidate's ethnic group is usually only a plurality rather than a majority, even among visible-minority citizens, suggesting that racialized affinity is, indeed, politically important, because most candidates cannot rely on their own ethnocultural group being demographically dominant, even at the riding level.

The analyses all point to the plausibility of affinity voting explored in earlier chapters. Party labels do not seem to automatically reduce ethnic-affinity effects, suggesting that affinity voting is likely in federal, provincial, and municipal elections. Similarly, the analysis of candidates in four federal elections shows that most visible-minority candidates face white opponents, as did the hypothetical candidates in the experiment. Visible minorities are widespread, running in some 25 percent of electoral districts, and a large number of visible-minority citizens have the opportunity to vote for them. Finally, most visible-minority candidates run in ridings where their ethnic group is a plurality – single ethnic groups do not dominate most ridings. Therefore, ethnic and racial affinity voting are likely to have a broad reach to large swaths of the population and in elections at all levels of government.

8
Conclusion

The conventional wisdom is that official multiculturalism in Canada has been a success and therefore that race and ethnicity divisions do not play a major role in electoral politics. After all, immigration and multiculturalism are widely supported by the public (Reitz 2011), accepted by all major political parties, and there is little or no evidence of explicit discrimination against racialized candidates in terms of voting (Black and Erickson 2006). Yet, by largely ignoring the decisions and preferences of racialized Canadians, we have missed an important way that race and ethnicity feature in politics. Race and ethnicity matter, because they matter to racialized Canadians themselves.

Racialized Canadians are more likely to support candidates of their own ethnic group and racialized candidates more generally, a finding that reveals new insights into how racial and ethnic identities are structured. The way that people identify at a given point in time emerges from a negotiation between long-term factors such as personal history and racial schema and short-term factors related to the immediate context. In the context of this study, this means that dominant social definitions of race and ethnicity constrain the identities that are plausible, and the electoral context makes one of these identities salient, with clear implications for affinity effects. The strong ethnic-affinity effects and more modestly sized racialized-affinity effects found in this study demonstrate that Canadians clearly identify with ethnic groups, as defined by Statistics Canada, but also that more general racialization – the division between white and nonwhite groups – also matters.

Understanding why voters support candidates of the same race and ethnicity sheds an important light on the meaning of citizenship and democracy. Some scholars theorize that affinity voting is primarily a heuristic for the ideological positions of the candidate, a way of making self-interested decisions about which candidate will be best. They argue that it is essentially an instrumental motivation, but there was little evidence to support this argument in the data. Instead, the key motivation was the voter's self-identity. Drawing on the rich literature of psychological theories of identity, a set of explanations linking self-identity and vote choice was developed. These explanations include in-group favouritism, bias in perceptions of candidate characteristics, and the persuasiveness of campaign messages.

Given the relevance of identity to understanding behaviour, it is important to know who identifies and with what group. Racialized Canadians identify with multiple racial and ethnic groups at different levels of specificity, including quite specific cultural, national, or ethnic groups; mid-level ethnic groups, as defined by Statistics Canada; and a higher-order racialized minority group. These identities are correlated, but lower-order identities seem to be stronger. The context is what determines which of these identities is active at a given point in time.

Five key results are worth highlighting. First, there is good evidence of co-ethnic affinity voting among multiple ethnic groups. Second, affinity voting can apply not just to the voter's own ethnic group but also to candidates of different racialized ethnic groups: that is, racialized affinity voting. Third, there is evidence of three levels of racial or ethnic identity. Fourth, there are substantial reasons to be skeptical of interest-based explanations for affinity voting. And fifth, ethnic and racialized affinity voting are strongly conditional on ethnic self-identity.

Affinity Effects in Electoral Politics
Race and ethnicity matter in Canadian politics. Racialized Canadians are more likely to support candidates of their own ethnic group as well as candidates from other ethnic groups (though the latter effect is smaller). One implication of these effects is that the demographic makeup of an electoral district may have a significant impact on the prospects of racialized candidates. Racialized candidates nominated in ridings with a high percentage of racialized voters may have a considerable advantage over those in primarily white ridings. The benefit from coethnic affinity voting will be largest where voters are of the same specific ethnicity as the candidate but will also exist to a lesser extent among all racialized voters. Affinity effects may compensate for lower support from white voters. Or, if there is little or no discrimination from white voters (e.g., Black and Erickson 2006), affinity effects may actually give racialized candidates in diverse electoral districts a distinct advantage over white candidates.

The same psychological mechanisms should also apply to other aspects of politics and beyond. In electoral politics, these aspects would include not only general elections but also nominations, fundraising, endorsements, and the actions of politicians and candidates between elections – all of increasing importance in the "permanent campaign," where candidates now continue to campaign between elections and ramp up their activities long before the official campaign period starts.

Among nonelectoral effects, these mechanisms could play an important role in the success or failure of advocacy groups, issue opinions, and social movements. For all of these areas, the key insight is that appeals by a member of one's own group are likely to be more successful and more persuasive. Lobbying efforts on in-group politicians are more likely to succeed, and people are more likely to be mobilized or persuaded by in-group members. Interestingly, this finding puts the historical tradition of appointing "representative" cabinets (e.g., Bakvis 1991; Kerby 2009; White 2005) in a new light: a racialized cabinet minister may, indeed, be more persuasive when communicating or campaigning for support from racialized citizens.

With a racialized Canadian as leader of a major party, these effects will probably be very large and influential. The practically unanimous support that Barack Obama received from African Americans may have been especially dramatic, but we should expect similar dynamics in Canada when, for example, the first South Asian Canadian becomes prime minister. These effects may be emerging even now with the 2017 election of Jagmeet Singh as leader of the federal NDP, the first visible-minority leader of a major federal party (and only the second to run, the first being Rosemary Brown in 1975). Singh was portrayed as a way for the NDP to appeal to "working- and middle-class immigrants and visible minorities" (Radwanski 2017), "ethnic minorities" (Jones 2017), and "minority voters in the suburbs" (Ivison 2017). The evidence presented here suggests that, all else being equal, Singh's leadership will lead to a substantial increase in support for the NDP by South Asian Canadians.

The extension of affinity affects to other ethnic-minority groups is also important in terms of political influence. If coethnic affinity voting was limited only to candidates of the same ethnicity, its influence would be limited. The ethnic diversity of racialized Canadians, both nationally and locally, means that most racialized candidates face electorates in which their own ethnic group is only a plurality among racialized voters. In other words, ethnic-affinity effects alone would affect a relatively small proportion of the electorate, thus limiting their political influence, even if the effect was very strong. However, it appears that affinity voting extends beyond specific ethnic groups; all else being equal, racialized voters are more likely to support candidates of different racialized ethnicities than a white candidate, greatly increasing the potential size of racialized coalitions and broadening the influence of affinity effects.

The effects of affinity voting should occur in partisan elections, as the party manipulations in Chapter 7 indicate. Previous research had suggested that party labels reduce or eliminate the effects of candidate ethnicity (Kam 2007), but in this study, candidate ethnicity had similar effects for candidates who were independent or affiliated with a party, suggesting that co-ethnic affinity voting will apply not only to municipal or other nonpartisan elections but also to provincial and federal elections. To be clear, affinity effects might be smaller in real elections for other reasons. In the experiments analyzed here, the respondents read biographies of the candidates and very likely noticed their ethnicities. By contrast, in real elections, some voters might know nothing about the local candidate. Note, however, that Fisher and colleagues (2015) found affinity effects between Pakistani-origin voters and local candidates in the United Kingdom in the 2011 election – so affinity effects clearly occur, even among local candidates in Westminster systems. The central finding here is that there is no psychological reason for partisanship to replace the effect of candidate ethnicity. "Good" heuristics like partisanship do not drive out "bad" heuristics like race. While previous research has found that party labels diminish the effects of race, it may be that negative affinity effects (i.e., discrimination) are reduced by party labels but that positive affinity effects are not. In any case, there is no reason to think the psychological effects of affinity will not apply in both partisan and nonpartisan contexts.

In the long run, the influence of race and ethnicity in Canadian politics will likely increase. In some ways, ethnic-affinity effects, as they occur in Canada, are a product of immigration, not simply because it creates ethnic diversity but because socialization in another country is in large part responsible for the strength of ethnocultural identities. Two key implications follow. The first is that the link to immigration implies a limit to the influence of affinity voting. Ethnic and racialized affinity voting are not a product of biology, nor even primarily of family history. Although the descendants of immigrants may continue to check off the same ethnicity box on the census, the further they are removed from immigration, the weaker the affinity effects will be. On the other hand, coethnic affinity voting is likely to grow as the percentage of Canadians who are immigrants increases. Given that immigration is likely to continue indefinitely – the percentage of immigrants has risen steadily since 1931 (HRSDC 2015) – ethnic and racialized affinity voting are likely to increase for the foreseeable future.

It is worth noting that the sample did not include respondents from Quebec (see Appendix A), but it is likely that the results can be generalized to candidates and voters in Quebec. To the extent that affinity voting is caused by the psychology of social-group identity, it is unlikely that it will operate in a fundamentally different way. Although it might be thought that higher levels of prejudice in Quebec (Lambert and Curtis 1983; Bilodeau, Turgeon, and Karakoç 2012) would affect affinity voting, the results of the racial-inequality model in the policy-interaction analysis in Chapter 7 do not support this supposition. However, it is notable that Quebec includes a particularly large number of racialized citizens that would fall into the "other" category, perhaps because of French-speaking Haitian and Lebanese immigrants.[1] In the data examined here, this category did not show statistically significant affinity effects. This might be due to problems with the terminology of group names, since there were other racialized-affinity effects (e.g., Chinese/South Asian, South Asian/Chinese). Nonetheless, it is possible that these groups might be exceptional in that black Canadians have especially low socioeconomic status and might experience greater discrimination from other racialized groups, while Muslim Canadians face a particular set of circumstances and attitudes.[2] This deserves further investigation and might produce different aggregate results in Quebec, but these results would relate to the composition of ethnic minorities rather than to residence in Quebec.

Cross-nationally, these affinity voting dynamics are very likely to occur in most democracies. Since the foundation of these effects is psychological, they are likely generalizable to a wide range of groups and countries. However, structural factors might influence the relative influence of mechanisms. One such factor might be the acceptance of an explicit link between ethnicity and access to government services. Some studies in Africa, for example, found interest-based effects (Wantchekon 2003; Bratton, Bhavnani, and Chen 2012), which are much more likely in systems where provision (or deprivation) of government resources to specific ethnic groups is very plausible; as a consequence, the election of coethnic legislators does have a clear impact on the voter's interests. Of course, some public policies like affirmative action could be interpreted this way, but it seems likely that the scale and explicitness of these links are far weaker in many developed countries. Because explicit links between ethnicity and government benefits are considered unacceptable in these countries, if not outright unconstitutional, it would not be surprising if the effect of self-interest was correspondingly weaker and identity effects stronger.

While much research in the United States has found conflict rather than affinity between racialized ethnic groups, it seems likely that it is the United States that is the outlier here, and the Obama coalition suggests that those results may no longer hold. Recall that Canada is comparable to many OECD countries on key indicators related to interminority conflict, such as levels of social prejudice and economic marginalization. While Canada is ahead of the United States on these measures and above the OECD average, it is not an outlier. Given this, it seems likely that we would find these kinds of ethnic- and racialized-affinity effects in a number of European countries and in other countries around the globe.

Identity and Interests

A major innovation of this study is its attention to the causes and motivations of affinity effects. Understanding voters' motivations helps us understand where and when affinity voting is likely and what the affinity effects mean for the act of voting and democracy more generally. To that end, a series of different interest-based explanations were described, and a largely novel set of identity-based explanations were elaborated. On this point, there are four key empirical claims. First, there is strong evidence that one major explanation for coethnic affinity voting, ideological stereotyping (McDermott 1998), is incorrect, at least in Canada. Second, four policy attitudes were tested, but there is little evidence that they are connected to affinity voting. Third, there are a number of persuasive pieces of evidence against general-interest explanations. Fourth, there is strong evidence that identity plays a crucial role in affinity voting. The apparent primacy of self-identity as a determinant of vote choice raises important questions about how we understand elections and democracy.

One of the earliest studies to explore the causes of coethnic affinity voting was by McDermott (1998), who argued that ideological stereotyping explains affinity voting among African Americans. The candidate's race tells voters about the candidate's ideological position, which enables voters to act on their ideological preferences (which they assume will match the candidate's position). This explanation was examined in Chapter 6 and, surprisingly, there was no evidence of ideological stereotyping of racialized candidates. There was good reason to expect ideological stereotyping as a considerable amount of evidence from the United States shows that racialized candidates are stereotyped as both Democrats and liberal (e.g., Jones 2014). In addition, racialized voters in Canada have a long history of supporting the Liberal Party (e.g., Blais 2005), and Canadian partisans have quite different opinions on diversity issues. Yet, here, respondents did not rate racialized candidates as more left-wing than white candidates nor as ideologically more similar to themselves. In fact, race and ethnicity seemed to be irrelevant to the perceived ideological positions of the candidates. This finding is quite strong evidence that affinity voting is not likely a result of ethnicity as a heuristic for ideology.

The lack of a relationship between candidate ethnicity and perceived ideology also suggests that other possible explanations that link ethnicity to ideology are less persuasive. For example, one explanation for why Republican voters are less likely to support minority candidates is because they view these candidates as ideologically liberal. Therefore, some argue that what appears to be discrimination may not be a result of prejudice against ethnic minorities but, rather, a result of ideological positions – a much less troublesome explanation (i.e., "principled conservatism"; for example, see Sniderman and Piazza 1993). The evidence here suggests that this kind of argument may not apply in Canada, even if it is true elsewhere; it seems quite unlikely that discrimination could be a product of perceived ideology, because there is simply no relationship between ethnicity and perceptions of the candidate's left-right position.

Specific policy attitudes also don't seem to lead to affinity voting. A series of models examining attitudes on immigration, racial inequality, government job creation, and crime policy all produced null results. There was some suggestion that immigration attitudes might be important, but they might well be expressions of symbolic attitudes. Conversely, the effect of ethnic identity is still strong, even controlling for policy attitudes. While further research might use other policy measures or manipulate policy positions to confirm the existence or lack of causal relationships, there was no solid evidence in this study that affinity voting is a product of policy attitudes.

Finally, there are at least four important pieces of evidence against general-interest accounts of affinity voting: 1) the lack of effect from cognitive group membership alone, 2) the noneffect of the self-interest manipulation, 3) the finding that low ethnic identifiers see candidates as acting in their own interest yet do not vote for them, and 4) the persistence of affinity effects even in the presence of party cues.

First, in separating the effects of identity and interests, a crucial distinction is between cognitive group membership and self-identification. Interests, I argue, are likely to be linked to cognitive ("objective") group membership rather than to self-identification because interests are, in large part, linked to the behaviour of others and to the social position of the individual rather than to internal psychological dispositions. For example, employment discrimination and eligibility for government programs are a function of objective membership, not the degree to which a person's self-identity is linked to the group. The fact that there were no affinity effects from objective group membership in the middle of the IDPG scale (i.e., when respondents are indifferent to the group in identity terms) is evidence against interests as an explanation for those affinity effects (see Chapter 6).

Another piece of evidence is the noneffect of the self-interest manipulation, which, rather than querying vote choice, instead asked if a candidate was in the respondent's or the respondent's family's financial self-interest. The test attempted to prime self-interest considerations and downplay other considerations, such as symbolic representation. In fact, no such priming effect was found: the treatment effects in the self-interest condition showed nearly identical point estimates to those in the vote-choice question. Given that we would expect larger effects when a key consideration is primed, this suggests that interests are, in fact, not a major consideration in voting for a racialized candidate.

These results were clarified by the interaction with the self-identification scale – it turns out that low identifiers are quite likely to say that a racialized candidate is in their interest but not to vote for that candidate. This finding is consistent with the interpretation that cognitive group membership drives perceptions of interest but not necessarily vote choice. The implication is that the vote-choice decision is quite different from the perception of interests, at least for respondents who do not strongly identify with their ethnic group.

The final strike against interest-based explanations is the persistence of affinity effects in the presence of party labels. Interest-based explanations are fundamentally about the policy positions and future actions of the candidates. However, party heuristics are probably a much better interest-based heuristic than ethnicity, in that they are a more accurate way of predicting a candidate's policy positions. Therefore, if we assume a relatively rational heuristic process, when given the opportunity, voters will replace candidate-ethnicity heuristics with party heuristics (as Kam 2007 suggests). In fact, this is not the case: coethnic-affinity effects appear to be just as strong when the candidates have party labels as when they are independent, implying that ethnic-affinity effects are caused by something other than the presumed policy positions of the candidate and, therefore, something other than the voters' self-interest.

Although there is little support for interest-based explanations, there is strong evidence in favour of the importance of ethnic self-identity. In examining the role of self-identification, this project goes considerably further than the existing research. The vast majority of studies on coethnic affinity voting ignore the issue of identification both in terms of measurement and theory. Instead, they simply use membership in a social group as the independent variable. That is, a citizen is black, or Chinese, or Latino, or white. Yet, I argue, this is a misspecification of the key concept. For many of the relevant effects, it is not mere group membership but rather self-identity that matters. While the two often go together, citizens understand the difference between their objective ethnocultural heritage, which is the correct answer on a census form, and the degree to which that group forms part of their self-identity. It is this self-identity that underlies many important psychological effects, in particular, in-group bias.

This project therefore adapted a widely used social-psychology measure, the Identification with a Psychological Group (IDPG) scale, which allows for measurement not only of the correct concept (self-identification with an ethnic group) but also of the degree to which people self-identify in that way. This theoretical innovation produced important empirical results, as it clearly demonstrated that ethnic self-identification plays a crucial role in coethnic affinity voting. Racialized Canadians who strongly self-identify with their ethnocultural background are far more likely to support a racialized candidate than those who identify weakly with their ethnocultural group.

This research demonstrates the importance of coethnic affinity voting, establishing both its psychological mechanisms and electoral effects. Citizens are more likely to support candidates of their own ethnic group, and for those who closely identify with their ethnic group, these effects can be very strong. Contrary to much previous research, it appears that affinity effects can apply to all racialized citizens and candidates rather than only to more narrow ethnic groups – in other words, rainbow coalitions are more plausible than previously suggested. In addition, this study draws on theoretical resources from social psychology, in particular social-identity theory, which detail the influential role that in-group bias can play in influencing behaviour. These perspectives help us to understand not only when and how ethnic groups influence electoral behaviour but also why they do so. Identity, rather than interests, appears to be the major motivating factor.

Distinguishing between Interests and Identities

Having made claims about the separate effects of interests and identity, some careful reflection is in order. As is so often the case in theoretical frameworks, these categories are something of a simplifying device. The fact that there is little evidence of interest-based effects certainly should not be taken as an argument that interests *never* matter – they certainly do in many situations. Instead, I aim to make two points. First, interests are not necessary. Contrary to what group-consciousness theory states, identity alone can produce affinity voting. The identity effects proposed here are quite different from mechanisms such as group interest in that the causal origin is entirely rooted in self-identification. Group-consciousness theory suggests that people are motivated by self-interest and that their identity needs to be linked to politics to have this effect. But for affinity voting, the candidates themselves link the identity to politics, and the motivation can be expressive or related to in-group bias. Second, self-interest and ideological stereotypes seem to play little or no part in the context of affinity voting among racialized Canadians for federal election candidates. Given the conventional wisdom that local members of Parliament have little control over government policy, perhaps voters are being quite sensible. The situation in question does not seem to meet Chong, Citrin, and Conley's (2001) conditions for self-interested behaviour, in that the benefits are not clear. The implication is that identity effects are likely to be strongest wherever the connection between vote choice and policy implementation is weak or unclear. Although this weak connection describes many political systems, in places where the link between candidate choice and policy outcomes is tighter, the explanations for affinity effects might differ.

In categorizing these effects, I have focused on the initial cause, but it is important to keep in mind that the causal pathways can be complex. Empirically, a person's self-identity might affect his or her perceptions of whether a candidate will act in his or her interests, or vice versa. From a modelling perspective, this means identities and interests could be either initial causes or mediators. The fact that there is not much evidence in this study in favour of interests militates against them as either an initial cause or as a mediator. But this might be less true in the long run if identities (or the long-term factors that influence the centrality of identity) are slowly shaped by interests through socialization, repeated elite influences, selection, or other effects. The argument here is not that voters are acting against their objective interests in the style of *What's the Matter with Kansas?* (Frank 2004) but rather that affinity voting is about identity rather than interests in the mind of the voter.

It is possible to interpret some of the identity-based explanations as interests. To some degree, this is a question of concept definition. Recall that in Chapter 2 interest-based explanations were defined as subjectively perceived, short- or medium-term, and relatively conscious. As noted, voters might perceive an in-group candidate as more honest; I classify this perception as an identity effect since it is caused by the voter's self-identity, though some might interpret it as kind of interest (i.e., having an honest member of Parliament). Alternatively, if symbolic representation has real psychological benefits, is it a kind of interest? There is some risk of conceptual hairsplitting here, but clearly there is more work to be done on these mechanisms. Regardless of how these explanations are categorized, they represent a shift away from assuming that affinity voting is a straightforward self-interest heuristic that relates to a candidate's future policy actions toward incorporating the deep and pervasive influence of self-identity.

Expressive Politics and Democracy

This research is a step forward in understanding the political behaviour of racialized Canadians, but it also has broad implications for electoral democracy. In one of the key debates in political science, the debate over instrumental versus expressive motivations, the evidence presented in this book comes down squarely on the side of expressive, identity-based politics. Politics is first and foremost who you are, not what you believe. On the surface, this might be deeply troubling for traditional interpretations of democracy. Democratic debate, so goes the usual story, is supposed to be about choosing the best public policy or producing a compromise between different interests. Elections should be fought over ideology and interests, because identity politics are often divisive and resistant to compromise or because they undercut more important issues such as economic redistribution and common national projects (e.g., Simon 1999; Rorty 1998; Gitlin 1995; Gutmann 2003). Similarly, studies of partisanship have demonstrated how partisan identities cause voters to ignore important information (Druckman, Peterson, and Slothuus 2013), increase polarization and anger (Mason 2015), bias economic judgments (Gerber and Huber 2009), and have many other negative effects. The effects of identity seem to undermine democratic choices.

If this is the case, then substantial identity effects uncovered in this study are seriously problematic. Identity effects – to the degree they stem from in-group bias and constitute unconscious, unreflective support of one's own group – are quite inimical to more demanding ways of understanding democracy. Certainly, in-group bias and the "cheering and booing" of expressive voting are not conducive either to deliberation or compromise. Moreover, it is much more difficult to normatively justify demands for descriptive representation when the connection to substantive representation is severed.

On the other hand, there are reasons to think we need not be so concerned about expressive politics. First, regardless of whether voters' motivations are normatively desirable, the outcome may still be desirable in that it leads to the policy outcomes voters want. Even if affinity voting is not a product of intentional heuristic use, it may nonetheless produce the same outcome: voters end up voting for candidates that are in their interest or who agree with them on policy. For affinity voting, descriptive and substantive representation must go together. Admittedly, there is little evidence of a role for policy attitudes (see, e.g., Table 6.1). Further analysis, such as substituting policy attitudes for the IDPG measure of ethnic identity, did not produce correlations with affinity voting (not shown). The analysis in this book does not suggest that voters are voting for descriptive representation and "accidentally" getting substantive representation. On the other hand, the data are limited and not designed to examine this issue, and there are a number of studies that do make the case for a link between descriptive and substantive representation, at least to some degree and in some circumstances (Bird 2010; Black 2016; Bowen and Clark 2014; Celis 2007; Hänni 2017; McEvoy 2016; Mackay 2010; Minta 2009; Preuhs 2006; Wängnerud 2009). If affinity voting leads to substantive representation despite a lack of intention by voters, this may not be the democratic ideal, but it does suggest that even if the motivations of expressive identity voting are problematic, the outcomes may be positive.

A more fundamental defence of identity-based voting is recognizing that it can lead to real psychological joy and pain, that it can affect the respect and standing of a group, and that symbolic victories can have real value all on their own. In-group bias, recall, is a product of the link between group attributions and self-esteem – the successes and failures of fellow group members impact our sense of self-worth. The victory of "one of our own" truly is a shared victory. There are real emotional effects of winning or losing elections. Pierce, Rogers, and Snyder (2016), for example, suggest that the emotional impact on partisans of losing an election is worse than the emotional impact of school shootings or terrorist attacks. This may seem hyperbolic – but was the elation of many African Americans over the election of Barack Obama any less profound? The key point is that we should recognize the very real identity-related psychological value (or harm) that elections can produce, rather than dismissing it simply because no policy change follows.

The argument that there is a real value to descriptive representation, quite separate from any links to substantive representation, is made by some theorists but has not had a great deal of influence on empirical studies of electoral behaviour. Mansbridge (1999), for example, suggests that symbolic representation creates social acceptance of the "ability to rule" – that is, general acceptance that these people are capable of managing and holding authority in society. Similarly, Philips (1995) argues that electing more blacks and women would be a good thing even if no policy changes ensued, because it would constitute public acknowledgment of the equal value of all. Being "at the table" is a sign of respect and recognition, and it may have value in and of itself, quite separate from more concrete dividends. Certainly, the value of symbolic respect and acknowledgment is widely recognized in other contexts, such as in the case of Quebec nationalism or Indigenous peoples. The recognition of the Québécois as a nation by Parliament in 2006, for example, was purely symbolic. Similarly, the recognition of Indigenous peoples in public ceremonies provides no concrete economic gains. Nonetheless, these are not just symbols: these gestures are powerfully meaningful and viewed as important in their own right. It would not be surprising if these symbolic actions, just like the election of racialized candidates, had electoral effects. Of course, the dynamics can be complex: the election of Obama did not necessarily lead to increased respect for black Americans by society in general – indeed, it may have led to a backlash (Tesler 2016). Success is not the same thing as acceptance by others. Nonetheless, the key point is that recognition and symbolic achievements motivate political actions and opinion precisely because they are important and meaningful to people, and so we should not readily dismiss them. This interpretation may not entirely ease concerns about deliberation and compromise, but it does show that the political effects of identity can be viewed in a more positive normative light.

Ethnic Identities

Given that identity is a crucial factor in affinity voting, which identities matter? The evidence shows that Canadians readily identify not only with their specific cultural or national groups but also with the ethnic categories used by the Canadian government: Arab, black, South Asian, and so on. It is not obvious that this should be the case: after all, many of them are artificial categories imposed by the state bureaucracy that do not always reflect the terms used in countries of origin or other self-chosen names of cultures or nationalities. Despite this, the IDPG scale using the Statistics Canada categories showed that many Canadians do identify with ethnic groups defined in this way. Moreover, the strong ethnic-affinity effects illustrated in Chapter 6 show not only that these identities affect behaviour but also that similar effects, of similar sizes, occur in multiple ethnic groups, suggesting that the role of identities in ethnic-affinity effects is broadly generalizable.

The multiplicity of identities makes studying their effects difficult; potentially, there are an infinite number of groups of varying sizes with which a person could identify, and narrower national or cultural categories are certainly influential. A similar issue arises when considering traditional racial or ethnic groups – why should people identify with them? People might instead identify only with their national-origin group rather than broader ethnic groups. For example, Espiritu (1992) and Masuoka (2006) look at pan-Asian identity (e.g., Asian American identity), as compared to Chinese, Japanese, Korean, or other national group identities. Similarly, Jones-Correa and Leal (1996) and Masuoka (2006) consider Hispanic and Latino and various South American and Central American national identities. Although debate about pan-ethnic identities continues, the general conclusion is that higher-order pan-ethnic identities are real but that lower order national identities are stronger (Okamoto and Mora 2014; Ashforth and Johnson 2001). The results here fit with this research in that lower-order identities had higher mean IDPG scores. However, these identity groups are also smaller in size, which makes them less influential politically. Therefore, it is particularly important that there are substantial affinity effects for "mid-range" groups such as the Statistics Canada categories, which are more specific than broad categories such as "racialized people "or "ethnic minorities" yet still represent a large enough percentage of the population to be politically influential.

Identification with ethnic categories should not be viewed as evidence that they are "real" categories of identification. Some surveys ask questions about identities by posing them in opposition, asking which group the respondent identifies with more. The 2010 British Ethnic Minority Election Study, for example, asked respondents if they identify more with their ethnic group or as British, while some Canadian Election Studies have asked if people identify more with their province or Canada. While these types of questions might be useful for determining the relative centrality of identity, or which identity is stronger, the answers do not suggest that one identity or another is any more real or more fundamental. People can and do identify with multiple groups. While it is more difficult to make a noncentral (weak) identity salient, given the right context, it can still be activated and have important effects on behaviour. From this perspective, it does not make sense to ask *which* group people identify with – their national group, their ethnicity, or, more broadly, as a minority – because they may well identify at multiple levels of specificity. Rather, these identities should be considered separately. Do people identify with the categories at all, and does identification affect their attitudes and behaviour? Clearly, Canadians do identify with both lower-order cultural groups and mid-level ethnic categories, and these identities do affect their behaviour.

Analysis of the determinants of ethnic self-identity showed that identities can endure for decades and adapt to different social contexts. Even decades later, the socialization people received in the country of origin had a powerful effect on their self-identity in Canada. Yet time spent in Canada did not seem to be connected with lower levels of cultural or ethnic identity. The interplay of history and experience is strikingly illustrated by the link between these levels of identity. For example, people living in the state of Gujarat, India, probably do not often think of themselves as South Asians but rather as Gujaratis, Indians, and so on. Yet, after immigrating to Canada and learning about the meaning of these categories – perhaps by reading the *South Asian Focus* newspaper published in Brampton, Ontario, or through contact with government-funded settlement organizations like the South Asian Women's Centre in Toronto – their pre-immigration experiences are linked with a new identity group. But those experiences were applied to the categories of identity determined by the state and the Canadian social context. Waters (2006) documents the experience of Caribbean immigrants being categorized as "black" after their immigration to the United States. The findings here suggest the same kind of process – that is, immigrants must reinterpret their identities in light of categories determined by the new state and society. In sum, ethnic identities are durable, and they can be reinterpreted and reapplied in new social contexts.

Racialized Identity

Evidence of support for candidates of different racialized ethnic groups sheds further light on the way that the racial schemas – the socially dominant definitions of racial and ethnic categories – are structured in Canada. Again, it is important to not make assumptions about who will be seen as in-group and out-group members: whether white candidates are seen as out-group members and other racialized candidates as in-group members is an empirical question, one that reflects how racial and ethnic categories are defined in a certain society and situation. Notably, early Chinese immigrants to the United States categorized themselves with whites rather than with blacks (McClain et al. 2006). It is certainly possible that the Chinese Canadians in this study would have categorized themselves with whites rather than with South Asians. Yet the evidence points toward a broad, superordinate racialized or minority identity.

There were two sources of evidence for the presence of a broader racialized identity: behavioural evidence and open-ended questions. The behavioural evidence is the support for candidates of other racialized ethnic groups. The results for racial affinity show that voters also show affinity effects for other racialized groups, not just their own ethnic group. That is, they act as if the racialized candidate is an in-group member. While there is no direct measure of racialized or minority identification, the implication for racialized affinity voting is that other racialized groups are seen as part of a superordinate, racialized in-group.

Responses to the open-ended question also provided support for identification with a broader racialized minority group. This question was asked after the candidate experiment, and it simply asked the voter why he or she supported that candidate. Respondents spontaneously and explicitly cited the candidate's minority and immigrant status, saying things such as "because he is an immigrant like me" and "because he is a minority."[3] Issues pertaining to causality make it difficult to demonstrate that this belief was the cause of the vote decision, but it is excellent evidence that at least some respondents were thinking in terms of these superordinate identity groups. Moreover, it is unclear what, precisely, the name of this broader group should be, but these are exactly the kind of generalized terms used in public discourse to refer to racialized Canadians.

To be sure, much work needs to be done on the effects of context. For weaker identities, context plays an especially important role in activating

identities. In these cases, the identity would be a result of the social definition of "racialized" as "nonwhite," combined with the choice between a
white and a racialized candidate. The analysis of candidate demographics in
Chapter 7 shows that, at least to date, it is quite common in federal electoral
districts to have a racialized candidate facing all white opponents. Even if
racialized identity is highly dependent on this particular context, it is still
one that is quite common in federal elections. On the other hand, where the
context is different – perhaps including multiple racialized candidates, one
of which is of the voter's own ethnic group – then the way the voter identifies
(the group he or she identifies with) might be different.

There may also be important exceptions to who is included in racialized
in-groups. The theory of motivated social positioning discussed in Chapter
2 suggests that lower-status groups might be rejected by mid-status racialized groups. For example, South Asians might show affinity effects toward
Chinese candidates but not toward black or Indigenous candidates. The key
here is the difference in status between groups, which might be a function
of the more general role that race and ethnicity play in social status in a
particular society. Alternatively, the distinction between immigrant and
nonimmigrant groups may be important – notably, this research does not
evaluate the place of Indigenous peoples despite the fact that they might
often be considered racialized. While there is no research on attitudes between Indigenous people and racialized immigrant communities, the very
nature of Indigenous identities is rooted in a long history in Canada that
might lead them to view racialized immigrants as having little relation to
their own identity group.

Multiple Identities

If people identify with multiple racial and ethnic identities, what is the relationship between these identities? It is important that we not treat some
identities as more "real" than others. Some identities may be stronger than
others, shape social life to a greater or lesser extent, or have their source in
daily social life or state coercion. Yet, when people actively identify with a
group, that identity, and its behavioural effects, is real, regardless.

Three levels of identity groups were considered: lower-order cultural,
mid-level ethnic, and higher-order racialized. These ethnic and racial groups
are not separate and unrelated. In fact, they are often viewed as concentric;
membership in more specific identity groups implies membership in more

general groups. In the data, identifying with a lower-order specific cultural group (e.g., Punjabi) was strongly correlated with identifying with a higher-order ethnic group (e.g., South Asian), but lower-order specific cultural groups had higher IDPG scores. This finding is consistent with nested-identity theory and research on pan-ethnicity, where nested identities are likely to be correlated, but lower-order identities tend to be stronger (more central).

Keeping in mind the distinction between membership and identity, we should recognize that a logically implied membership does not necessarily or immediately result in a sense of emotional attachment. But in the long run, membership and identification tend to come together, so identification with lower- and higher-order groups will be correlated. Just as Waters (2001) and Roth (2012) found that immigrants learn to fit their previous identities into the new racial schemas of their new countries, they also develop affective attachments to these categories, which result in group identities that – in the right context – influence behaviour.

The argument here is that the ethnicity of the two candidates helps determine which identity matters for a given decision. The principle of meta-contrast, of comparative similarity, determines which of the candidates is the in-group candidate. However, even if the minority candidate is the in-group candidate, which identity is activated? This is less clear, but it seems likely that it would be the stronger, more central identity. Therefore, the weaker effects for racialized affinity suggest that the corresponding identity (higher-order racialized identity) is less central to the self-identity. However, since it encompasses a much larger group of people, racialized identity is still of great political and social consequence.

Politics and the Structure of Ethnic and Racial Identities

In recent decades, Canada and most established democracies around the world have seen massive changes in the racial and ethnic composition of their populations. These identities play a crucial role in politics, and the changing demographics brought about by global immigration mean that these identities will shift and reform even as they grow in importance.

Understanding when identities matter requires recognizing the role of context. Identity is fluid and dynamic, but not random. The way that issues or campaigns are constructed can alter the way that people identify at a given point in time and with reference to a given topic. Police violence is perceived to be disproportionately targeted at black people (Black Experience

Project 2017), which means that black identity – rather than lower-order Caribbean or higher-order racialized identities – will be more likely to be activated and influence behaviour. In Olivia Chow's campaign for mayor of Toronto, she explicitly framed herself as an immigrant rather than as Chinese (Besco, Gerrits, and Matthews 2016), perhaps attempting to activate a broader identity that included more voters than her ethnic group. The context that frames a choice determines which identities matter, making it a crucial point of political contestation. Understanding who is affected by an identity requires focusing on its centrality rather than on who "objectively" belongs in the group. Given the same context, some people will actively identify, and others will not, depending on how central the identity is to their self-conceptualization. This centrality has wide-ranging origins in people's history and experiences. A crucial source of ethnic identity is socialization in another country: immigrants, particularly those who immigrated at an older age, have stronger ethnic identities. This means that, given the long-standing trend of growing numbers of immigrants in Canada, these identity effects will likely grow but will be tempered by smaller effects in subsequent generations.

Understanding how much identities matter requires knowing the relative size of groups. The incredible diversity of immigrant groups means that even though identification with specific cultural and national groups might be strong, they are often simply too small to have much political influence. The exception is Chinese-origin Canadians, who constitute a very large and relatively homogeneous group in terms of identity. Smaller groups can certainly matter in some circumstances, such as nomination meetings or as activists in organizations with a relatively small number of committed people. In wider areas, however, these specific identities will be less consequential. This makes it all the more important for Canadians to identify with middle-range categories, such as "South Asian," since they are large enough to be politically influential on a broad scale.

Identities are often linked: nested identities include higher- and lower-order identities in which membership in one implies membership in the other. For immigrants, some identities have to be learned: Jamaicans learn they are black (Waters 2001, 2006), and Sri Lankans learn that in Canada they are South Asian. None of these identities are more "real" than others, but racial schemas in Canada are different than in other countries, and immigrants need to learn these new definitions before they identify with these new groups. These identities do not necessarily conflict. In fact, identifying with a lower-order ethnic group seems to be correlated with identifying with higher-order groups.

Racial and ethnic identities matter, not only in elections but in nominations, leadership races, social movements, and many other parts of our social and political world. These identity groups are deeply influential in politics, but this influence depends on the nature and structure of these identities. How these groups are defined, who identifies with them, and when these identities matter are essential to their political influence. Understanding this process is far more complex than simply focusing on group membership, but there is now little doubt that we need to take the direct effects of self-identity on political choices seriously.

Appendices

Appendix A: Sample Information

This survey was conducted using an online panel in March 2011, through Abingdon Research. As is usual, the panel was recruited using multiple methods, including online and random-digit dialing. Respondents were selected by using the demographic questions in the survey as screening questions. Quotas limited white respondents to 1,000 and visible-minority respondents to 1,500, with 50 percent male and 40 percent Ontario respondents. The survey did not include respondents from Quebec because of the difficulty in validating the translation of questions and treatments for equivalent effects and because of considerably higher recruitment costs.

Table A.1 shows the demographic information for racialized respondents of the 2011 Canadian Election Study (CES) and the sample used in this study. In general, the study's sample is fairly representative. The median age of racialized respondents in the study's sample is forty-three – slightly, but not much, younger than that of the CES, which has a median age of forty-six for racialized respondents. The census data is not included, since including children makes the median age considerably different. However, we can compare the percentage of older respondents, which is necessary, given that a web panel might well underrepresent older Canadians. It appears, though, that there is good representation of older respondents in the study sample – approximately 10 percent of racialized Canadians are over sixty-five (Statistics Canada 2013a), compared to 14 percent in the sample.[1] Here, the CES is comparable – 15 percent of racialized respondents are over sixty-five.

There is also a higher proportion of immigrants as a percentage of racialized respondents in the study sample (65 percent) than in the CES (54 percent). This difference is particularly important given that immigrants may well show stronger affinity effects than native-born, racialized Canadians.

TABLE A.1

Demographics of racialized respondents

	Sample	CES	Census
Immigrant (%)	65	54	65
Household income	$72,000	$78,000	$68,000
Age (median)	42	46	–
Over 65 (%)	14	15	10

NOTES: Census data exclude First Nations respondents. Census age data not comparable since they include children.
SOURCE: 2011 Census, 2011 Canadian Election Study.

However, comparing this difference to census data, it is the CES that may underrepresent immigrants, since census data put the percentage of immigrants among racialized minorities in Canada at 65.1 percent (Statistics Canada 2011). On this measure, the sample is quite representative.

The sample does have somewhat more educated respondents than the CES. It has considerably more respondents with university degrees and fewer respondents with only a high school education. Table A.2 shows education by category. Only 39 percent of racialized respondents over the age of fifteen

TABLE A.2

Educational attainment of racialized respondents

	Web sample	CES
Less than high school	0.3	2.6
Some high school	1.3	4.4
High school diploma	5.7	17.8
Some college	6.5	4.7
College diploma	15.4	14.9
Some university	10.9	13.7
Undergraduate degree	38.9	28.9
Graduate or professional degree	21.2	13.1

NOTES: Cell entries are rounded percentages of total racialized respondents.
Web sample mean = Some university
CES mean = Completed technical/community college
Web sample median = Completed undergraduate degree
CES median = Completed undergraduate degree
SOURCE: 2011 Census, 2011 Canadian Election Study.

TABLE A.3

Ethnocultural background of respondents

	n	%		n	%
Arab	44	1.8	Latin American	80	3.2
Black	165	6.6	South Asian	290	11.6
Chinese	679.	27.1	Southeast Asian	54	2.2
Filipino	88	3.5	West Asian	10	0.4
Japanese	64	2.6	First Nations	17	0.7
Korean	27	1.1	White	984	39.3

NOTE: The survey question reads "Not a visible minority" rather than "white."

in the census had a university degree (Statistics Canada 2013b) as compared to 60 percent of the sample, a 21 percentage-point difference. However, even the CES overestimates education levels compared to census data, which puts the average number of racialized respondents with at least a bachelor's degree at 41 percent.

In addition, the ethnicity of respondents in the sample differs from the population; specifically, among racialized respondents, South Asian respondents are underrepresented, and Chinese respondents are overrepresented. (Of course, in the sample as a whole, all racialized groups are overrepresented by design.) As Table A.3 shows, 11.6 percent of the sample identified as South Asian, but South Asians are, in fact, the largest racialized ethnic group in Canada, at 25 percent of the racialized population. Conversely, 27 percent of respondents identified as having Chinese origins, but the 2011 National Household Survey puts the Chinese Canadian population at only 21 percent of the visible minority population (Statistics Canada 2011). If coethnic affinity voting is quite different for respondents of different ethnicities, then these representativeness issues would be a serious problem. However, as Chapter 5 shows, affinity voting is largely dependent on self-identification with an ethnic group rather than specific ethnicity. Thus, the difference in ethnocultural origins should be noted, but it does not undermine the key findings.

The sample had a broad geographic base, with respondents from every province except Quebec. Unfortunately, urban-rural data were not available. As Table A.4 shows, the overall majority of respondents, and 63 percent of the racialized respondents, are from Ontario. Nonetheless, the western provinces have respectable numbers of respondents, with about 10 percent of racialized respondents from Alberta and 20 percent from British Columbia. These results are not surprising, since a large proportion of racialized Canadians live in the greater Toronto and Vancouver areas, although Ontario is still somewhat overrepresented. Nonetheless, since we have no particular reason to expect important interactions between provincial residence and the effects of ethnicity, the imperfect geographic representation is unlikely to pose a serious problem for the analysis.

TABLE A.4

Geographic distribution

	White	Racialized
Newfoundland and Labrador	16	8
Nova Scotia	45	27
Prince Edward Island	4	1
New Brunswick	25	12
Ontario	593	958
Manitoba	50	42
Saskatchewan	32	26
Alberta	95	151
British Columbia	124	293

NOTE: Cell entries are frequencies.

TABLE A.5

Factor structure and assignment

	Candidate condition			
Biography version	White	Chinese	South Asian	Total
Conservative Candidate 2	127 (5%)	128 (5%)	127 (5%)	382
Liberal Candidate 2	128 (5%)	126 (5%)	126 (5%)	380
Independent candidates	437 (18%)	440 (18%)	436 (18%)	1,313
Self-interest prime	141 (6%)	144 (6%)	142 (6%)	427
Total	833	838	831	2,502

NOTES: Cells show number of respondents. The approximate (rounded) likelihood of assignment is in brackets. White and racialized respondents are included.

TABLE A.6

Candidate experiment and respondent ethnicity

Respondent ethnicity	Candidate condition		
	White	Chinese	South Asian
Chinese	184	199	181
South Asian	82	78	81
Other racialized respondent	154	143	156

NOTE: Cell entries are frequencies.

TABLE A.7

Cell assignments for self-interest and independent vote-choice questions

	White	Chinese	South Asian	Other racialized respondents
Self-interest	167	115	49	96
Vote	521	351	151	290

NOTE: Cell entries are number of respondents.

TABLE A.8

Cell assignment for party labels

Respondent ethnicity	Candidate 2 party labels		
	Liberal	Conservative	Independent
White	149	147	521
Chinese	100	113	351
South Asian	43	47	151
Other racialized	90	73	290
Total	382	380	1,313

NOTE: Cell entries are respondent frequencies.

Appendix B: Candidate Data

The candidate data were collected using Elections Canada lists of candidate information and publicly available data, such as websites and media reports, during 2011–12. These data should be regarded as estimates: there are, no doubt, some errors, and the coding is not based on self-identification by candidates. However, a comparison to data collected by Jerome Black (2013) indicates a low level of divergence. The 2004 election showed the greatest divergence from the present data set: Black's data set has thirteen more visible-minority candidates than the present data set, out of a total of 999 candidates. In 2006 and 2008, the difference in visible-minority counts is only one and three, respectively, suggesting a relatively low error rate, between 1.3 percent and 0.03 percent, even dating back almost ten years. In addition, there may be errors in individual coding despite similarities in the total number. However, Black generously provided detailed data for 2011, and there were only four instances of divergent coding (of 999 candidates), indicating strong consistency of method and results. There also may well be errors in the coding of specific ethnicities, rather than just visible-minority status. Nonetheless, the close convergence of the two data sets is encouraging, and the error rate seems to be in the low single-digit percentages.

Appendix C: Detailed Model Results

TABLE C.1

Coethnic and racialized affinity

Variables	Model 3.1	
Coethnic affinity	0.28*	(0.17)
Racialized affinity	0.23*	(0.14)
Income	−0.27	(0.20)
Education	0.32	(0.29)
Age	−0.00	(0.01)
Gender (man)	0.23*	(0.12)
Religion (non-Christian)	−0.43***	(0.15)
Religion (no religion)	−0.29*	(0.16)
Immigrant	−0.02	(0.13)
Constant	−0.20	(0.34)
Observations	1,125	

NOTES: Standard errors are in parentheses.
* $p < .1$.   ** $p < .05$.   *** $p < .01$.

TABLE C.2

Specific ethnic groups

Variables	Model 3.2	
Chinese respondent	0.07	(0.22)
South Asian respondent	0.36	(0.23)
South Asian candidate	−0.31	(0.30)
Chinese candidate	−0.46*	(0.24)
Chinese candidate* South Asian respondent	0.23	(0.40)
Chinese candidate* Other racialized respondent	0.09	(0.34)
South Asian candidate* South Asian respondent	0.00	(0.40)
South Asian candidate* Other racialized respondent	−0.03	(0.33)
Income	−0.32	(0.20)
Education	0.27	(0.29)
Age	−0.00	(0.01)
Gender (man)	0.23*	(0.12)
Religion (non-Christian)	−0.30*	(0.15)
Religion (no religion)	−0.19	(0.18)
Immigrant	−0.06	(0.13)
Constant	0.04	(0.37)
Observations	1,125	

NOTES: Standard errors are in parentheses.
* $p < .1$.   ** $p < .05$.   *** $p < .01$.

TABLE C.3

Coethnic and racialized affinity, with IDPG scale

Variables	Model 5.1	
Coethnic affinity	−0.57	(0.45)
Racialized affinity	−1.00*	(0.55)
IDPG	−0.74	(0.52)
Coethnic affinity* IDPG	1.30*	(0.69)
Racialized affinity* IDPG	2.09**	(0.86)
Income	−0.27	(0.20)
Education	0.32	(0.29)
Age	0.00	(0.01)
Gender (man)	0.24*	(0.12)
Religion (non-Christian)	−0.46***	(0.15)
Religion (no religion)	−0.30*	(0.17)
Immigrant	−0.02	(0.13)
Constant	0.25	(0.46)
Observations	1,125	

NOTES: Logistic regression, with vote for Candidate 2 as dependent variable. Standard errors are in parentheses.

$* p < .1.$ $** p < .05.$ $*** p < .01.$

TABLE C.4

Specific ethnic groups, with IDPG scale

Variables	Model 5.2	
South Asian respondent	−1.71**	(0.81)
Other racialized respondent	−0.80	(0.80)
Chinese candidate	0.11	(0.85)
South Asian candidate	−0.95	(0.79)
Chinese candidate* South Asian respondent	0.84	(1.30)
Chinese candidate* Other racialized respondent	1.15	(1.18)
South Asian candidate* South Asian respondent	0.05	(1.22)
South Asian candidate* Other racialized respondent	1.42	(1.11)
IDPG	−0.79	(0.87)
Chinese candidate* IDPG	2.96**	(1.31)
South Asian candidate* IDPG	1.90	(1.25)
South Asian respondent* IDPG	−0.68	(1.33)
Other racialized respondent* IDPG	0.85	(1.24)
Chinese candidate* South Asian respondents* IDPG	−1.09	(1.99)
Chinese candidate* Other racialized respondents* IDPG	−1.77	(1.86)
South Asian candidate* South Asian respondents* IDPG	−0.07	(1.89)
South Asian candidate* Other racialized respondents* IDPG	−2.37	(1.72)
Income	−0.33	(0.21)
Education	0.30	(0.30)
Age	−0.00	(0.01)
Gender (man)	0.26**	(0.12)
Religion (non-Christian)	−0.33**	(0.16)
Religion (no religion)	−0.19	(0.19)
Immigrant	−0.06	(0.13)
Constant	0.48	(0.62)
Observations	1,125	

NOTES: Logistic regression, with vote for Candidate 2 as dependent variable. Standard errors are in parentheses.
$* p < .1.$ $** p < .05.$ $*** p < .01.$

TABLE C.5

Ideological position and distance

Variables	Model 6.1 Party and ideology	Model 6.2 Ideological position	Model 6.4 Ideological distance	Model 6.6 Ideology and political knowledge
Racialized candidate	-0.04 (0.04)	0.01 (0.02)	0.00 (0.01)	-0.02 (0.04)
Racialized respondent	-0.19*** (0.04)			
Liberal	-0.05 (0.03)			
Independent	-0.05 (0.04)			
Self-interest	0.13** (0.05)			
Liberal* Racialized respondent	0.03 (0.04)			
Independent* Racialized respondent	0.03 (0.05)			
Self-interest* Racialized respondent				
Political knowledge				-0.03 (0.04)
Political knowledge* Racialized candidate				0.04 (0.05)
Income	-0.03 (0.02)	-0.03 (0.02)	-0.01 (0.02)	-0.03 (0.02)
Education	0.04 (0.03)	0.02 (0.03)	0.06** (0.03)	0.02 (0.04)
Age	-0.00 (0.00)	-0.00 (0.00)	-0.00 (0.00)	-0.00 (0.00)
Gender (man)	0.02 (0.01)	0.04** (0.01)	-0.01 (0.01)	0.04** (0.01)
Religion (non-Christian)	0.02 (0.02)	-0.02 (0.02)	-0.02 (0.02)	-0.02 (0.02)
Religion (no religion)	0.00 (0.02)	-0.03 (0.02)	-0.02 (0.02)	-0.03 (0.02)
Immigrant	0.02 (0.02)	0.01 (0.02)	-0.03** (0.01)	0.01 (0.02)
Constant	0.63*** (0.05)	0.58*** (0.04)	0.19*** (0.04)	0.60*** (0.05)
Observations	751	711	711	711
R-squared	0.05	0.02	0.02	0.02

NOTES: OLS regression. Dependent variables are perceived candidate ideological position and distance between candidate and respondent. Higher is further right and more distance. Racialized respondents only. Standard errors are in parentheses.

* $p < .1$.   ** $p < .05$.   *** $p < .01$.

TABLE C.6

Ideological position and distance, specific ethnicities

Variables	Model 6.3 Ideological position		Model 6.5 Ideological distance	
Chinese candidate	0.04	(0.03)	0.02	(0.02)
South Asian candidate	0.03	(0.03)	0.04*	(0.02)
South Asian respondent	0.01	(0.04)	0.09***	(0.03)
Other racialized respondent	0.01	(0.03)	0.06**	(0.03)
Chinese candidate* South Asian respondent	0.01	(0.05)	−0.09**	(0.04)
Other racialized respondent	−0.07*	(0.04)	−0.03	(0.04)
South Asian candidate* South Asian respondent	−0.05	(0.05)	−0.08*	(0.04)
Other racialized respondent	−0.05	(0.04)	−0.02	(0.04)
Income	−0.04*	(0.02)	−0.01	(0.02)
Education	0.02	(0.03)	0.07**	(0.03)
Age	−0.00	(0.00)	−0.00	(0.00)
Gender (man)	0.03**	(0.01)	−0.01	(0.01)
Religion (non-Christian)	−0.01	(0.02)	−0.03*	(0.02)
Religion (no religion)	−0.02	(0.02)	−0.04**	(0.02)
Immigrant	0.01	(0.02)	−0.03**	(0.01)
Constant	0.58***	(0.04)	0.16***	(0.04)
Observations	711		711	
R-squared	0.03		0.05	

NOTES: OLS regression. Dependent variables are perceived candidate ideological position and distance between candidate and respondent. Higher is further right and more distance. Racialized respondents only. Standard errors are in parentheses.

* $p < .1$.   ** $p < .05$.   *** $p < .01$.

TABLE C.7

Self-interest

Variables	Model 6.10	
Liberal	0.39	(0.34)
Independent	0.12	(0.28)
Self-interest	−0.05	(0.34)
Racialized candidate	0.12	(0.30)
Liberal* Racialized candidate	0.20	(0.42)
Independent* Racialized candidate	0.16	(0.34)
Self-interest* Racialized candidate	0.25	(0.42)
Income	−0.28	(0.18)
Education	0.37	(0.27)
Age	−0.00	(0.00)
Gender (man)	0.20*	(0.11)
Religion (non-Christian)	−0.36***	(0.13)
Religion (no religion)	−0.15	(0.15)
Immigrant	−0.05	(0.12)
Constant	−0.42	(0.38)
Observations	1,355	

NOTES: Logistic regression, with vote for Candidate 2 as the dependent variable. Racialized respondents only. Standard errors are in parentheses.
* $p < .1$. ** $p < .05$. *** $p < .01$.

TABLE C.8

Self-interest and the IDPG scale

Variables	Model 6.11 Self-Interest and IDPG	
Racialized candidate	−0.58	(0.94)
IDPG	−1.17	(1.27)
Racialized candidate* IDPG	1.17	(1.50)
Liberal	0.97	(1.26)
Independent	−0.27	(0.88)
Self-interest	−1.24	(1.10)
Liberal* Racialized candidate	−0.09	(1.49)
Independent* Racialized candidate	−0.29	(1.07)
Self-interest* Racialized candidate	2.07	(1.32)
Liberal* IDPG	−0.86	(1.98)
Independent* IDPG	0.66	(1.41)
Self-interest* IDPG	2.01	(1.77)
Liberal* Racialized candidate* IDPG	0.40	(2.32)
Independent* Racialized candidate* IDPG	0.69	(1.70)
Self-interest* Racialized candidate* IDPG	−3.02	(2.09)
Income	−0.30	(0.19)
Education	0.38	(0.27)
Age	−0.00	(0.00)
Gender (man)	0.21*	(0.11)
Religion (non-Christian)	−0.36***	(0.13)
Religion (no religion)	−0.15	(0.15)
Immigrant	−0.05	(0.12)
Constant	0.28	(0.83)
Observations	1,355	

NOTES: OLS regression, with ideological placement of Candidate 2 as dependent variable. Standard errors are in parentheses.

* $p < .1$. ** $p < .05$. *** $p < .01$.

Table C.9

Party manipulations

Variables	Model 7.1		Model 7.2	
Racialized candidate	−0.86*	(0.51)	−0.57	(0.94)
IDPG	−0.47	(0.62)	−1.12	(1.27)
Racialized candidate* IDPG	1.85**	(0.79)	1.16	(1.51)
Party	0.64	(0.73)		
Racialized candidate* Party	0.25	(0.89)		
IDPG* Party	−0.92	(1.15)		
IDPG* Racialized candidate* Party	−0.53	(1.38)		
Liberal			1.01	(1.26)
Independent			−0.26	(0.88)
Liberal* Racialized candidate			−0.13	(1.49)
Independent* Racialized candidate			−0.29	(1.07)
Liberal* IDPG			−0.93	(1.98)
Independent* IDPG			0.65	(1.41)
Self-Interest* IDPG			0.46	(2.32)
Liberal* Racialized candidate* IDPG			0.70	(1.70)
Income	−0.28	(0.20)	−0.31	(0.20)
Education	0.31	(0.29)	0.31	(0.29)
Age	0.00	(0.01)	−0.00	(0.01)
Gender (man)	0.24**	(0.12)	0.24*	(0.12)
Religion (non-Christian)	−0.46***	(0.15)	−0.46***	(0.15)
Religion (no religion)	−0.30*	(0.17)	−0.30*	(0.17)
Immigrant	−0.02	(0.13)	−0.02	(0.13)
Constant	0.07	(0.51)	0.38	(0.84)
Observations	1,125		1,125	

NOTES: Logistic regression, with vote for Candidate 2 as the dependent variable. Racialized respondents only. Standard errors are in parentheses.

* $p < .1$.   ** $p < .05$.   *** $p < .01$.

Notes

CHAPTER 2: FRAMING AND EXPLAINING AFFINITY VOTING

1 If party identifiers voting for their party's candidates is considered a kind of affinity voting this would be an exception, although it is not usually described that way.

2 The different factors in group consciousness are formulated various ways by different authors, and sometimes beliefs about status and collective action are described as single factor.

3 Interestingly, Dawson (1994) explicitly discusses social-identity theory and cites Turner et al. (1987) but does not draw the conclusion that identity alone can influence behaviour.

4 One solution to this disagreement between social-identity theory and group-consciousness theory on the implications of group status might be permeability. When people can exit a low-status group, the effect on behaviour is low. Since racial and ethnic groups are generally difficult to exit, especially in situations where there are high levels of prejudice and discrimination, these groups would have stronger effects then low-status groups in general (Tajfel and Turner 1979, Lalond and Silverman 1994). Nonetheless, this issue is not addressed in the literature on group consciousness.

5 There is a question of causality here: people who are more politicized might be more likely to notice and report discrimination. But since experimental treatments manipulating discrimination are ethically fraught, there is not much research of this kind and, as far as I know, none that looks at group consciousness.

6 It should be noted that many of the more recent findings show mixed or null effects (for a review, see Chong and Rogers 2005), but group consciousness remains an important theoretical paradigm.

7 Note that these studies focus on groups we might today consider white – Barry and Kalin, for example, ask about Ukrainian and German Canadians, among other groups. Nonetheless, ethnicity defines the key social group.

8 In cases with multiple racialized candidates, it is likely that the narrower identity would prevail – that is, ethnic affinity. Nonetheless, as Chapter 7 shows, these cases are relatively uncommon. These dynamics might be especially interesting in single transferable voting systems, where second choices matter.

9 This measure is calculated in annualized equivalent disposable income, in 2008 US dollars.

10 Joe Ghiz, of Lebanese decent, was the premier of Prince Edward Island from 1986 to 1993, and his son Robert was elected in 2007. Ujjal Dosanjh, a Sikh born in India, became premier of British Columbia after winning the BC NDP leadership in 2000 but lost the subsequent election. There are no election studies associated with these party leaders.

CHAPTER 3: COETHNIC AND RACIALIZED AFFINITY IN CANADA

1 For example, as Chapter 7 shows, the 2011 election included visible-minority candidates in seventy-seven ridings. There were some 250 minority respondents in the 2011 Canadian Election Study, on average 0.8 per riding. We could therefore project sixty-two visible-minority respondents living in ridings with visible-minority candidates. Other elections have fewer racialized candidates and voters, so even with the assumption of a concentration of visible-minority voters, the numbers are still very small.

2 The order of presentation of the candidates' biographies was randomized across respondents, but the content of the candidate biographies was not manipulated. Only the name of Candidate 2 varied; his biography was the same in all conditions. As a result, we could not examine the effect of the biographies themselves. A test with a student sample, however, showed no interaction between the content of the biographies and the variables of interest.

3 Quebec is the exception, where candidate photos on signs are used widely. As described below, however, the data for this study were collected outside Quebec.

4 Covariates reduce the unexplained variation and hence the size of confidence intervals but do not change the basic results. Including covariates leads to some missing respondents, which generally changes little, although the Chinese respondent–South Asian candidate effect is 5 percentage points smaller than in Table 3.1. Therefore, that result ought to be treated with caution. All other estimates of affinity-voting effects are only 1 percentage point different, and none change signs. Note that these differences do not change the confirmation or rejection of hypotheses in the following chapters.

5 Collinearity between interaction and main effect terms is sometimes raised as an issue, especially in three-way interactions, as used in later chapters. It can increase standard errors, but they will still be the correct standard errors. See Brambor and colleagues (2006) for a discussion of this issue.

CHAPTER 4: THE IMPORTANCE OF SELF-IDENTIFICATION

1 As noted by Huddy (2002), this term can lead to the awkward construction that identification (readiness) is a good predictor of identification (in the moment). But, here, I follow the convention in many studies (e.g. Kelly and Kelly 1994; Veenstra and Haslam 2000; Ellemers, Kortekaas, and Ouwerkerk 1999; and Barreto 2010), as well as more general discourse in political science and beyond.

2 For example, an influential piece by Miller et al. (1981) on group consciousness draws on data from the 1972 and 1976 American National Election Study which asked of sixteen groups, "Which of these groups do you feel particularly close to – people who are most like you in their ideas and interests and feelings about things" – with response categories ranging from "very close" to "not close at all." The language of "close to," however, continues to be consistent.

3 Space considerations allowed only for a three-statement scale. The statement dropped was "[Group's] successes are my successes." Some pretesters listed this statement as being the least related to self-identity. For example, one person noted that it seems to suggest benefitting from stereotypes.

4 After discussion with community members, it was decided that "Asian," rather than "East Asian," was a more natural-sounding category and would be easily understood in this context.

5 Using this measure in the affinity-voting analysis in Chapter 5 leads to results with similar point estimates, but the results are not significant (not shown). Given the substantially smaller sample size, this is not surprising. Of course, respondents who gave a sensible answer were not randomly selected – they may have been more interested or more attentive. The implications are unclear: they may be more likely to pay attention to the treatment but also more likely to have strong opinions and, therefore, be unaffected.

CHAPTER 5: ETHNIC IDENTITY AND VOTER BEHAVIOUR

1 Respondents were required to provide an answer but could give responses such as "I don't know." Encouraging for the validity of the whole survey, only 1.15 percent of respondents provided an unintelligible response, suggesting that almost all respondents took the questions seriously.

2 While there is little research on social status as such, these groups are clearly among the most marginalized. For example, black Canadians have the lowest rates of university education and highest-rates of low-income status of any visible-minority group, and Indigenous people are worse off still (using low income cut-off, Statistics Canada 2016).

CHAPTER 6: THE ROLE OF INTERESTS, IDEOLOGY, AND POLICY

1 This manipulation is examined at greater length in Chapter 7.

2 The responses in the 2008 Canadian Election Study are quite similar to this sample, though slightly higher. For example, 47 percent of Chinese respondents "somewhat agree," compared to 44 percent in this study; 20 percent in the Canadian Election Study "strongly agree," compared to 16 percent in this sample. It should be noted that examining the effects of racial inequality and discrimination are not easy. Among other issues, perceptions of discrimination are affected by group identification (Operario and Fisk 2001). Similarly, people tend to minimize personal discrimination while exaggerating group-level discrimination because of how it reflects on themselves (Taylor et al. 1990).

3 It seems Clinton first used that precise phrase when responding to an AIDS activist (*New York Times* 1992), but the phrase became emblematic of his broader approach. See Dickerson 2011 for a discussion, including similar strategies by other politicians.

CHAPTER 7: AFFINITY VOTING IN FEDERAL ELECTIONS

1 This is the same manipulation used to validate the measure for perceived ideological position of candidates in Chapter 6.

CHAPTER 8: CONCLUSION

1 For example, South Asians are about 25 percent of the visible-minority population across Canada but only 11 percent inside Quebec. Conversely, the categories "Arabic" and "black" constitute 5 percent and 15 percent of the population across Canada, respectively, but only 17 percent and 29 percent in Quebec (Statistics Canada 2017).

2 Black Canadians have the lowest educational achievement and nearly the lowest income of any visible-minority group (Statistics Canada 2015). Certainly, not all Lebanese or Arabic people are Muslim, but many are, and it is often assumed that they must be Muslim, so they likely receive similar treatment.

3 In fact, there was no reference to the candidate being an immigrant, but it is often assumed that nonwhite Canadians are immigrants.

APPENDIX A: SAMPLE INFORMATION

1 Since this survey only accepted respondents aged eighteen or over, to provide an adequate, if imperfect, comparison, the Statistics Canada data were altered by dropping the lowest category ("Under 15"), merging the top two categories ("65–75" and "75 and over") and then recalculating the percentage over sixty-five.

References

Aberson, Christopher L., Michael Healy, and Victoria Romero. 2000. "Ingroup Bias and Self-Esteem: A Meta-analysis." *Personality and Social Psychology Review* 4 (2): 157–73.

Abrams, Dominic, and Michael A. Hogg. 1990. *Social Identity: Constructive and Critical Advances.* Exeter: Simon and Schuster.

Abu-Laban, Yasmeen. 2014. "Reform by Stealth." In *The Multiculturalism Question: Debating Identity in 21st-Century Canada,* edited by Jack Jedwab, 149–72. Montreal and Kingston: McGill-Queen's University Press.

Achen, Christopher H., and Larry M. Bartels. 2016. *Democracy for Realists: Why Elections Do Not Produce Responsive Government.* Princeton, NJ: Princeton University Press.

Allen, P.T., and Geoffrey M. Stephenson. 1983. "Inter-group Understanding and Size of Organization." *British Journal of Industrial Relations* 21 (3): 312–29. https://doi.org/10.1111/j.1467-8543.1983.tb00138.x.

Allport, Gordon Willard. 1954. *The Nature of Prejudice.* Oxford, England: Addison-Wesley.

Ansolabehere, Stephen, and Brian F. Schaffner. 2014. "Does Survey Mode Still Matter? Findings from a 2010 Multi-mode Comparison." *Political Analysis* 22 (3): 285–303. https://doi.org/10.1093/pan/mpt025.

Archer, Keith, and Faron Ellis. 1994. "Opinion Structure of Party Activists: The Reform Party of Canada." *Canadian Journal of Political Science* 27 (2): 277–308.

Ashforth, Blake E., and Scott Johnson. 2001. "Which Hat to Wear? The Relative Salience of Multiple Identities in Organizational Contexts." In *Social Identity Processes in Organizational Contexts,* edited by Michael A. Hogg and Deborah J. Terry, 31–48. New York: Psychology Press/Taylor and Francis.

Ashforth, Blake E., and Fred Mael. 1989. "Social Identity Theory and the Organization." *Academy of Management Review* 14 (1): 20–39. https://doi.org/10.2307/258189.

Ashforth, Blake E., Kristie M. Rogers, and Kevin G. Corley. 2011. "Identity in Organizations: Exploring Cross-Level Dynamics." *Organization Science* 22 (5): 1144–56.

Ashmore, Richard D., Kay Deaux, and Tracy McLaughlin-Volpe. 2004. "An Organizing Framework for Collective Identity: Articulation and Significance of Multidimensionality." *Psychological Bulletin* 130 (1): 80–114.

Bakvis, Herman. 1991. *Regional Ministers: Power and Influence in the Canadian Cabinet.* Toronto: University of Toronto Press.

Balakrishnan, T.R., and Feng Hou. 1999. "Socioeconomic Integration and Spatial Residential Patterns of Immigrant Groups in Canada." *Population Research and Policy Review* 18 (3): 201–17.

Baldwin, Andrew, Laura Cameron, and Audrey Kobayashi, eds. 2011. *Rethinking the Great White North: Race, Nature, and the Historical Geographies of Whiteness in Canada*. Vancouver: UBC Press.

Barreto, Matt. 2007. "Sí Se Puede! Latino Candidates and the Mobilization of Latino Voters." *American Political Science Review* 101 (3): 425–44.

–. 2010. *Ethnic Cues: The Role of Shared Ethnicity in Latino Political Participation*. Ann Arbour, MI: University of Michigan Press.

Barreto, Matt A., and Francisco I. Pedraza. 2009. "The Renewal and Persistence of Group Identification in American Politics." *Electoral Studies* 28 (4): 595–605.

Bauder, Harald, and Bob Sharpe. 2002. "Residential Segregation of Visible Minorities in Canada's Gateway Cities." *Canadian Geographer/Le Géographe canadien* 46 (3): 204–22. https://doi.org/10.1111/j.1541-0064.2002.tb00741.x.

Bauer, Nichole M. 2018. "Untangling the Relationship between Partisanship, Gender Stereotypes, and Support for Female Candidates." *Journal of Women, Politics and Policy* 39 (1): 1–25.

Baumeister, Roy F., and Mark R. Leary. 1995. "The Need to Belong: Desire for Interpersonal Attachments as a Fundamental Human Motivation." *Psychological Bulletin* 117 (3): 497.

Bean, Clive, and Anthony Mughan. 1989. "Leadership Effects in Parliamentary Elections in Australia and Britain." *American Political Science Review* 83 (4): 1165–79.

Bem, Sandra Lipsitz. 1981. "Gender Schema Theory: A Cognitive Account of Sex Typing." *Psychological Review* 88 (4): 354.

Berelson, Bernard R., Paul F. Lazarsfeld, and William N. McPhee. 1954. *Voting: A Study of Opinion Formation in a Presidential Campaign*. Chicago: University of Chicago Press.

Berinsky, Adam J., Tesalia Rizzo, Leah R. Rosenzweig, and Elisha Heaps. 2018. "Attribute Affinity: US Natives' Attitudes Toward Immigrants." *Political Behavior*: 1–24. https://doi.org/10.1007/s11109-018-9518-9.

Bergami, Massimo, and Richard P. Bagozzi. 2000. "Self-Categorization, Affective Commitment and Group Self-Esteem as Distinct Aspects of Social Identity in the Organization." *British Journal of Social Psychology* 39 (4): 555–77.

Bergh, Johannes, and Tor Bjørklund. 2011. "The Revival of Group Voting: Explaining the Voting Preferences of Immigrants in Norway." *Political Studies* 59 (2): 308–27. https://doi.org/10.1111/j.1467-9248.2010.00863.x.

Berry, J.W., and Rudolf Kalin. 1979. "Reciprocity of Inter-ethnic Attitudes in a Multicultural Society." *International Journal of Intercultural Relations* 3 (1): 99–111. https://doi.org/10.1016/0147-1767(79)90048-8.

Besco, Randy. 2015. "Rainbow Coalitions or Inter-minority Conflict? Racial Affinity and Diverse Minority Voters. *Canadian Journal of Political Science* 48 (2): 305–28.

–. 2018. "Friendly Fire: Electoral Discrimination and Ethnic Minority Candidates." *Party Politics*. OnlineFirst. https://doi.org/10.1177/1354068818761178.

Besco, Randy, Bailey Gerrits, and J. Scott Matthews. 2016. "White Millionaires and Hockey Skates: Racialized and Gendered Mediation in News Coverage of a Canadian Mayoral Election." *International Journal of Communication* 10 (20): 4641–60.

Bilodeau, Antoine. 2008. "Immigrants' Voice through Protest Politics in Canada and Australia: Assessing the Impact of Pre-migration Political Repression." *Journal of Ethnic and Migration Studies* 34 (6): 975–1002. https://doi.org/10.1080/1369183 0802211281.

Bilodeau, Antoine, and Mebs Kanji. 2010. "The New Immigrant Voter, 1965–2004: The Emergence of a New Liberal Partisan?" In *Perspectives on the Canadian Voter: Puzzles of Influence and Choice,* edited by Laura Stephenson and Cameron Anderson. Vancouver: UBC Press.

Bilodeau, Antoine, Luc Turgeon, and Ekrem Karakoç. 2012. "Small Worlds of Diversity: Views toward Immigration and Racial Minorities in Canadian Provinces." *Canadian Journal of Political Science* 45 (3): 579–605.

Bird, Karen. 2010. "Patterns of Substantive Representation among Visible Minority MPs: Evidence from Canada's House of Commons." In *The Political Representation of Immigrants and Minorities,* edited by Karen Bird, Thomas Saalfeld, and Andreas M. Wüst, 227–49. New York: Routledge.

–. 2015. "'We Are Not an Ethnic Vote!' Representational Perspectives of Minorities in the Greater Toronto Area." *Canadian Journal of Political Science* 48 (2): 249–79.

–. 2016. "What Accounts for the Local Diversity Gap? Supply and Demand of Visible Minority Candidates in Ontario Municipal Politics." In *Just Ordinary Citizens? Towards a Comparative Portrait of the Political Immigrant,* edited by Antoine Bilodeau, 180–200. Toronto: University of Toronto Press.

Bird, Karen, Samantha D. Jackson, R. Michael McGregor, Aaron A. Moore, and Laura B. Stephenson. 2016. "Sex (and Ethnicity) in the City: Affinity Voting in the 2014 Toronto Mayoral Election." *Canadian Journal of Political Science* 49 (2): 359–83.

Bittner, Amanda. 2011. *Platform or Personality? The Role of Party Leaders in Elections.* Oxford: Oxford University Press.

Black, Jerome. 2016. "Who Represented Minorities? Question Period, Minority MPs, and Constituency Influence in the Canadian Parliament." In *Just Ordinary Citizens? Towards a Comparative Portrait of the Political Immigrant,* edited by Antoine Bilodeau, 201–23. Toronto: University of Toronto Press.

Black, Jerome H. 1987. "The Practice of Politics in Two Settings: Political Transferability among Recent Immigrants to Canada." *Canadian Journal of Political Science* 20 (4): 731–53.

–. 2008. "Ethnoracial Minorities in the 38th Parliament: Patterns of Change and Continuity." In *Electing a Diverse Canada,* edited by Caroline Andrew, John Biles, Myer Siemiatycki, and Erin Tolley, 229–54. Vancouver: UBC Press.

–. 2013. "Racial Diversity in the 2011 Federal Election: Visible Minority Candidates and MPs." *Canadian Parliamentary Review* 36 (3): 21–26.

Black, Jerome H., and Lynda Erickson. 2006. "Ethno-racial Origins of Candidates and Electoral Performance: Evidence from Canada." *Party Politics* 12 (4): 541–61. https://doi.org/10.1177/1354068806064733.

Black, Jerome H., and Bruce M. Hicks. 2006. "Visible Minority Candidates in the 2004 Federal Election." *Canadian Parliamentary Review* 29 (2): 26–31.

Black Experience Project. 2017. *The Black Experience Project in the GTA: Overview Report*. https://www.theblackexperienceproject.ca/wp-content/uploads/2017/07/Black-Experience-Project-GTA-OVERVIEW-REPORT-4.pdf.

Blais, André. 2005. "Accounting for the Electoral Success of the Liberal Party in Canada." *Canadian Journal of Political Science/Revue canadienne de science politique* 38 (4): 821–40. https://doi.org/10.1017/S0008423905050304.

Blais, André, Elisabeth Gidengil, Agnieszka Dobrzynska, Neil Nevitte, and Richard Adeau. 2003. "Does the Local Candidate Matter? Candidate Effects in the Canadian Election of 2000." *Canadian Journal of Political Science/Revue canadienne de science politique* 36 (3): 657–64. https://doi.org/10.1017/S0008423903778810.

Blumer, Herbert. 1958. "Race Prejudice as a Sense of Group Position." *Pacific Sociological Review* 1(1): 3–7.

Bobo, Lawrence, and Vincent L. Hutchings. 1996. "Perceptions of Racial Group Competition: Extending Blumer's Theory of Group Position to a Multiracial Social Context." *American Sociological Review* 61 (6): 951–72. https://doi.org/10.2307/2096302.

Bobo, Lawrence, and James R. Kluegel. 1993. "Opposition to Race-Targeting: Self-Interest, Stratification Ideology, or Racial Attitudes?" *American Sociological Review* 58 (4): 443–64. https://doi.org/10.2307/2096070.

Bowen, Daniel C., and Christopher J. Clark. 2014. "Revisiting Descriptive Representation in Congress: Assessing the Effect of Race on the Constituent-Legislator Relationship." *Political Research Quarterly* 67 (3): 695–707.

Brambor, Thomas, William Roberts Clark, and Matt Golder. 2006. "Understanding Interaction Models: Improving Empirical Analyses." *Political Analysis* 14 (1): 63–82.

Bratton, Michael, Ravi Bhavnani, and Tse-Hsin Chen. 2012. "Voting Intentions in Africa: Ethnic, Economic or Partisan?" *Commonwealth and Comparative Politics* 50 (1): 27–52. https://doi.org/10.1080/14662043.2012.642121.

Brennan, Geoffrey, and James Buchanan. 1984. "Voter Choice: Evaluating Political Alternatives." *American Behavioral Science* 28 (2): 185–201.

Brennan, Geoffrey, and Loren Lomasky. 1997. *Democracy and Decision: The Pure Theory of Electoral Preference*. Cambridge: Cambridge University Press.

Breton, Charles. 2015. "Making National Identity Salient: Impact on Attitudes toward Immigration and Multiculturalism." *Canadian Journal of Political Science* 48 (02): 357–81.

Brewer, Marilynn B. 2003. "Optimal Distinctiveness, Social Identity, and the Self." In *Handbook of Self and Identity*, edited by Mark R. Leary, and June Price Tangney, 480–91. New York. Guilford Press.

–. 1999. "The Psychology of Prejudice: Ingroup Love or Outgroup Hate?" *Journal of Social Issues* 55 (3): 429–44. https://doi.org/10.1111/0022-4537.00126.

Brewer, Marilynn B., and Madelyn Silver. 1978. "Ingroup Bias as a Function of Task Characteristics." *European Journal of Social Psychology* 8 (3): 393–400.

–. 2000. "Group Distinctiveness, Social Identification, and Collective Mobilization." In *Self, Identity, and Social Movements*, edited by Sheldon Stryker, Timothy J. Owens, and Robert W. White, 153–71. Minneapolis: University of Minnesota Press.

Browning, Rufus P., Dale Rogers Marshall, and David Tabb. 1984. *Protest Is Not Enough: The Struggle of Blacks and Hispanics for Equality in Urban Politics.* Berkeley: University of California Press.

–. 1990. "Can Blacks and Latinos Achieve Power in City Government? The Settings and the Issues." In *Racial Politics in American Cities,* edited by Rufus P. Browning, Dale Rogers Marshall, and David H. Tabb, 10–25. Harlow: Longman.

Buchanan, James M. 1954. "Individual Choice in Voting and the Market." *Source Journal of Political Economy* 62 (4): 334–43.

Burke, Peter J., and Jan E. Stets. 2009. *Identity Theory.* Oxford: Oxford University Press, 2009.

Cameron, James E. 2004. "A Three-Factor Model of Social Identity." *Self and Identity* 3 (3): 239–62.

Campbell, Angus, Philip E. Converse, Warren E. Miller, and Donald E. Stokes. 1960. *The American Voter.* New York: John Wiley and Sons. https://doi.org/10.2307/1952653.

Carey, John M., and Matthew Soberg Shugart. 1995. "Incentives to Cultivate a Personal Vote: A Rank Ordering of Electoral Formulas." *Electoral Studies* 14 (4): 417–39. https://doi.org/10.1016/0261-3794(94)00035-2.

Carroll, Susan J., and Wendy S. Strimling. 1983. *Women's Routes to Elective Office: A Comparison with Men's.* Rutgers: Rutgers University Center for the American Woman and Politics, Eagleton Institute of Politics.

Castonguay, Alex. 2013. "The Inside Story of Jason Kenney's Campaign to Win Over Ethnic Votes." *Maclean's,* February 2.

CBC News. 2008. "Sherwood Park Conservatives Split over Nomination Process." September 15. https://www.cbc.ca/news/canada/edmonton/sherwood-park-conservatives-split-over-nomination-process-1.744468.

Celis, Karen. 2007. "Substantive Representation of Women: The Representation of Women's Interests and the Impact of Descriptive Representation in the Belgian Parliament (1900–1979)." *Journal of Women, Politics and Policy* 28 (2): 85–114.

Chang, Linchiat, and Jon A. Krosnick. 2010. "Comparing Oral Interviewing with Self-Administered Computerized Questionnaires: An Experiment." *Public Opinion Quarterly* 74 (1): 154–67. https://doi.org/10.1093/poq/nfp090.

Charles, Camille Zubrinsky. 2003. "The Dynamics of Racial Residential Segregation." *Annual Review of Sociology* 29 (1): 167–207. https://doi.org/10.1146/annurev.soc.29.010202.100002.

Chong, Dennis, Jack Citrin, and Patricia Conley. 2001. "When Self-Interest Matters." *Political Psychology* 22 (3): 541–70. https://doi.org/10.1111/0162-895x.00253.

Chong, Dennis, and Reuel Rogers. 2005. "Racial Solidarity and Political Participation." *Political Behavior* 27 (4): 347–74.

Cialdini, Robert B., and Melanie R. Trost. 1998. "Social Influence: Social Norms, Conformity and Compliance." In *The Handbook of Social Psychology: Fourth Edition,* vol. 2, edited by Daniel T. Gilbert, Susan T. Fiske, and Gardner Lindzey, 151–92. New York: McGraw-Hill.

Citrin, Jack, Donald Philip Green, and David O Sears. 1990. "White Reactions to Black Candidates: When Does Race Matter?" *Public Opinion Quarterly* 54 (1): 74–96. https://doi.org/10.1086/269185.

CityNews. 2016. "Toronto Immigration Organization Launches Anti-racism Ad Campaign." June 14. www.citynews.ca/2016/06/14/toronto-immigration-organization-launches-anti-racism-ad-campaign.

Clarke, Simon, and Garner, Steve. 2009. *White Identities: A Critical Sociological Approach.* London: Pluto Press.

Converse, Philip E. 1964. "The Nature of Belief Systems in Mass Publics." In *Ideology and Discontent,* edited by David Apter. New York: The Free Press of Glencoe.

Crandall, Christian S., and Amy Eshleman. 2003. "A Justification-Suppression Model of the Expression and Experience of Prejudice." *Psychological Bulletin* 129 (3): 414–46.

Cunningham, Robert. 1971. "The Impact of the Local Candidate in Canadian Federal Elections." *Canadian Journal of Political Science* 4 (2): 287–90.

Cutler, Fred. 2002. "The Simplest Shortcut of All: Sociodemographic Characteristics and Electoral Choice." *Journal of Politics* 64 (2): 466–90. https://doi.org/10.1111/1468-2508.00135.

Dahl, Robert A. 1961. *Who Governs? Democracy and Power in an American City.* New Haven, CT: Yale University Press.

Dawson, Michael C. 1994. *Behind the Mule: Race and Class in African American Politics.* Princeton, NJ: Princeton University Press.

Deshpandé, Rohit, Wayne D. Hoyer, and Naveen Donthu. 1986. "The Intensity of Ethnic Affiliation: A Study of the Sociology of Hispanic Consumption." *Journal of Consumer Research* 13 (2): 214–20.

Deshpandé, Rohit, and Douglas Stayman. 1994. "A Tale of Two Cities: Distinctiveness Theory and Advertising Effectiveness." *Journal of Marketing Research* 31 (1): 57–64. https://doi.org/10.2307/3151946.

DeSipio, Louis, and Carole Jean Uhlaner. 2007. "Immigrant and Native: Mexican American Presidential Vote Choice across Immigrant Generations." *American Politics Research* 35 (2): 176–201.

Dhamoon, Rita Kaur. 2011. "Considerations on Mainstreaming Intersectionality." *Political Research Quarterly* 64 (1): 230–43.

Dickerson, John. 2011. "The Problem with Presidential Empathy. May 12. www.cbsnews.com/news/the-problem-with-presidential-empathy. Last accessed March 8, 2019.

Dolan, Kathleen. 2008. "Is There a 'Gender Affinity Effect' in American Politics? Information, Affect, and Candidate Sex in US House Elections." *Political Research Quarterly* 61 (1): 79–89.

Downs, Anthony. 1957. *An Economic Theory of Democracy.* New York: Harper and Row.

Driedger, Leo. 1989. *The Ethnic Factor: Identity in Diversity.* Toronto: McGraw-Hill Ryerson.

Druckman, James N., Erik Peterson, and Rune Slothuus. 2013. "How Elite Partisan Polarization Affects Public Opinion Formation." *American Political Science Review* 107 (1): 57–79. https://doi.org/10.1017/S0003055412000500.

Dyer, Richard. 1988. "White." *Screen* 29 (4): 44–65.

Eckstein, Harry. 1975. "Case Study and Theory in Political Science." In *Handbook of Political Science,* edited by Fred Greenstein and Nelso Polsby, 79–138. Reading, MA: Addison-Wesley.

Ellemers, Naomi, Paulien Kortekaas, and Jaap W. Ouwerkerk. 1999. "Self-Categorisation, Commitment to the Group and Group Self-Esteem as Related but Distinct Aspects of Social Identity." *European Journal of Social Psychology* 29: 371–89. https://doi.org/10.1002/(SICI)1099-0992(199903/05)29:2/33.3.CO;2-L.

Enelow, James M., and Melvin J. Hinich. 1982. "Ideology, Issueism and the Spatial Theory of Elections." *American Political Science Review* 76 (3): 493–501. https://doi.org/10.2307/1963727.

Espiritu, Yen Le. 1992. *Asian American Panethnicity: Bridging Institutions and Identities.* Philadelphia, PA: Temple University Press.

Evans, Geoffrey. 2000. "The Continued Significance of Class Voting." *Annual Review of Political Science* 3(1): 401–17.

Farley, Reynolds, and William H. Frey. 1994. "Changes in the Segregation of Whites from Blacks during the 1980s: Small Steps toward a More Integrated Society." *American Sociological Review* 59 (1): 23–45. https://doi.org/10.1126/science.135.3503.554.

Feldman, Saul D. 1979. "Nested Identities." In *Studies in Symbolic Interaction*, vol. 2, edited by N.K. Denzin, 399–418. Greenwich, CT: JAI Press.

Ferree, Karen E. 2006. "Explaining South Africa's Racial Census." *Journal of Politics* 68 (4): 803–15. https://doi.org/10.1111/j.1468-2508.2006.00471.x.

Ferree, Karen E., and Jeremy Horowitz. 2007. *Identity Voting and the Regional Census in Malawi.* Afrobarometer Working Paper 72.

Fiorina, Morris P. 1976. "The Voting Decision: Instrumental and Expressive Aspects." *The Journal of Politics* 38 (2): 390–413.

Fischer, Alastair J. 1996. "A Further Experimental Study of Expressive Voting." *Public Choice* 88 (1–2): 171–84. https://doi.org/10.1007/BF00130417.

Fisher, Stephen D., Anthony F. Heath, David Sanders, and Maria Sobolewska. 2015. "Candidate Ethnicity and Vote Choice in Britain." *British Journal of Political Science* 45 (4): 883–905.

Foreman, Peter, and David Whetten. 2002. "Members' Identification with Multiple-Identity Organizations." *Organization Science* 13 (6): 618–35.

Fraga, Bernard L. 2016. "Candidates or Districts? Reevaluating the Role of Race in Voter Turnout." *American Journal of Political Science* 60 (1): 97–122.

Frank, Thomas. 2004. *What's the Matter with Kansas? How Conservatives Won the Heart of America.* New York: Macmillan Press.

Frankenberg, Ruth, 1993. *White Women, Race Matters: The Social Construction of Whiteness.* Minneapolis: University of Minneapolis Press.

Gaertner, Samuel L., and J.F. Dovidio. 2000. *Reducing Intergroup Bias: The Common Ingroup Identity Model.* Philadelphia, PA: Psychology Press.

Gaertner, Samuel L., John F. Dovidio, Phyllis A. Anastasio, Betty A. Bachman, and Mary C. Rust. 1993. "The Common Ingroup Identity Model: Recategorization and the Reduction of Intergroup Bias." *European Review of Social Psychology* 4 (1): 1–26. https://doi.org/10.1080/14792779343000004.

Garramone, Gina M. 1985. "Effects of Negative Political Advertising: The Roles of Sponsor and Rebuttal." *Journal of Broadcasting & Electronic Media* 29 (2): 147–59.

Garzia, Diego 2017. "Voter Evaluation of Candidates and Party Leaders." In *The Sage Handbook of Electoral Behaviour*, edited by Kai Arzheimer, Jocelyn Evans, and Michael S. Lewis-Beck, 633–53. London: Sage.

Gay, Claudine. 2001. "The Effect of Black Congressional Representation on Political Participation." *American Political Science Review* 95 (3): 589–602.

–. 2004. "Putting Race in Context: Identifying the Environmental Determinants of Black Racial Attitudes." *American Political Science Review* 98 (4): 547–62.

–. 2006. "Seeing Difference: The Effect of Economic Disparity on Black Attitudes toward Latinos." *American Journal of Political Science* 50 (4): 982–97. https://doi.org/10.1111/j.1540-907.2006.00228.x.

Gerber, Alan S., and Gregory A. Huber. 2009. "Partisanship and Economic Behavior: Do Partisan Differences in Economic Forecasts Predict Real Economic Behavior?" *American Political Science Review* 103 (3): 407–26. https://doi.org/10.1017/S0003055409990098.

Gershon, Sarah. 2012 "When Race, Gender, and the Media Intersect: Campaign News Coverage of Minority Congresswomen." *Journal of Women, Politics & Policy* 33 (2): 105–25.

Ghosh, Sutama. 2013. "'Am I a South Asian, Really?' Constructing 'South Asians' in Canada and Being South Asian in Toronto." *South Asian Diaspora* 5 (1): 35–55.

Gidengil, Elizabeth, and André Blais. 2007. "Are Party Leaders Becoming More Important to Vote Choice in Canada?" In *Political Leadership and Representation in Canada: Essays in Honour of John C. Courtney*, edited by Hans J. Michelmann, Donald C. Story, and Jeffrey S. Steeves, 39–59. Toronto: University of Toronto Press.

Gidengil, Elizabeth, Matthew Hennigar, André Blais, and Neil Nevitte. 2005. "Explaining the Gender Gap in Support for the New Right: The Case of Canada." *Comparative Political Studies* 38 (10): 1171–95. https://doi.org/10.1177/0010414005279320.

Gilens, Martin. 1996. "'Race Coding' and White Opposition to Welfare." *American Political Science Review* 90 (3): 593–604. https://doi.org/10.2307/2082611.

Gitlin, Todd. 1995. *The Twilight of Common Dreams: Why America Is Wracked by Culture Wars*. New York: Holt Press.

Goette, Lorenz, David Huffman, and Stephan Meier. 2006. "The Impact of Group Membership on Cooperation and Norm Enforcement: Evidence Using Random Assignment to Real Social Groups." *American Economic Review* 96 (2): 212–16. https://doi.org/10.1257/000282806777211658.

Goodyear-Grant, Elizabeth, and Julie Croskill. 2011. "Gender Affinity Effects in Vote Choice in Westminster Systems: Assessing 'Flexible' Voters in Canada." *Politics and Gender* 7 (2): 223–50. https://doi.org/10.1017/S1743923X11000079.

Goodyear-Grant, Elizabeth, and Erin Tolley. 2017. "Voting for One's Own: Racial Group Identification and Candidate Preferences." *Politics, Groups, and Identities* 7 (1): 131–47. https://doi.org/10.1080/21565503.2017.1338970.

Goren, Paul, Christopher M. Federico, and Miki Caul Kittilson. 2009. "Source Cues, Partisan Identities, and Political Value Expression." *American Journal of Political Science* 53 (4): 805–20.

Green, Donald P., and Alan S. Gerber. 2015. *Get Out the Vote: How to Increase Voter Turnout*. Washington, D.C.: Brookings Institution Press.

Green, Donald P., Bradley Palmquist, and Eric Schickler. 2004. *Partisan Hearts and Minds: Political Parties and the Social Identities of Voters*. New Haven, CT: Yale University Press.

Greene, Steven. 1999. "Understanding Party Identification: A Social Identity Approach." *Political Psychology* 20 (2): 393–403. https://doi.org/10.1111/0162-895X.00150.

–. 2002. "The Social-Psychological Measurement of Partisanship." *Political Behavior* 24 (3): 171–97. https://doi.org/10.1023/A:1021859907145.

–. 2004. "Social Identity Theory and Party Identification." *Social Science Quarterly* 85 (1): 136–53.

Grier, Sonya A., and Rohit Deshpandé. 2001. "Social Dimensions of Consumer Distinctiveness: The Influence of Social Status on Group Identity and Advertising Persuasion." *Journal of Marketing Research* 38 (2): 216–24. https://doi.org/10.1509/jmkr.38.2.216.18843.

Gutmann, Amy. 2003. *Identity in Democracy*. Princeton, NJ: Princeton University Press.

Hagendoorn, Louk. 1995. "Intergroup Bias in Multiple Group Systems: The Perception of Ethnic Hierarchies." *European Review of Social Psychology* 6 (1): 199–228.

Hagendoorn, Louk, Rian Drogendijk, Sergey Tumanov, and Joseph Hraba. 1998. "Interethnic Preferences and Ethnic Hierarchies in the Former Soviet Union." *International Journal of Intercultural Relations* 22 (4): 483–503.

Hamlin, Alan, and Colin Jennings. 2011. "Expressive Political Behaviour: Foundations, Scope and Implications." *British Journal of Political Science* 41 (3): 645–70.

Hänni, Miriam. 2017. "Presence, Representation, and Impact: How Minority MPs Affect Policy Outcomes." *Legislative Studies Quarterly* 42 (1): 97–130.

Harell, Allison, Stuart Soroka, and Kiera Ladner. 2013. "Public Opinion, Prejudice and the Racialization of Welfare in Canada." *Ethnic and Racial Studies* 37 (14): 1–16.

Harmon-Jones, Eddie, Joel Armstrong and James M. Olson. 2018. "The Influence of Behavior on Attitudes." In *The Handbook of Attitudes*, edited by Dolores Albarracín and Blair T. Johnson, 404–49. Abingdon: Routledge.

Hawkesworth, Mary. 2003 "Congressional Enactments of Race-Gender: Toward a Theory of Raced-Gendered Institutions." *American Political Science Review* 97 (4): 529–50.

Heath, Anthony F., Stephen D. Fisher, Gemma Rosenblatt, David Sanders, and Maria Sobolewska. 2013. *The Political Integration of Ethnic Minorities in Britain*. Oxford: Oxford University Press.

Heimlich, Russell. 2010. "Latinos' Perception of Discrimination." *Pew Research Center*, November 2. https://www.pewresearch.org/daily-number/latinos-perceptions-of-discrimination.

Herring, Mary, Thomas B. Jankowski, and Ronald E. Brown. 1999. "Pro-black Doesn't Mean Anti-white: The Structure of African-American Group Identity." *Journal of Politics* 61 (2): 363–86. https://doi.org/10.2307/2647508.

Hersh, Eitan D. 2015. *Hacking the Electorate: How Campaigns Perceive Voters*. Cambridge: Cambridge University Press.

Higgins, E. Tory. 1989. "Knowledge Accessibility and Activation: Subjectivity and Suffering from Unconscious Sources." In *Unintended Thought*, edited by James S. Uleman, and John A. Bargh, 75–123. New York: Guilford Press.

Hogg, Michael, and Dominic Abrams. 1988. *Social Identifications: A Social Psychology of Intergroup Relations and Group Processes*. London: Routledge.

–. 1990. "Social Motivation, Self-esteem and Social Identity." *Social Identity Theory: Constructive and Critical Advances* 28: 47.

Hornsey, Matthew J. 2008. "Social Identity Theory and Self-Categorization Theory: A Historical Review." *Social and Personality Psychology Compass* 21 (10): 204–22. https://doi.org/10.1111/j.1751-9004.2007.00066.x.

Horowitz, Donald. 1985. *Ethnic Groups in Conflict*. Berkeley: University of California Press.

Huddy, Leonie. 2001. "From Social to Political Identity: A Critical Examination of Social Identity Theory." *Political Psychology* 22 (1): 127–56. https://doi.org/10.1111/162-95X.00230.

–. 2002. "Context and Meaning in Social Identity Theory: A Response to Oakes." *Political Psychology* 23 (4): 825–38. https://doi.org/10.1111/0162-895X.00309.

Huddy, Leonie, and Nadia Khatib. 2007. "American Patriotism, National Identity, and Political Involvement." *American Journal of Political Science* 51 (1): 63–77. https://doi.org/10.1111/j.1540-907.2007.00237.x.

Huddy, Leonie, Lilliana Mason, and Lene Aarøe. 2015. "Expressive Partisanship: Campaign Involvement, Political Emotion, and Partisan Identity." *American Political Science Review* 109 (1): 1–17. https://doi.org/10.1017/S0003055414000604.

Human Resource and Skills Development Canada. 2015. "Canadians in Context – Immigration." Accessed July 28, 2015. https://www4.hrsdc.gc.ca/.3ndic.1t.4r@-eng.jsp?iid=38.

Ivison, John. 2017. "NDP Leadership Race about to Heat Up as Party Searches for a New Voice." *National Post*, July 17. https://www.nationalpost.com/opinion/john-ivison-ndp-leadership-race-about-to-heat-up-as-party-searches-for-a-new-voice.

Iyengar, Shanto, and Donald R. Kinder. 1987. *News that Matters: Agenda-Setting and Priming in a Television Age*. Chicago: University of Chicago Press.

Iyengar, Shanto, Gaurav Sood, and Yphtach Lelkes. 2012. "Affect, Not Ideology: Social Identity Perspective on Polarization." *Public Opinion Quarterly* 76 (3): 405–31.

Jackson, Jay W. 2002. "Intergroup Attitudes as a Function of Different Dimensions of Group Identification and Perceived Intergroup Conflict." *Self and Identity* 1 (1): 11–33.

Jackson, Jesse. 1984. Speech to the 1984 Democratic Convention, San Francisco, July 18. *American Rhetoric*. https://www.americanrhetoric.com/speeches/jessejackson1984dnc.htm.

Jackson, Linda A., Linda A. Sullivan, Richard Harnish, and Carole N. Hodge. 1996. "Achieving Positive Social Identity: Social Mobility, Social Creativity, and Permeability of Group Boundaries." *Interpersonal Relations and Group Processes* 70 (2): 241–54. https://doi.org/10.1037/0022-3514.70.2.241.

Jacobson, Matthew Frye. 1999. *Whiteness of a Different Color*. Cambridge, MA: Harvard University Press.

James, Carl E. 1999. *Seeing Ourselves: Exploring Race, Ethnicity, and Culture*. Revised Edition. Toronto: Thompson.

Janis, Irving L., and Bert T. King. 1954. "The Influence of Role Playing on Opinion Change." *The Journal of Abnormal and Social Psychology* 49 (2): 211.

Jenkins, Richard W. 2002. "How Campaigns Matter in Canada: Priming and Learning as Explanations for the Reform Party's 1993 Campaign Success." *Canadian Journal of Political Science* 35 (02): 383–408. https://doi.org/10.1017/S0008423902 778281.

Jennings, M. Kent, Laura Stoker, and Jake Bowers. 2009. "Politics across Generations: Family Transmission Reexamined." *Journal of Politics* 71 (3): 782–99.

Johnson, James H. Jr., and Melvin L. Oliver. 1989. "Inter-ethnic Minority Conflict in Urban America: The Effects of Economic and Social Dislocations." *Urban Geography* 10 (5): 449–63. https://doi.org/10.2747/0272-3638.10.5.449.

Johnston, Richard. 2008. "Polarized Pluralism in the Canadian Party System: Presidential Address to the Canadian Political Science Association." *Canadian Journal of Political Science* 41 (4): 815–34.

Johnston, Richard, André Blais, Henry E. Brady, and Jean Crête. 1992. *Letting the People Decide: Dynamics of a Canadian Election.* Montreal and Kingston: McGill-Queen's University Press.

Jones, Allison. 2017. "Ontario Politician Jagmeet Singh Launches Bid for Federal NDP Leadership." *Globe and Mail,* May 15. https://www.theglobeandmail.com/news/politics/ontario-politician-jagmeet-singh-launches-bid-for-federal-ndp-leadership/article35001559/.

Jones, Philip, and Nils Soguel. 2010. "Fiscal Federalism at the Ballot Box: The Relevance of Expressive Voting." *Review of Law and Economics* 6 (3): 469–88. https://doi.org/10.2202/1555-5879.1536.

Jones, Philip Edward. 2014. "Revisiting Stereotypes of Non-White Politicians' Ideological and Partisan Orientations." *American Politics Research* 42 (2): 283–310. https://doi.org/10.1177/1532673X13498266.

Jones-Correa, Michael., and David L. Leal. 1996. "Becoming 'Hispanic': Secondary Panethnic Identification among Latin American-Origin Populations in the United States." *Hispanic Journal of Behavioral Sciences* 18 (2): 214–54.

Junn, Jane, and Natalie Masuoka. 2008. "Asian American Identity: Shared Racial Status and Political Context." *Perspectives on Politics* 6(4): 729–40.

Kalin, Rudolf, and John W. Berry. 1996. "Interethnic Attitudes in Canada: Ethnocentrism, Consensual Hierarchy and Reciprocity." *Canadian Journal of Behavioural Science* 28 (4): 253.

Kam, Cindy D. 2007. "Implicit Attitudes, Explicit Choices: When Subliminal Priming Predicts Candidate Preference." *Political Behavior* 29 (3): 343–67. https://doi.org/10.1007/s11109-007-9030-0.

Kam, Cindy D., and Donald R. Kinder. 2007. "Terror and Ethnocentrism: Foundations of American Support for the War on Terrorism." *Journal of Politics* 62 (2): 320–38. https://doi.org/10.1111/j.1468-2508.2007.00534.x.

Kamloops This Week. 2005. "Flawed Candidacy System." May 25. https://www.kamloopsthisweek.com/flawed-candidacy-system.

Kan, Kamhon, and C.C. Yang. 2001. "On Expressive Voting: Evidence from the 1988 U.S. Presidential Election." *Public Choice* 108 (3–4): 295–312. https://doi.org/10.1023/A:1017556626815.

Karnig, Albert, and Susan Welch. 1980. *Black Representation and Urban Policy.* Chicago: University of Chicago Press.

Kaufmann, Karen M. 2003. "Cracks in the Rainbow: Group Commonality as a Basis for Latino and African-American Political Coalitions." *Political Research Quarterly* 56 (2): 199–210. https://doi.org/10.1177/106591290305600208.

Kay, Fiona, and Richard Johnston, eds. 2011. *Social Capital, Diversity, and the Welfare State.* Vancouver: UBC Press.

Kelley, Ninette, and Michael J. Trebilcock. 1998. *The Making of the Mosaic: A History of Canadian Immigration Policy.* Toronto: University of Toronto Press.

Kelly, Caroline, and John Kelly. 1994. "Who Gets Involved in Collective Action?: Social Psychological Determinants of Individual Participation in Trade Unions." *Human Relations* 47 (1): 63–88.

Kerby, Matthew. 2009. "Worth the Wait: Determinants of Ministerial Appointment in Canada, 1935–2008." *Canadian Journal of Political Science* 42 (3): 593–611.

Kester, Karen, and Sheila K. Marshall. 2003. "Intergenerational Similitude of Ethnic Identification and Ethnic Identity: A Brief Report on Immigrant Chinese Mother-Adolescent Dyads in Canada." *Identity: An International Journal of Theory and Research* 3 (4): 367–73. https://doi.org/10.1207/S1532706XID0304_04.

Key, V.O. Jr. 1949. *Southern Politics in State and Nation.* New York: Alfred A. Knopf.

Kinder, Donald R. 2003. "Belief Systems after Converse." In *Electoral Democracy,* edited by Michael MacKuen and George Rabinowitz, 13–47. Ann Arbor: University of Michigan Press.

Kinder, Donald R., and Lynn M. Sanders. 1996. *Divided by Color: Racial Politics and Democratic Ideals.* Chicago: University of Chicago Press.

King, David C., and Richard E. Matland. 2003. "Sex and the Grand Old Party: An Experimental Investigation of the Effect of Candidate Sex on Support for a Republican Candidate." *American Politics Research* 31 (6): 595–612. https://doi.org/10.1177/1532673X03255286.

Klandermans, Bert. 2002. "How Group Identification Helps to Overcome the Dilemma of Collective Action." *American Behavioral Scientist* 45 (5): 887–900.

Kluegel, James R., and Eliot R. Smith. 1986. *Beliefs about Inequality: Americans' Views of What Is and What Ought to Be.* New York: Aldine de Gruyter.

Krashinsky, Michael, and William J. Milne. 1983. "Some Evidence on the Effect of Incumbency in Ontario Provincial Elections." *Canadian Journal of Political Science/Revue canadienne de science politique* 16 (3): 489–500. https://doi.org/10.2307/3227392.

–. 1986. "The Effect of Incumbency in the 1984 Federal and 1985 Ontario Elections." *Canadian Journal of Political Science* 19 (2): 337–43. https://doi.org/10.1017/S0008423900054056.

Kreuter, Frauke, Stanley Presser, and Roger Tourangeau. 2008. "Social Desirability Bias in CATI, IVR, and Web Surveys: The Effects of Mode and Question Sensitivity." *Public Opinion Quarterly* 72 (5): 847–65. https://doi.org/10.1093/poq/nfn063.

Kuklinski, James H., Ellen Riggle, Victor Ottati, Norbert Schwarz, and Robert S. Wyer Jr. 1991. "The Cognitive and Affective Bases of Political Tolerance Judgments." *American Journal of Political Science* 35 (1): 1–27. https://doi.org/10.2307/2111436.

Kunda, Ziva. 1990. "The Case for Motivated Reasoning." *Psychological Bulletin* 108 (3): 480–98. https://doi.org/10.1037/0033-2909.108.3.480.

Lalonde, Richard N., and Randy A. Silverman. 1994. "Behavioral Preferences in Response to Social Injustice: The Effects of Group Permeability and Social Identity Salience." *Journal of Personality and Social Psychology* 66 (1): 78.

Lambert, Ronald D., and James E. Curtis. 1983. "Opposition to Multiculturalism among Québécois and English-Canadians." *Canadian Review of Sociology and Anthropology* 20 (2): 193–206.

Lau, Richard R., and David P. Redlawsk. 2001. "Advantages and Disadvantages of Cognitive Heuristics in Political Decision Making." *American Journal of Political Science* 45 (4): 951–71. https://doi.org/10.2307/2669334.

–. 2006. *How Voters Decide: Information Processing in Electoral Campaigns*. Cambridge: Cambridge University Press.

Lawless, Jennifer L. 2004. "Politics of Presence? Congresswomen and Symbolic Representation." *Political Research Quarterly* 57(1): 81–99.

Layman, Geoffrey C. 1997. "Religion and Political Behavior in the United States: The Impact of Beliefs, Affiliations, and Commitment from 1980 to 1994." *Public Opinion Quarterly* 61 (2): 288–316.

Lazarsfeld, Paul F., Bernard Berelson, and Hazel Gaudet. 1944. *The People's Choice: How the Voter Makes Up His Mind in a Presidential Campaign*. New York: Columbia University Press.

Lee, Taeku. 2008. "Race, Immigration, and the Identity-to-Politics Link." *Annual Review of Political Science* 11: 457–78.

Levitt, Peggy, and Mary Waters. 2001. *The Changing Face of Home: The Transnational Lives of the Second Generation*. New York: Russel Sage Foundation.

Lien, Pei-te. 1994. "Ethnicity and Political Participation: A Comparison between Asians and Mexican Americans." *Political Behavior* 19: 237–64.

Lien, Pei-te, M. Margaret Conway, and Janelle Wong. 2004. *The Politics of Asian Americans: Diversity and Community*. New York: Routledge.

Long, Karen, and Russell Spears. 1997. "The Self-Esteem Hypothesis Revisited: Differentiation and the Disaffected." In *The Social Psychology of Stereotyping and Group Life*, edited by Russell Spears, Penelope J. Oakes, Naomi Ellemers, and S. Alexander Haslam, 296–317. Oxford: Blackwell.

Lopez, Ian Haney. 1997. *White by Law: The Legal Construction of Race*. New York: NYU Press.

Lun, Janetta, Selin Kesebir, and Shigehiro Oishi. 2008. "On Feeling Understood and Feeling Well: The Role of Interdependence." *Journal of Research in Personality* 42 (6): 1623–28.

Mackay, Fiona. 2010. "Gendering Constitutional Change and Policy Outcomes: Substantive Representation and Domestic Violence Policy in Scotland." *Policy and Politics* 38 (3): 369–88.

Mael, Fred A., and Cathie E. Alderks. 1993. "Leadership Team Cohesion and Subordinate Work Unit Morale and Performance." *Military Psychology* 5 (3): 141–58. https://doi.org/10.1207/s15327876mp0503_1.

Mael, Fred, and Blake E. Ashforth. 1992. "Alumni and Their Alma Mater: A Partial Test of the Reformulated Model of Organizational Identification." *Journal of Organizational Behavior* 13 (2): 103–23. https://doi.org/10.1002/job.4030130202.

Mael, Fred A., and Lois E. Tetrick. 1992. "Identifying Organizational Identification." *Educational and Psychological Measurement* 52 (4): 813–24.

Malhotra, Neil, and Jon A. Krosnick. 2007. "The Effect of Survey Mode and Sampling on Inferences about Political Attitudes and Behavior: Comparing the 2000 and 2004 ANES to Internet Surveys with Nonprobability Samples." *Political Analysis* 15 (3): 286–323. https://doi.org/10.1093/pan/mpm003.

Malka, Ariel, and Yphtach Lelkes. 2010. "More Than Ideology: Conservative-Liberal Identity and Receptivity to Political Cues." *Social Justice Research* 23 (2): 156–88. https://doi.org/10.1007/s11211-010-0114-3.

Mansbridge, Jane. 1999. "Should Blacks Represent Blacks and Women Represent Women? A Contingent 'Yes.'" *Journal of Politics* 61 (3): 628–57. https://doi.org/10.2307/2647821.

Mantler, Gordon K. 2013. *Power to the Poor: Black-Brown Coalition and the Fight for Economic Justice, 1960–1974.* Chapel Hill: UNC Press Books.

Manzano, Sylvia, and Gabriel R. Sanchez. 2010. "Take One for the Team? Limits of Shared Ethnicity and Candidate Preferences." *Political Research Quarterly* 63 (3): 568–80. https://doi.org/10.1177/1065912909333130.

Marques, José M., Vincent Y. Yzerbyt, and Jacques-Philippe Leyens. 1988. "The 'Black Sheep Effect': Extremity of Judgments towards Ingroup Members as a Function of Group Identification." *European Journal of Social Psychology* 18 (1): 1–16. https://doi.org/10.1002/ejsp.2420180102.

Marschall, Melissa J., and Dietlind Stolle. 2004. "Race and the City: Neighborhood Context and the Development of Generalized Trust." *Political Behavior* 26 (2): 125–53. https://doi.org/10.1023/B:POBE.0000035960.73204.64.

Marwah, Inder, Phil Triadafilopoulos, and Steve White. 2013. "Immigration, Citizenship and Canada's New Conservative Party." In *Conservatism in Canada,* edited by David Rayside and James Farney, 95–119. Toronto: University of Toronto Press.

Mason, Lilliana. 2013. "The Rise of Uncivil Agreement: Issue versus Behavioral Polarization in the American Electorate." *American Behavioral Scientist* 57 (1): 140–59. https://doi.org/10.1177/0002764212463363.

–. 2015. "'I Disrespectfully Agree': The Differential Effects of Partisan Sorting on Social and Issue Polarization." *American Journal of Political Science* 59 (1): 128–45. https://doi.org/10.1111/ajps.12089.

Massey, Douglas S., and Nancy A. Denton. 1988. "The Dimensions of Residential Segregation." *Social Forces* 67 (2): 281–315. https://doi.org/10.1093/sf/67.2.281.

Masuoka, Natalie. 2006. "Together They Become One: Examining the Predictors of Pan-ethnic Group Consciousness among Asian Americans and Latinos." *Social Science Quarterly* 85 (5): 993–1011. https://doi.org/10.1111/j.1540-6237.2006.00412.x.

Mattes, Robert. 1995. *The Election Book: Judgement and Choice in South Africa's 1994 Election.* Cape Town: Idasa.

McCall, George J., and J.L. Simmons. 1966. *Identities and Interactions*. New York: Free Press.

McClain, Paula D., Niambi M. Carter, Victoria M. DeFrancesco Soto, Monique L. Lyle, Jeffrey D. Grynaviski, Shayla C. Nunnally, Thomas J. Scotto, J. Alan Kendrick, Gerald F. Lackey, and Kendra Davenport Cotton. 2006. "Racial Distancing in a Southern City: Latino Immigrants' Views of Black Americans." *Journal of Politics* 68 (3): 571–84. https://doi.org/10.1111/j.1468-2508.2006.00446.x.

McClain, Paula D., Jessica D. Johnson Carew, Eugene Walton, and Candis S. Watts. 2009. "Group Membership, Group Identity, and Group Consciousness: Measures of Racial Identity in American Politics?" *Annual Review of Political Science* 12: 471–85.

McConnaughy, Corrine M., Ismail K. White, David L. Leal, and Jason P. Casellas. 2010. "A Latino on the Ballot: Explaining Coethnic Voting among Latinos and the Response of White Americans." *Journal of Politics* 72 (4): 1199–211.

McConnell, Eileen D., and Edward A. Delgado-Romero. 2004. "Latino Panethnicity: Reality or Methodological Construction?" *Sociological Focus* 37 (4): 297–312.

McDermott, Monika L. 1998. "Race and Gender Cues in Low-Information Elections." *Political Research Quarterly* 51 (4): 895–918.

McEvoy, Caroline. 2016. "Does the Descriptive Representation of Women Matter? A Comparison of Gendered Differences in Political Attitudes between Voters and Representatives in the European Parliament." *Politics and Gender* 12 (4): 754–80.

McGarty, Craig, Ana-Maria Bliuc, Emma F. Thomas, and Renata Bongiorno. 2009. "Collective Action as the Material Expression of Opinion-based Group Membership." *Journal of Social Issues* 65 (4): 839–57.

McGregor, R. Michael, Aaron Moore, Samantha Jackson, Karen Bird, and Laura B. Stephenson. 2017. "Why So Few Women and Minorities in Local Politics?: Incumbency and Affinity Voting in Low Information Elections." *Representation* 53 (2): 135–52.

Medrano, Juan Díez, and Paula Gutiérrez. 2001. "Nested Identities: National and European Identity in Spain." *Ethnic and Racial Studies* 24 (5): 753–78.

Meier, Kenneth J., Paula D. McClain, J.L. Polinard, and Robert D. Wrinkle. 2004. "Divided or Together? Conflict and Cooperation between African Americans and Latinos." *Political Research Quarterly* 57 (3): 399–409.

Meier, Kenneth J., and Joseph Stewart. 1991. "Cooperation and Conflict in Multiracial School Districts." *Journal of Politics* 53 (4): 1123–33.

Merolla, Jennifer L., Abbylin H. Sellers, and Derek J. Fowler. 2013. "Descriptive Representation, Political Efficacy, and African Americans in the 2008 Presidential Election." *Political Psychology* 34 (6): 863–75.

Miller, Arthur H., Patricia Gurin, Gerald Gurin, and Oksana Malanchuk. 1981. "Group Consciousness and Political Participation." *American Journal of Political Science* 25 (3): 494–511. https://doi.org/10.2307/2110816.

Minescu, Anca, Louk Hagendoorn, and Edwin Poppe. 2008. "Types of Identification and Intergroup Differentiation in the Russian Federation." *Journal of Social Issues* 64 (2): 321–42.

Minta, Michael D. 2009. "Legislative Oversight and the Substantive Representation of Black and Latino Interests in Congress." *Legislative Studies Quarterly* 34 (2): 193–218.

Minushkin, Susan, and Mark Hugo Lopez. 2008. *The Hispanic Vote in the 2008 Democratic Presidential Primaries*. Washington, DC: Pew Hispanic Center.

Modood, Tariq. 1994. "Political Blackness and British Asians." *Sociology* 28 (4): 859–76.

Monteith, Margo J., and C. Vincent Spicer. 2000. "Contents and Correlates of Whites' and Blacks' Racial Attitudes." *Journal of Experimental Social Psychology* 36 (2): 125–54.

Morris, R.C. 2013. "Identity Salience and Identity Importance in Identity Theory." *Current Research in Social Psychology* 21 (8): 23–36.

Mullen, Brian, John F. Dovidio, Craig Johnson, and Carolyn Copper. 1992. "In-Group-Out-Group Differences in Social Projection." *Journal of Experimental Social Psychology* 28 (5): 422–40.

Mutz, Diane. 2011. *Population-Based Survey Experiments*. Princeton, NJ: Princeton University Press.

New York Times. 1992. "The 1992 Campaign Verbatim; Heckler Stirs Clinton Anger: Excerpts From the Exchange." p. 1001009 of the National edition. March 28. Digitized version available at: www.nytimes.com/1992/03/28//us/1992-campaign-verbatim -heckler-stirs-clinton-anger-excerpts-exchange.html. Last accessed March 8, 2019.

Nunnally, Jum C., and Ira H. Bernstein. 1967. *Psychometric Theory*. Vol. 226. New York: McGraw-Hill.

Oakes, Penelope J. 1987. "The Salience of Social Categories." In *Rediscovering the Social Group: A Self-Categorization Theory,* edited by John Turner, 117–41. Cambridge, MA: Basil Blackwell.

–. 1996. "The Categorization Process: Cognition and the Group in the Social Psychology of Stereotyping." In *Social Groups and Identities: Developing the Legacy of Henri Tajfel,* edited by W. Peter Robinson, 95–120. Oxford: Butterworth-Heinemann.

–. 2002. "Psychological Groups and Political Psychology: A Response to Huddy's 'Critical Examination of Social Identity Theory.'" *Political Psychology* 23 (4): 809–24.

OECD (Organisation for Economic Co-operation and Development). 2012. *Settling In: OECD Indicators of Immigrant Integration 2012*. http://www.oecd-ilibrary. org/social-issues-migration-health/settling-in-oecd-indicators-of-immigrant -integration-2012_9789264171534-en.

Oishi, Shigehiro, Jamie Schiller, and E. Blair Gross. 2013. "Felt Understanding and Misunderstanding Affect: The Perception of Pain, Slant, and Distance." *Social Psychological and Personality Science* 4 (3): 259–66.

Okamoto, Dina, and G. Cristina Mora. 2014. "Panethnicity." *Annual Review of Sociology* 40: 219–39.

Oliver, J. Eric, and Janelle Wong. 2003. "Intergroup Prejudice in Multiethnic Settings." *American Journal of Political Science* 47 (4): 567–82.

Olsen, Marvin E. 1970. "Social and Political Participation of Blacks." *American Sociological Review* 35 (4): 682–97.

Olson, Joel. 2008. "Whiteness and the Polarization of American Politics." *Political Research Quarterly* 61 (4): 704–18.

Operario, Don, and Susan T. Fiske. 2001. "Ethnic Identity Moderates Perceptions of Prejudice: Judgments of Personal versus Group Discrimination and Subtle versus Blatant Bias." *Personality and Social Psychology Bulletin* 27 (5): 550–61.

Pantoja, Adrian D., and Gary M. Segura. 2003. "Does Ethnicity Matter? Descriptive Representation in Legislatures and Political Alienation among Latinos." *Social Science Quarterly* 84 (2): 441–60.

Parenti, Michael. 1967. "Ethnic Politics and the Persistence of Ethnic Identification." *American Political Science Review* 61 (3): 717–26.

Patrikios, Stratos. 2013. "Self-Stereotyping as 'Evangelical Republican': An Empirical Test." *Politics and Religion* 6 (4): 800–22.

Petty, Richard E., and John T. Cacioppo. 1986. *Communication and Persuasion: Central and Peripheral Routes to Attitude Change.* New York: Springer-Verlag.

Pew Research Center. 2009. *Dissecting the 2008 Electorate: Most Diverse in U.S. History.* http://www.pewhispanic.org/2009/04/30/dissecting-the-2008-electorate-most -diverse-in-us-history/.

–. 2013. *King's Dream Remains an Elusive Goal; Many Americans See Racial Disparities.* www.pewsocialtrends.org/2013/08/22/kings-dream-remains-an-elusive-goal -many-americans-see-racial-disparities/.

Phelan, Julie E., and Laurie A. Rudman. 2010. "Reactions to Ethnic Deviance: The Role of Backlash in Racial Stereotype Maintenance." *Journal of Personality and Social Psychology* 99(2): 265.

Philips, Anne. 1995. *The Politics of Presence.* Oxford: Oxford University Press.

Philpot, Tasha S., and Hanes Walton. 2007. "One of Our Own: Black Female Candidates and the Voters Who Support Them." *American Journal of Political Science* 51 (1): 49–62. https://doi.org/10.1111/j.1540-907.2007.00236.x.

Pierce, Lamar, Todd Rogers, and Jason A. Snyder. 2016. "Losing Hurts: The Happiness Impact of Partisan Electoral Loss." *Journal of Experimental Political Science* 3 (1): 44–59. https://doi.org/10.1017/XPS.2015.8.

Piliavin, Jane A. 1987. "Age, Race, and Sex Similarity to Candidates and Voting Preference." *Journal of Applied Social Psychology* 17 (4): 351–68.

Pornpitakpan, Chanthika. 2004. "The Persuasiveness of Source Credibility: A Critical Review of Five Decades' Evidence." *Journal of Applied Social Psychology* 34 (2): 243–81. https://doi.org/10.1111/j.1559-1816.2004.tb02547.x.

Preuhs, Robert R. 2006. "The Conditional Effects of Minority Descriptive Representation: Black Legislators and Policy Influence in the American States." *Journal of Politics* 68 (3): 585–99.

Price, Vincent, and Mei-Ling Hsu. 1992. "Public Opinion about AIDS Policies: The Role of Misinformation and Attitudes toward Homosexuals." *Public Opinion Quarterly* 56 (1): 29–52. https://doi.org/10.1086/269294.

Pulido, Laura. 2006. *Black, Brown, Yellow, and Left: Radical Activism in Los Angeles.* Berkeley: University of California Press.

Radwanski, Adam, 2017. "Jagmeet Singh Poses Unique Threat for the Trudeau Liberals." *Globe and Mail,* May 14. https://www.theglobeandmail.com/news/politics/jagmeet -singh-poses-unique-threat-for-the-trudeau-liberals/article34983533/.

Rahn, Wendy M. 1993. "The Role of Partisan Stereotypes in Information Processing about Political Candidates." *American Journal of Political Science* 37 (2): 472–96. https://doi.org/10.2307/2111381.

Rahn, Wendy M., John H. Aldrich, Eugene Borgida, and John L. Sullivan. 1993. "A Social-Cognitive Model of Candidate Appraisal." In *Controversies in Voting Behavior,* edited by Richard G. Niemi, 187–206. Washington, DC: Congressional Quarterly.

Reeves, Keith. 1997. *Voting Hopes or Fears? White Voters, Black Candidates and Racial Politics in America.* New York: Oxford University Press.

Reis, Harry T., Edward P. Lemay Jr, and Catrin Finkenauer. 2017. "Toward Understanding Understanding: The Importance of Feeling Understood in Relationships." *Social and Personality Psychology Compass* 11 (3): 1–22.

Reitz, Jeffrey G. 2011. *Pro-immigration Canada: Social and Economic Roots of Popular Views.* Montreal: Institute for Research on Public Policy.

Reitz, Jeffrey G., and Rupa Banerjee. 2007. "Racial Inequality, Social Cohesion and Policy Issues in Canada." In *Diversity, Recognition and Shared Citizenship in Canada,* edited by Stuart N. Soroka, Richard Johnston, and Keith Banting, 561–600. Montreal: Institute for Research on Public Policy.

Riketta, Michael. 2005. "Organizational Identification: A Meta-analysis." *Journal of Vocational Behavior* 66 (2): 358–84. https://doi.org/10.1016/j.jvb.2004.05.005.

Rocha, Rene R., Caroline J. Tolbert, Daniel C. Bowen, and Christopher J. Clark. 2010. "Race and Turnout: Does Descriptive Representation in State Legislatures Increase Minority Voting?" *Political Research Quarterly* 63 (4): 890–907.

Rogers, Todd, and Don Moore. 2015. "It's Close but We're Losing: The Motivating Power of Under-Confidence." *Academy of Management Proceedings* 1: 15388.

Rorty, Richard. 1998. *Achieving Our Country: Leftist Thought in Twentieth-Century America.* Cambridge, MA: Harvard University Press.

Rosenberg, Morris. 1979. *Conceiving the Self.* New York: Basic Books.

Roth, Wendy. 2012. *Race Migrations: Latinos and the Cultural Transformation of Race.* Palo Alto, CA: Stanford University Press.

Rubin, Mark, and Miles Hewstone. 1998. "Social Identity Theory's Self-esteem Hypothesis: A Review and Some Suggestions for Clarification." *Personality and Social Psychology Review* 2 (1): 40–62.

Rudman, Laurie A., and Kimberly Fairchild. 2004. "Reactions to Counterstereotypic Behavior: The Role of Backlash in Cultural Stereotype Maintenance." *Journal of Personality and Social Psychology* 87(2): 157.

Rumbaut, Rubén G. 2005. "Assimilation, Dissimilation, and Ethnic Identities: The Experience of Children of Immigrants in the United States." in *Ethnicity and Causal Mechanisms,* edited by Michael Rutter and Marta Tienda, 301–44. Cambridge: Cambridge University Press.

Saito, Leland T. 1998. *Race and Politics: Asian Americans, Latinos, and Whites in a Los Angeles Suburb.* Urbana: University of Illinois Press.

Sanchez, Gabriel R. 2008. "Latino Group Consciousness and Perceptions of Commonality with African Americans." *Social Science Quarterly* 89 (2): 428–44. https://doi.org/10.1111/j.1540-6237.2008.00540.x.

Sanchez, Gabriel R., and Natalie Masuoka. 2010. "Brown-Utility Heuristic? The Presence and Contributing Factors of Latino Linked Fate." *Hispanic Journal of Behavioral Sciences* 32 (4): 519–31. https://doi.org/10.1177/0739986310383129.

Sanchez, Gabriel R., and Edward D. Vargas. 2016. "Taking a Closer Look at Group Identity: The Link between Theory and Measurement of Group Consciousness and Linked Fate." *Political Research Quarterly* 69 (1): 160–74.

Schleicher, Andreas. 2006. "Where Immigrant Students Succeed: A Comparative Review of Performance and Engagement in PISA 2003." *Intercultural Education* 17 (5): 507–16. https://doi.org/10.1080/14675980601063900.

Schuessler, Alexander A. 2000. "Expressive Voting." *Rationality and Society* 12 (1): 87–119. https://doi.org/10.1177/104346300012001005.

Sears, David O. 1983. "The Person-Positivity Bias." *Journal of Personality and Social Psychology* 44 (2): 233–50. https://doi.org/10.1037/0022-3514.44.2.233.

Sears, David O., and Jack Citrin. 1982. *Tax Revolt: Something for Nothing in California*. Cambridge, MA: Harvard University Press.

Sears, David O., and Carolyn L. Funk. 1990. "The Limited Effect of Economic Self-Interest on the Political Attitudes of the Mass Public." *Journal of Behavioral Economics* 19 (3): 247–71. https://doi.org/10.1016/0090-5720(90)90030-B.

Shah, Baiju R., Maria Chiu, Shubarna Amin, Meera Ramani, Sharon Sadry, and Jack V. Tu. 2010. "Surname Lists to Identify South Asian and Chinese Ethnicity from Secondary Data in Ontario, Canada: A Validation Study." *BMC Medical Research Methodology* 10 (1): 42. https://doi.org/10.1186/1471-2288-10-42.

Sherif, Muzafer. 1966. *In Common Predicament: Social Psychology of Intergroup Conflict and Cooperation*. Boston: Houghton-Mifflin.

Shingles, Richard D. 1981. "Black Consciousness and Political Participation: The Missing Link." *American Political Science Review* 75 (1): 76–91.

Sidanius, James, Shana Levin, Colette Van Laar, and David O. Sears. 2008. *The Diversity Challenge: Social Identity and Intergroup Relations on the College Campus*. New York: Russell Sage Foundation.

Sigelman, Carol K., Lee Sigelman, Barbara J. Walkosz, and Michael Nitz. 1995. "Black Candidates, White Voters: Understanding Racial Bias in Political Perceptions." *American Journal of Political Science* 39 (1): 243–65. https://doi.org/10.2307/2111765.

Sigelman, Lee, and Carol K. Sigelman. 1982. "Sexism, Racism and Ageism in Voting Behavior: An Experimental Analysis." *Social Psychology Quarterly* 45 (4): 263–69. https://doi.org/10.2307/3033922.

Sigelman, Lee, and Susan Welch. 1984. "Race, Gender, and Opinion toward Black and Female Presidential Candidates." *Public Opinion Quarterly* 48 (2): 467–75. https://doi.org/10.1086/268843.

Simien, Evelyn M. 2005. "Race, Gender, and Linked Fate." *Journal of Black Studies* 35 (5): 529–50. https://doi.org/10.1177/0021934704265899.

Simon, William H. 1999. "Three Limitations of Deliberation: Identity Politics, Bad Faith, and Indeterminacy." In *Deliberative Politics: Essays on Democracy and Disagreement*, edited by Stephen Macedo, 49–57. Oxford: Oxford University Press.

Simpson, Brent, and Michael W. Macy. 2004. "Power, Identity, and Collective Action in Social Exchange." *Social Forces* 82 (4): 1373–1409.

Slovic, Paul, Melissa L. Finucane, Ellen Peters, and Donald G. MacGregor. 2007. "The Affect Heuristic." *European Journal of Operational Research* 177 (3): 1333–52. https://doi.org/10.1016/j.ejor.2005.04.006.

Sniderman, Paul M., Aloysius Hagendoorn, and Louk Hagendoorn. 2007. *When Ways of Life Collide: Multiculturalism and its Discontents in the Netherlands.* Princeton: Princeton University Press.

Sniderman, Paul M., Louk Hagendoorn, and Markus Prior. 2004. "Predisposing Factors and Situational Triggers: Exclusionary Reactions to Immigrant Minorities." *American Political Science Review* 98 (1): 35–49. https://doi.org/10.1017/S000305540 400098X.

–. 2009. *When Ways of Life Collide: Multiculturalism and Its Discontents in the Netherlands.* Princeton, NJ: Princeton University Press.

Sniderman, Paul, and T. Piazza. 1993. *The Scar of Race.* Cambridge, MA: Harvard University Press.

Sniderman, Paul M., and Philip E. Tetlock. 1986. "Symbolic Racism: Problems of Motive Attribution in Political Analysis." *Journal of Social Issues* 42 (2): 129–50. https://doi.org/10.1111/j.1540-4560.1986.tb00229.x.

Soroka, Stuart, Richard Johnston, Will Kymlicka, and Keith Banting. 2013. "Ethnic Diversity and Social Solidarity in Canada." Canadian Election Study Working Papers Series, Working Paper No. 2013–03. https://ces-eec.sites.olt.ubc.ca/files/2014/07/SJKBCES.pdf.

Soroka, Stuart N., Richard Johnston, and Keith Banting. 2008. "Ties That Bind? Social Cohesion and Diversity in Canada." In *Diversity, Recognition and Shared Citizenship in Canada,* edited by Keith Banting, Thomas J. Courchene, and Leslie Seidle, 561–600. Montreal: McGill-Queen's University Press.

Spears, Russell, Bertjan Doosje, and Naomi Ellemers. 1999. "Commitment and the Context of Social Perception." In *Social Identity,* edited by Naomi Ellemers, Russell Spears, and Bertjan Doosje, 59–83. Oxford: Blackwell.

Spivak, Gayatri Chakravorty. 1987. *In Other Worlds: Essays in Cultural Politics.* London: Routledge.

Statistics Canada. 2011. "Immigration and Ethnocultural Diversity in Canada." 2011 National Household Survey. Catalogue no. 99-010-X2011001.

–. 2013a. National Household Survey Data Table. 99-010-X2011030. Release date May 8, 2013.

–. 2013b. National Household Survey Data Table. 99-010-X2011038. Release date December 11, 2013.

–. 2017. Data Table, 2016 Census. Catalogue no. 98-400-X2016286. Release date: November 29, 2017.

Statistics Canada Individuals File, 2016 Census of Population (Public Use Microdata Files). 98M0001X. February 5, 2019.

Stephenson, Laura, and Jean Crête. 2011. "A Comparison of Internet and Telephone Surveys for Studying Political Behavior." *International Journal of Public Opinion Research* 23: 24–55.

Stets, Jan E., and Peter J. Burke. 2000. "Identity Theory and Social Identity Theory." *Social Psychology Quarterly* 63 (3): 224–37.

Stokes, Atiya Kai. 2003. "Latino Group Consciousness and Political Participation." *American Politics Research* 31 (4): 361–78.

Stokes, Donald E. 1966. "Some Dynamic Elements of Contests for the Presidency." *American Political Science Review* 60 (1): 19–28.

Stokes-Brown, Atiya Kai. 2006. "Racial Identity and Latino Vote Choice." *American Politics Research* 34 (5): 627–52. https://doi.org/10.1177/1532673X06289156.

Street, Alex. 2014. "Representation Despite Discrimination: Minority Candidates in Germany." *Political Research Quarterly* 67 (2): 374–85.

Stryker, Sheldon. 1980. *Symbolic Interactionism: A Social Structural Version.* Menlo Park, CA: Benjamin/Cummings.

Tajfel, Henri. 1981. *Human Groups and Social Categories.* Cambridge: Cambridge University Press.

Tajfel, Henri, Michael G. Billig, Robert P. Bundy, and Claude Flament. 1971. "Social Categorization and Intergroup Behaviour." *European Journal of Social Psychology* 1 (2): 149–77. http://garfield.library.upenn.edu/classics1992/A1992GZ34400001.pdf.

Tajfel, Henri, and John C. Turner. 1979. "An Integrative Theory of Intergroup Conflict." Reprinted in *Organizational Identity: A Reader,* edited by Mary Jo Hatch, and Majken Schultz, 56–65. Oxford: Oxford University Press.

–. 1986. "The Social Identity Theory of Intergroup Behavior." *Psychology of Intergroup Relations* 2 (1): 204–22. https://doi.org/10.1111/j.1751-9004.2007.00066.x.

Tate, Katherine. 1994. *From Protest to Politics: The New Black Voters in American Elections.* Cambridge, MA: Harvard University Press.

Taylor, Donald M., Stephen C. Wright, Fathali M. Moghaddam, and Richard N. Lalonde. 1990. "The Personal/Group Discrimination Discrepancy: Perceiving My Group, but Not Myself, to Be a Target for Discrimination." *Personality and Social Psychology Bulletin* 16 (2): 254–62.

Taylor, Shelley E. 1981. "A Categorization Approach to Stereotyping." In *Cognitive Processes in Stereotyping and Intergroup Behavior,* edited by Hamilton, David L. London: Psychology Press.

Tedin, Kent L., and Richard W. Murray. 1994. "Support for Biracial Political Coalitions among Blacks and Hispanics." *Social Science Quarterly* 75 (4): 772–89.

Tesler, Michael. 2016. *Post-racial or Most-racial? Race and Politics in the Obama Era.* Chicago: University of Chicago Press.

Theiss-Morse, Elizabeth. 2009. *Who Counts as an American? The Boundaries of National Identity.* Cambridge: Cambridge University Press.

Thompson, Debra. 2012. "Making (Mixed-)Race: Census Politics and the Emergence of Multiracial Multiculturalism in the United States, Great Britain and Canada." *Ethnic and Racial Studies* 35 (8): 1409–26. https://doi.org/10.1080/01419870.2011.556194.

–. 2015. "Through, Against and Beyond the Racial State: The Transnational Stratum of Race." *Cambridge Review of International Affairs* 26 (1): 133–51.

–. 2016. *The Schematic State: Race, Transnationalism, and the Politics of the Census.* Cambridge: Cambridge University Press.

Tolley, Erin. 2015. *Framed: Media and the Coverage of Race in Canadian Politics.* Vancouver: UBC Press.

Tong, Eddie M.W., and Weining C. Chang. 2008. "Group Entity Belief: An Individual Difference Construct Based on Implicit Theories of Social Identities." *Journal of Personality* 76 (4): 707–32.

Torres, Maria de los Angeles. 1988. "From Exiles to Minorities: The Politics of Cuban-Americans." In *Latinos and the Political System,* edited by F. Chris Garcia. Notre Dame, IN: University of Notre Dame Press.

Tossutti, Livianna S., and Tom Pierre Najem. 2002. "Minorities and Elections in Canada's Fourth Party System: Macro and Micro Constraints and Opportunities." *Canadian Ethnic Studies* 34 (1): 85–111.

Transue, John E. 2007. "Identity Salience, Identity Acceptance, and Racial Policy Attitudes: American National Identity as a Uniting Force." *American Journal of Political Science* 51 (1): 78–91.

Turner, John C. 1978. "Social Categorization and Social Discrimination in the Minimal Group Paradigm." In *Differentiation between Social Groups: Studies in the Social Psychology of Intergroup Relations,* edited by Henri Tajfel, 102–40. London: Academic Press.

Turner, John C., Michael A. Hogg, Penelope J. Oakes, Stephen D. Reicher, and Margaret S. Wetherell. 1987. *Rediscovering the Social Group: A Self-Categorization Theory.* Cambridge, MA: Basil Blackwell.

Turner, John C., Penelope J. Oakes, S. Alexander Haslam, and Craig McGarty. 1994. "Self and Collective: Cognition and Social Context." *Personality and Social Psychology Bulletin* 20 (5): 454–63. https://doi.org/10.1177/0146167294205002.

Ujimoto, K. Victor. 1999. "Studies of Ethnicity Identity, Ethnic Relations, and Citizenship." In *Race and Ethnic Relations in Canada,* edited by Peter Li, 253–90. Oxford: Oxford University Press.

Veenstra, Kristine, and S. Alexander Haslam. 2000. "Willingness to Participate in Industrial Protest: Exploring Social Identification in Context." *British Journal of Social Psychology* 39 (2): 153–72.

Verba, Sidney, and Norman H. Nie. 1972. *Participation in America.* New York: Harper and Row.

Verge, Tània. 2015. "The Symbolic Impact of Women's Representation on Citizens' Political Attitudes: Measuring the Effect through Survey Experiments." European Conference on Politics and Gender, Uppsala, June 11, 2015.

Verkuyten, Maykel. 2005. *The Social Psychology of Ethnic Identity.* East Sussex, UK: Taylor and Frances.

Walsh, Penny E., and Jessi L. Smith. 2007. "Opposing Standards within the Cultural Worldview: Terror Management and American Women's Desire for Uniqueness versus Inclusiveness." *Psychology of Women Quarterly* 31 (1): 103–13. https://doi.org/10.1111/j.1471-6402.2007.00335.x.

Wängnerud, Lena. 2009. "Women in Parliaments: Descriptive and Substantive Representation." *Annual Review of Political Science* 12: 51–69.

Wantchekon, Leonard. 2003. "Clientelism and Voting Behavior: Evidence from a Field Experiment in Benin." *World Politics* 55 (3): 399–422. https://doi.org/10.1353/wp.2003.0018.

Waters, Mary. 1999. *Black Identities: West Indian Immigrant Dreams and American Realities.* Cambridge, MA: Harvard University Press.

–. 2006. "Optional Ethnicities: For Whites Only?" In *Identity and Belonging: Rethinking Race and Ethnicity in Canadian Society,* edited by Sean P. Hier and B. Singh Bolaria, 137–46. Toronto: Canadian Scholars' Press.

Waters, Mary C., and Philip Kasinitz. 2012. "Discrimination, Race Relations and the Second Generation." *Social Research* 77 (1): 101–32.

Wattenberg, Martin P. 1991. *The Rise of Candidate-centered Politics: Presidential Elections of the 1980s.* Cambridge, MA: Harvard University Press.

Weaver, Vesla M. 2012. "The Electoral Consequences of Skin Color: The 'Hidden' Side of Race in Politics." *Political Behavior* 34 (1): 159–92. https://doi.org/10.1007/s11109-010-9152-7.

Wheeler, S. Christina., Richard E. Petty, and George Y. Bizer. 2005. "Self-Schema Matching and Attitude Change: Situational and Dispositional Determinants of Message Elaboration." *Journal of Consumer Research* 31 (4): 787–97. https://doi.org/10.1086/426613.

White, Clovis L., and Peter J. Burke. 1987. "Ethnic Role Identity among Black and White College Students: An Interactionist Approach." *Sociological Perspectives* 30 (3): 310–31. https://doi.org/10.2307/1389115.

White, Stephen, Neil Nevitte, André Blais, Elisabeth Gidengil, and Patrick Fournier. 2008. "The Political Resocialization of Immigrants: Resistance or Lifelong Learning?" *Political Research Quarterly* 61 (2): 268–81.

White, Graham. 2005. *Cabinets and First Ministers.* Vancouver: UBC Press.

Wiener, Yoash. 1982. "Commitment in Organizations: A Normative View." *Academy of Management Review* 7 (3): 418–28. https://doi.org/10.5465/AMR.1982.4285349.

Wilson, David C., and Darren Davis. 2017. "African Americans' Racial Resentment Toward Whites: Meaning, Measurement, and Theory." Paper presented at the 2018 National Conference of Black Political Scientists Annual Meeting, Chicago, November 17.

Winter, Nicholas. 2008. *Dangerous Frames: How Ideas about Race and Gender Shape Public Opinion.* Chicago: University of Chicago Press.

Wolbrecht, Christina, and David E. Campbell. 2007. "Leading by Example: Female Members of Parliament as Political Role Models." *American Journal of Political Science* 51 (4): 921–39.

Wolfinger, Raymond E. 1965. "The Development and Persistence of Ethnic Voting." *American Political Science Review* 59 (4): 896–908.

Wong, Janelle S., Pei-Te Lien, and M. Margaret Conway. 2005. "Group-Based Resources and Political Participation among Asian Americans." *American Politics Research* 33 (4): 545–76.

Index

and, 160–61; federal election affinity voting experiment's support for, 143, 149; lack of research on, 61; need for better measures in racialized affinity voting, 74; overview of coethnic affinity voting, 37–44; overview of racialized affinity voting, 48–53; positive and negative implications of, 161–63; role of self-esteem in, 99; tenets of, 20; vs self-interest, 128–29. *See also* ethnic identities; racial identities; self-identification; self-identification and affinity voting experiment; self-identification experiment

ideological stereotyping: approach to, 17–18; as explanation for interest-based coethnic affinity voting, 31–33, 44; as explanation for interest-based racialized affinity voting, 46–47, 53; in self-identification and affinity voting experiment, 107–8, 109(t); tenets of, 11. *See also* interest-based affinity voting experiment: ideological stereotyping component; stereotyping of candidates' attributes

IDPG scale. *See* Identification with a Psychological Group (IDPG) Scale

immigrants: African Americans and, 45; candidate survey experiment and, 73–74, 171, 172(t), 188n3; discrimination by, 112–13; discrimination and prejudice against, 56, 57(t); economic outcomes of Canadian, 54–55, 58, 186n9; identity of Latino, 51; Indigenous peoples' views of, 167; mentioned in experiments' open-ended questions, 109–10, 126, 133, 166, 188n3; shifting identities of, 20–21, 165, 168, 169; studies using IDPG scale on, 83

immigration: affinity voting as product of, 154–55; policies on, 122–24, 125(t), 127; political parties' positions on, 149; as variable in self-identification experiment, 88–91, 94, 96–97. *See also* country of origin

income levels, 54, 88, 90, 186n9, 187n2, 188n2

independent Canadian candidates: in candidate survey experiment, 68, 174(t); in federal election affinity voting experiment, 139–42, 148, 175(t), 184(t); in interest-based affinity voting experiment, 115–17, 126(t), 180(t), 182(t)–83(t)

independent voters, 83–84

Indigenous candidates, 111, 145

Indigenous peoples, 163, 167, 187n2

inequality, 35, 36. *See also* racial inequality policies

in-group bias: affective self-identification as cause of, 79; approach to, 16, 160; defined, 38; in federal election affinity voting experiment, 143; as identity- vs interest-based explanation, 161; role in identity-based coethnic affinity voting, 38–41, 42, 43; role of group identity in, 96; role in identity-based racialized affinity voting, 51; role in interest-based racialized affinity voting, 46–47; self-esteem and, 38–41, 43, 162–63; in self-identification and affinity voting experiment, 108, 112–13; in social-identity theory, 20, 38

in-groups: in common-intergroup-identity model, 51; fluidity of membership in, 166, 168; inclusion vs exclusion from racialized, 167; and influence of affinity effects beyond voting, 153; of racialized vs ethnic peoples, 52; role of normalization and racialization in broadening, 23; sanctions amongst, 21; in social-identity theory, 12

instrumental politics, 4, 10, 11–12

integration, 55

interest-based affinity voting experiment, 114–36; approach to, 114; challenges of, 135–36; federal election affinity voting experiment's lack of support for, 143, 149–50; hypotheses, 117, 120, 123, 129, 131; ideological stereotyping